The Christian Writer's Book

—

A Practical Guide to Writing

ABOUT THE AUTHORS

DON M. AYCOCK is Editor of Special Projects at the Brotherhood Commission, an agency of the Southern Baptist Convention. He was educated at the University of Southwestern Louisiana, Louisiana College, Southern Baptist Theological Seminary, and Mansfield College of Oxford University before earning the Th.D. degree in systematic theology from the New Orleans Baptist Theological Seminary. He has also served as a visiting professor of homiletics at the Midwestern Baptist Theological Seminary. While serving for many years in the pastorate (in Kentucky and Louisiana), Don wrote more than a dozen books and published a wide variety of articles and Sunday school lessons. He is active in several civic organizations, is founder of the Louisiana Christian Writers Guild, and is a contributing editor for the *Journal of the American Academy of Ministry*. Don speaks widely across the country at various writing conferences, and has been listed in *Personalities of America, Directory of Distinguished Americans, Contemporary Authors*, and the *Directory of International Biography*. He and his wife Carla have twin sons, Ryan and Christopher, and they live in Memphis.

LEONARD GEORGE GOSS is Vice President of Editorial and Editor in Chief for Crossway Books, a division of Good News Publishers. He is a native of San Diego, California, and is an alumnus of Phoenix College, Arizona State University, the School of Religion of the Tempe Religious Conference, the University of Windsor, and Trinity Evangelical Divinity School. Active on a national scale as a public speaker on writing, editing, and publishing topics, he has spoken at many writing guilds and conferences. Len has been honored by being listed in several biographical reference titles, including *Who's Who in the Midwest, Who's Who of Emerging Leaders in America, Who's Who in Religion, Who's Who in Finance and Industry, Who's Who in Advertising, Notable American Men, Men of Achievement*, and the *Dictionary of International Biography*. He is a member of several associations, including the Evangelical Theological Society, the Conference on Faith and History, The New York C. S. Lewis Society, The Southern California C. S. Lewis Society, and The Lewis Carroll Society of North America. Len is married to Carolyn J. Stanford, and they live near Chicago. They have two adult sons, Joseph Stanford and David Leonard.

Together **AYCOCK** and **GOSS** have coauthored *Writing Religiously: A Guide to Writing Nonfiction Religious Books* and coedited *Inside Religious Publishing: A Look Behind the Scenes*.

The Christian Writer's Book

—

A Practical Guide to Writing

DON M. AYCOCK & LEONARD G. GOSS

All Scripture verses unless otherwise indicated are taken from the King James version of the Bible.

The Christian Writer's Book: A Practical Guide to Writing
by Don M. Aycock & Leonard G. Goss
ISBN: 0-88270-695-0
Library of Congress Catalog Card Number: 96-84820
Copyright © 1996 by **BRIDGE-LOGOS Publishers**

Published by:
BRIDGE-LOGOS Publishers
North Brunswick Corporate Center
1300 Airport Road, Suite E
North Brunswick, NJ 08902

To My Small Family: Carla, my wife, and
Chris and Ryan, my teenage sons; and
To My Larger Family: The readers of this
book and some of my other work.
Thanks, folks. You keep me going.

(DMA)

———————————————————

To My Mother
Sylvia
To the Memory of My Father
J o e
To My Parents In-Law
Jim and Thelma
To My Wife
Carolyn
and
To My Sons
Joseph and David

(LGG)

To request that either Don or Len do speaking
engagements or seminars, please contact:

BRIDGE-LOGOS *Publishers*
North Brunswick Corporate Center
1300 Airport Road, Suite E
North Brunswick, NJ 08902

CONTENTS

FOREWORD

For the past thirty-five years, I have had the rewarding pleasure of encouraging writers to get into print. Most of these people have had their eyes set on authoring a book. Were I to hazard a guess as to the number of people in the United States who at this moment are engaged in trying to write a book, it would be in the millions. Those I have met are eager, diligent, conscientious, charming, and—for the most part—doomed to disappointment.

In discussing the making of books with aspiring writers in many parts of the world, I have often come across those with a subtle distinction that seems to make an enormous difference. They may have a brilliant "idea" and they may not; they may have a literary background and they may not; but there is an air about them. It is a professional air, an approach to the writing business that makes me realize that my advice is really not needed; they either know what they're doing or very soon will know. They approach writing as they would sheep farming or pilot training or practical nursing. Whatever their tactics of the moment, their strategy is sound. In a very short time they will be published.

These people are not usually attracted by the glamour of the literary set. They don't expect to storm the market with a best seller. As Christians, they are motivated to serve the Lord—but so are the unsuccessful ones! What makes the difference is that these people are out to learn the craft from top to bottom. They subscribe to the right journals, attend the right conferences, seek out the right people, study the trends, and seek to meet the current demands of the readership. They think of themselves as professional writers.

This book by Don Aycock and Len Goss, if carefully studied, might well be the means of turning amateur writers into pros. It is carefully designed to bring the neophyte into the fraternity. It is loaded with practical suggestions and guidelines for writers, quotes scores of contemporary editors and publishers, and contains standard information that is often difficult to come by. The result is that this volume is a fine writer's resource textbook and teaching manual; but it is more than that. As you will learn on the first page, it is an intimate, often delightful reading experience. I wish you joy and Godspeed as you read—and write.

—Sherwood Eliot Wirt

PREFACE

Enthusiasts for the new electronic technology have predicted the demise of the book. But the authors of *The Christian Writer's Book* do not believe that anyone should be writing a premature obituary for the poor and lowly book. Books will be here for a long time. They have been and will continue to be the most versatile and user-friendly communications package in existence. You can move from front to back, or from back to front, or you can dive into a book at any place. You can go at any speed. You can snuggle up with a book in front of a fire, or in bed, or take one to the beach, or on a vacation to the mountains. Books are tactile in a way that a computer is not. We were told that binding pages together to make books would go out of fashion when the personal computer was developed. But books as we know them have been alive since Johann Gutenberg invented typographic printing in the 1400s, and they will be alive for a long while to come. Our education will continue to be built around books. The structure of our national life will continue to rest on our books of law, politics, religion, history, geography, and biography. Books will continue to be the main source of our reservoir of knowledge about faith, memory, wisdom, morality, poetry, philosophy, history, and science.

The power of the book is immense and terrible; books influence individual thought and debate, as well as national conscience and policy. Daniel Boorstin has said that our civilization is a product of "the Culture of the Book." In short, it is true that books in their traditional form will continue to encompass us in a thousand ways. People are still motivated by ideas, and books are the principle means by which ideas are given currency and made effective.

But the present state of book publishing is precarious. On the one hand, people who produce books are still able to be in a position of influence on what is read and are sometimes even able to influence the flow of important ideas. So there is so much we can do. In book publishing, we can have a creative and constructive influence that could be multiplied a thousand times in our world. Some publishers are still aware that books can have something to do with spiritual values. They use the print media to present the Gospel because the print media is still the best way to do that, having fewer layers than other media between the intention and the realization of the Christian message.

On the other hand, in book publishing our sense of business may be taking over our sense of critical judgment. It may well be that what we feel comfortable producing in Christian book publishing is changing. We are not the only ones who have noticed, but in Christian publishing today many seem unconcerned about the *right* choice of what to publish. Rather, they are concerned only with sales and with bringing their wares to the market. This is the jackpot syndrome. When George Bernard Shaw once said of publishing that "there is probably no other trade in which there is so little relationship between profits and actual value," he was not thinking about Christian book publishing in the 90's—but he could have been. Some book publishers virtually have become a subset of the electronic media. Some of them are in fact owned or have been owned by non-Christian conglomerate media companies. Why is this troublesome? With the media takeover of book publishing, the distribution of books is increasingly in the hands of fewer and fewer people, and the battle is to get the books on the bookstore shelves. That is the only thing that matters. Many bookstores now stock only those titles that are guaranteed to sell quickly—and so they take the popular titles, titles with well-known author's names on them, titles that have broad appeal. As many have noted, the current state of affairs is that not *only* does the post-Christian *culture* demonstrate an utter contempt for serious books, but Christian publishers and booksellers *themselves* sometimes demonstrate the same contempt when they disguise moral responsibility with marketing-oriented camouflage. When a publishing house exists for one reason and one reason only—to make money for their owners—and when they do this by exploiting trends and publishing fads, it is a grim time to be in Christian publishing, and it is a grim time to be a Christian writer.

All of this makes it almost amazing that the number of Christians who write books is increasing. In a way, this should not be surprising. God has given us the gift of books. We write them and publish them to please ourselves and others who, like us, love and want books. And we publish them because people depend on books to build a strong foundation. Books have the depth to let thinkers develop their thoughts and engage in dialog with others. They enable one generation to leave a heritage for the next. In short, the world needs the value of books, and people who write them enjoy their association with books and ideas and with people who love books and ideas. For the bibliophile, books are not luxuries, but absolute necessities.

And God has given us the gift of words. At their best, words are windows into the soul of another person—the writer. Perhaps this is why the printed word holds such a permanent place in the ranks of human achievement. What do these windows to the soul admit? Among other things, knowledge, inspiration, challenge, motivation, hope, and plain fun to millions who read and to a smaller number who write. Do you doubt it? Visit a bookstore and watch the ravenous looks in the patrons' eyes as they relish each title and devour each cover.

Saul Bellow has written that there is "an immense, painful longing for a broader, more flexible, fuller, more coherent, more comprehensive account of what we human beings are, who we are, and what this life is for." *That* is why we write and publish—to help readers discover what this life is for. The real business of Christian writing and publishing is promoting ideas. It is no exaggeration to say that we hold in our hands the power to mold minds, and we work in this field with a deep sense of responsibility. We try to offer answers to readers through writing and publishing in the same way the Gospels tell us Jesus offered answers to his hearers on the vital religious, political, and social issues of his day—by mooring them in stories of personal accountability. Through stories the entire Bible conveys the good news that God has entered into the story of His creation. Our challenge as Christian writers and publishers is to pursue excellence in promoting that Story.

Our whole purpose in writing this book is to share our excitement regarding Christian books on an intimate, personal basis with other Christian writers. We have picked up tips, pointers, ideas, no-nos, maybes and musts about writing books along the way. We want to make these available to you. There is no *one* way to do it. But there are some generally accepted principles and methods of going about the writing of books and getting those books published. If we can help you make even a single step in your journey toward writing and publishing your book, then our purpose will be served, and our own book worthwhile.

1

WORDS AND THE WORD: Some Musings on Christian Writing

In The Beginning . . .

A story was told of a meeting between a theologian and an astronomer. The astronomer said to the theologian, "I don't understand why you theologians fuss so much about things like predestination and supralapsarianism, about the communicable and the incommunicable attributes of God, of imputed or infused grace, and the like. To me Christianity is very simple—it's the Golden Rule: 'Do unto others as you would have others do unto you'."

The theologian thought about that for a moment and then replied, "I think I see what you mean. I get lost in all your talk about exploding novas, the expanding universe, theories of entropy, black holes, and the like. To me astronomy is very simple—it's 'Twinkle, twinkle, little star. . . '."

The urge to reduce every discipline to simplest terms is understandable but sometimes laughable. Astronomy has its world view, its technical language, and its methods of accomplishing its work. So does theology. Theological methodology is a branch of systematic theology which seeks to understand how theology does its work. This chapter is not on theological method, thankfully. But Christian writers need to be aware that theology is not our enemy.

Theology troubles us though. We might be tempted to think of it as a needless encumbrance to our work, the same way high school kids think math is the most useless subject ever invented. Most people do not like to do the necessary reflection to dissect and analyze a subject. Someone once said, "I hate botany but I love flowers." We could translate that as, "I hate theology but I love God."

Botany and theology are not the same, however. Botany is characterized by its subject—flora. But theology is characterized by its object—God. The word *theology* is literally *Theos logos*, "thinking about God". Theology is not just the narrow contemplation of God and "religious" concepts. Medieval theologians supposedly debated about how many angels could sit on the head of a pin. Who cares? Theology is an awareness of otherness; it provides the perspective from which Christians think and write.

One contemporary theologian has written that theology is "involved in the practical task of acquiring an understanding of life and world."[1] This same theologian says, "Theology is not or ought not to be a haven for all inarticulate sputterings about human life or Christian faith nor the sort of lunatic asylum where everyone does his or her own thing without facing the responsibility of giving an account for such speaking, writing, or gesticulating which is, or purports to be, of theological significance."[2] The Christian writer will give such an account. Did not Jesus say, "But I tell you that men will have to give account on the day of judgment for every careless word they have spoken [or written?]" (Matthew 12:36)?

This chapter is not a full-scale theology for writers. In order to pique your curiosity about some elements of writing that go beyond form and style, this opening chapter will give you some stories about writing and open some windows to let in some fresh air and light. We will gather pollen from many flowers to make this honey. At the end of the chapter you will not have a systematic theology of Christian writing. But maybe what you will have is a renewed sense of appreciation for your calling as a writer and a new perspective from which to work.

We all have a theology whether we are aware of it or not. The Christian writer is influenced by his or her concept of God, relationship to Christ, involvement or lack of it in a church, and so on. The question is not "Do I have a theology?" but rather, "Is my theology a good one or a defective one?" Martin Luther, C. S. Lewis, Billy Graham, Frank Peretti, Beverly LaHaye, and Oral Roberts all have a theology. You do, too, even if you are someone who says you hate theology.

The fundamental conviction in this chapter is that Christian writers need a sound, biblical understanding of human life and of God's will. That is theology. You need not have a Ph.D. degree in systematic theology in order to write, but you do need to possess a well-rounded basis from which to write. Please understand that we are *not* pleading for writers to sound "orthodox" by peppering their manuscripts with religious-sounding words. There is no doubt too much of that already. But as writers we have to take great care with the words we do use. Words are words. There are no "Christian words" but only words that can be used to convey Christian meaning. The late H. Grady Davis once said, "A Christian may use language for a Christian purpose, but, as there is no such thing as 'Christian' wood or stone or metal, so there can be no such thing as 'Christian' or 'sacred' or 'holy' language. Even in the Bible, especially in the Bible, language is human, true to the reality of human life." Yes, there are holy usages of language in the Bible but mostly it is everyday language that is filled with new meaning and infused with grace.

One obvious reason for this need for writers to have a sound theology is because there is so much ignorance about the basics of our faith. A Church of England Publication listed the following children's answers to church school questions:

* Noah's wife was called Joan of Ark.
* The fifth commandment is: Humor thy father and thy mother.
* Lot's wife was a pillar of salt by day, but a ball of fire by night.
* When Mary heard she was to be the mother of Jesus, she went off and sang the Magna Carta.
* Salome was a woman who danced naked in front of Harrods.
* Holy acrimony is another name for marriage.
* Christians can have only one wife. This is called monotony.
* The Pope lives in a vacuum.
* Today wild beasts are confined to Theological Gardens.
* Iran is the Bible of the Moslems.
* A republican is a sinner mentioned in the Bible.
* Abraham begat Isaac and Isaac begat Jacob and Jacob begat twelve partridges.
* The natives of Macedonia did not believe, so St. Paul got stoned.
* The first commandment was when Eve told Adam to eat the apple.[3]

Pure nonsense? Give a biblical/theological test to nearly anyone you know and you will likely get similar results. Christian writers cannot afford the luxury of ignorance but often we are ignorant anyway. We are like Columbus in search of the new world. He did not know where he was going when he left Spain, did not know were he was when he arrived at the new world, and did not know where he had been after he returned home.

Carl F. H. Henry, founding editor of *Christianity Today*, once said that theology is important because "an empty head committed to Christ will sooner or later be vulnerable to other commitments. Unless one can give a reason for the hope he has, he soon will be whiplashed by illusionary hopes."[4]

Could this lack of a theological foundation account for some of the items in contemporary Christian bookstores? One writer said that, "Evangelicals are generally afraid to compete in the marketplace of ideas with the modern secularist. They would rather separate themselves from the 'world' to avoid the embarrassment of intellectual defeat. They still prefer their devotional, self-help publications to decisive refutations of the naked illogic of unbelief."[5] This writer continues, "Instead of the great classics in defense of the faith . . . what are the stores selling? Little Prudy Dottie Dimple's joybells quiet-time books, how-to-be-blessed-out-of-your-socks manuals, and ball-point pens with suitable Bible verses inscribed thereon."

Writers do not need to become professional theologians. The point is that our message of the Gospel is too important to leave it to "I'll-just-let-the-Spirit-move-me" whims. Someone has observed that too many people who have said, "I have half a mind to write a book," do so!

...Was The Word . . .

Which of these two statements is true? Words are tools that can move the world and shape consciences for Christ. Words are cheap little gimmicks that can be spun any way to produce the maximum effect desired by the writer. Both are true. Words can be used to influence wills and shape consciences toward Christ, but they can also be used to manipulate people for a writer's selfish purpose. The better Christian writers aim for the former and not the latter.

Have you noticed the devaluation of words lately? There is a terrible inflation in the economy of language, and words are worth much less now than before. The National Council of Teachers of English (NCTE) speaks of "verbal pollution." This is doublespeak that tries to convey a simple idea by using high sounding words. The NCTE offers the following examples. In some regions, a gas bill is now called an "energy document." A stock market crash can be merely a "fourth-quarter equity retreat." Chrysler does not lay off 5,000 workers but rather calls the move a "career alternative enhancement program." And did you know that jumping off a building could lead to "sudden deceleration trauma" upon landing?

Even everyday objects and actions are not immune to this doublespeak. Zippers are "interlocking slide fasteners," toothbrushes are "home plaque removal instruments," and a spanking is an "intensive adverse intervention." Janitors are now "entropy control engineers." The military is into this mess, too. War is now "lethal intervention," an event that could lead to "excess mortality."[6]

The federal government is probably more guilty than anyone else. A second example of verbal inflation is from a government lawyer who took the line from the Lord's Prayer which goes, "Give us this day our daily bread," and phrased it in "governmentese." "We respectfully petition, request, and entreat that due and adequate provision be made, this day and the date hereinafter subscribed, for the satisfying of these petitioners' nutritional requirements and for the organizing of such methods of allocation and distribution as may be deemed necessary and proper to assure the reception by and for said petitioners of such quantities of baked cereal products as shall, in the judgment of the aforesaid petitioners, constitute a sufficient supply thereof."

Biblical language knows no such devaluation. What is striking about the language of the Bible is its sparseness and its frugality. Words are never multiplied at the expense of the Word. Instead, words are the servants of the Word. The prophet Jeremiah knew this fact. He once complained that God had tricked and deceived him. But after the complaint Jeremiah said, "But if I say, 'I will not mention him or speak any more in his name,' his word is in my heart like a fire, a fire shut up in my bones. I am weary of holding it in; indeed, I cannot" (Jeremiah 20:9).

The Word is God's creative act. In Genesis God spoke and creation came into being. In the prophets the Word defies every effort to silence it, as with Jeremiah, or with false prophets. "'Is not my word like fire,' declares the LORD, 'and like a hammer that breaks a rock in pieces?'" (Jeremiah 23:29). In Isaiah the word is like rain that falls to earth to nourish the seeds in the soil. The Lord says of his word, "So is my word that goes out from my mouth: It will not return to me empty, but will accomplish what I desire and achieve the purpose for which I sent it" (Isaiah 55:11).

Finally, the Word of God became flesh in Jesus of Nazareth. As John's gospel puts it, "In the beginning was the Word, and the Word was with God, and the Word was God. He was with God in the beginning" (John 1:1-2). Death and the grave could not silence him. This Word is the supreme power at work in the world, a power to which all knees will ultimately bend (Philippians 2:10-11). Christian writers are servants of the Word with our words.

When all is said and done, our message is something given to us. We do not invent it. While we have great latitude to be creative in finding ways to communicate the Gospel, the central message is still something given to us. As King David once prayed, "Everything comes from you, and we have given you only what comes from your hand" (1 Chronicles 29:14b). While the core message is given to us, the means of communicating it is not. When one of the authors was in seminary he was a professor's assistant in homiletics class. His job was to grade student sermons. Several students became very upset with him because he gave them less than an "A" on their sermon outlines. They would say, "God gave me this sermon! How can you give me a 'C'?" He sometimes wanted to say, "I think God can spell better than this." What the students meant was easily understood. They felt a sense of inspiration in formulating the idea of the sermon. What they did not realize was that while the central idea may have been inspirational, the communicating of that idea required hard work. It is a difficult lesson to learn, and most of us are still learning it. Writing—whether sermons, articles, or books—is difficult work. The old adage is still true that writing is 10 percent inspiration and 90 percent perspiration.

We owe a debt to our readers to convey this message in clear, compelling language. The problem with much popular Christian writing is banality. The problem with much scholarly Christian writing is obscurity. Why can't there be both clarity and art? The answer is that there *can* be if Christian writers are willing to work on both the message and the form of communicating it.

Clarity is essential. John Wesley, a co-founder of the Methodist denomination, published a book of sermons in 1746. He wrote in his introduction: "I design plain truth for plain people; therefore, of set purpose, I abstain from all nice and philosophical speculations; from all perplexed and intricate reasonings; and, as far as possible, from even the show of learning. I labor to avoid all words which are not easy to be understood, all which are not used in common life; and, in particular, those kinds of technical terms that so frequently occur in Bodies of Divinity; those modes of speaking which men of reading are intimately acquainted with, but which to common people are an unknown tongue."[7] As Paul put it, "But in church I would rather speak five intelligible words to instruct others than ten thousand words in a tongue. Brothers, stop thinking like children. In regard to evil be infants, but in your thinking be adults" (1 Corinthians 14:19-20).

Being "adult" in our thinking does not mean being obscure, pseudo-intellectual, or showy in our use of language. Some theological literature is like a black hole. It is so dense that no light can escape from it. Why not instead have a jack-in-the-box style that contains a surprise and a delight? One reason C. S. Lewis continues to be so popular and well-loved is that he paid the price of thinking deeply while clothing his thought in bright garments. Everyone is more attracted to a party costume than a funeral shroud.

By way of personal example, one of the authors earned the Doctor of Theology degree in the field of systematic theology. At the time he pursued his degree and wrote his dissertation he was also the pastor of a church. He would sit in his doctoral seminars at the theological seminary and discuss great books and write scholarly papers. But when he went back home to his parish the people did not want or think they needed purely academic theology. They had no interest in anyone reciting great recipes. They just wanted to know if there was anything to eat.

During the time he was writing his dissertation he felt a strong internal need to write something of a completely different vein. He was captivated by Galatians 5:22—"the fruit of the Spirit is love, joy, peace," and so on. He preached sermons on the fruit of the Spirit and also wrote a book about it entitled *Walking Straight In A Crooked World*.[8] The book just seemed to tumble out, and writing it was a joy.

Shortly after it was published, he was invited to speak at a writers conference in Tacoma, Washington. The invitation came partly because of another recently-published book, *Writing Religiously*.[9] It was a general conference and he was the token religious person. He led a workshop and also shared in a panel discussion. On that panel were editors from several prestigious secular magazines, editors from several large book publishing houses, and five successful literary agents from New York. When the discussion turned to religious writing, the editors and agents seemed to snort in contempt. They said they thought religious writing was junk, and none of them would touch it. One agent in particular seemed to be proud of her refusal to consider anything so far beneath her like inspirational writing. The truth is, these cultured despisers of religious writing were partially right.

That evening the conference officials invited him to take a dinner cruise on Puget Sound. One of the hostesses at the conference came up to him and said, "I just read your book, *Walking Straight In A Crooked World*. I thought you said you wrote religious stuff." He stared at her for a moment and said, "I do. That book is a religious book." She said, "No it's not!

I wouldn't be caught dead reading a religious book, but I read yours and loved it. I read it all the way through. I like your style. But it's not a religious book." They talked about it some more and he realized she had a prejudice against anything labeled "religious." She thought everything in that area was designed to force particular opinions down unwilling throats. For her, along with the agents and editors on the panel discussion, religious literature was propaganda, merely an ugly stepchild of legitimate publishing.

That experience shows the perspective many people have on Christian writing. They think of it as boring, shallow tripe with no real connection to contemporary life. Christian writers may be like the gnat in a story Aesop told. A gnat landed on the horn of a bull and then apologized. The bull said, "It doesn't matter. Actually, I didn't even know you were there." Are we Christian writers just gnats swarming around the horns of "real" publishers? Definitely not! But we do have a reputation of being uninformed, unintelligible, and uninteresting. Those three sins are unforgivable to secular publishers. Thankfully, they are finally becoming unforgivable to religious publishers, too.

... And The Word Was With God ...

How do we Christian writers move beyond drivel and trivia to works of significance? In a word, the answer lies in passion. To have passion is to be committed to our work the way a lover is committed to his beloved. This precludes writing that is as cold as an iceberg or as speculative as the stock market. Great writers are passionate people. This is not meant in a sexual sense. This passion is something deeply felt and believed. When it emerges on the page it is alive and moves. Such writing is sometimes a guard dog that snaps at our heels while we run away. At other times it is a lap dog that snuggles next to us and warms us with its breath. Passionate writing, though, is never a stuffed puppy to be tossed around at will.

Sherwood Anderson has said that a real writer is a lover. Consider his counsel.

> The disease we all have and that we have to fight against all our lives is, of course, the disease of self. I am pretty sure that writing may be a way of life in itself. It can be that, because it continually forces us away from self toward others. Let any man, or woman, look too much upon his own life, and everything becomes a mess. I think the whole glory of writing lies in the fact that it forces us out of ourselves and into the lives of others. In the end the real writer becomes a lover.[10]

Writing does something. It changes the writer and also the reader. The story—whatever you are writing about—is both a personal offering and a sacred act. The late Jewish philosopher and writer Martin Buber used to tell a story about a rabbi whose grandfather had been a pupil of the founder of Hasidism, the Baal Shem Tov. This rabbi was once asked to tell a story. He said, "A story ought to be told so that it is itself a help." Then he told this story. "My grandfather was paralyzed. Once he was asked to tell a story about his teacher and he told how the holy Baal Shem Tov used to jump and dance when he was praying. My grandfather stood up while he was telling the story and the story carried him away so much that he had to jump and dance to show how the master had done. From that moment, he was healed. That is how stories ought to be told."[11]

The passionate storyteller jumps and dances while telling a tale of jumping and dancing. The passionate writer pours herself into her work and emerges as a different person. J. B.

Priestley referred to this as being "engrossed by an art." He compared himself with other earlier writers and concluded:

> The difference between us was not ability, but in the fact that while at heart they did not really much care about authorship, but merely toyed with the fascinating idea of it, I cared like blazes. And I suspect that in any form of art, it is this caring like blazes, while you are still young, that counts. Because you care and the dream never fades, other things, looking like those gifts of the gods, are added unto you. The very passion of the heart draws power. In some mysterious fashion, I suspect, you orient your being so that such gifts as observation, invention, and imagination are pulled your way. . . .
>
> A mere desire for the rewards, no matter how constant and burning that desire may be, will not do the trick. You have to be fascinated from the first by the art itself, engrossed and spellbound, and not simply dazzled by the deceptively superior life of its successful practitioners. In this matter you have, in short, to be pure in heart before you can be blessed.[12]

He "cared like blazes." That is passion, and that is what Christian writers need. It is an internal heat that strikes sparks and warms the words in service of the Word.

Where does the source of our writing originate? Is it simply that we do market research and find something that will sell? Market research is critical, but that does not produce writing that is both timely and timeless. The poet Robert Frost was often asked about the sources of his poems. He answered his questioners this way.

> A poem is never a put-up job, so to speak. It begins as a lump in the throat, a sense of wrong, a homesickness, a lovesickness. It is never a thought to begin with. It is at its best when it is a tantalizing vagueness. It finds its

thought and succeeds, or doesn't find it and comes to nothing. I suppose it finds it lying around with others not so much to its purpose in a more or less full mind.[13]

That lump in the throat or sense of wrong is like Jeremiah's fire in his bones and like Paul's "woe is me if I preach not the gospel." Christian writing will improve when our works are less commissioned by the market place and more compelled by the living God.

Passion—another name for love—gives writers not only a voice but also eyes and ears. Conventional wisdom says that love helps us overlook the faults in others. That is only half true. Love helps us genuinely see and hear other people. A very wise seminary professor wrote a book about preaching and said that preachers, like writers, must learn to see and hear. Pay attention to his council and substitute "writer" in place of "pastor" and "writes" instead of "preaches."

When a pastor preaches, he doesn't sell patent medicine; he writes prescriptions. Others may hurl epithets at the "wealthy" but the pastor knows a lonely and guilt-ridden man confused by the Bible's debate with itself over prosperity: Is prosperity a sign of God's favor or disfavor? Others may display knowledge of "poverty programs" but the pastor knows what a bitter thing it is to be somebody's Christmas project. He sees a boy resisting his mother's insistence that he wear the nice sweater that came in the charity basket. He can see the boy wear it until out of Mother's sight, but not at school out of fear that he may meet the original owner on the playground. There are conditions worse than being cold. Others may discuss "the problem of geriatrics" but the pastor has just come from the local rest home and he still sees worn checkerboards, faded bouquets, large print King James Bibles, stainless steel trays, and dim eyes staring at an empty parking lot reserved for visitors. Others may analyze "the trouble with the youth today" but the pastor sees a fuzzy-lipped boy,

awkward, noisy, wishing he were absent, not a man, not
a child, preoccupied with ideas that contradict his fourteen
years' severe judgment against the girls.[14]

Are you awake and seeing? There is little room for
theological Rip Van Winkles.

... And The Word Was God. ...

Writers are lovers and lovers are seers. That is what made
Jesus, the Word, so effective with words. He was passionate
about what he said, not that he shouted all the time but rather
that he was totally present in his encounters with people. Think
about his life as portrayed in the gospels.

Jesus was observant of everyday life. He communicated
with wit and humor, giving us pictures of religious leaders who
strained out gnats and swallowed a camel, and blind people
leading blind people. He turned potentially embarrassing
situations into object lessons through his repartee: a coin with
Caesar's image enabled him to teach the disciples to give to
Caesar the things that are Caesar's and to God the things that
are God's.

Jesus spun homey images: a woman looking for a lost
coin; a father waiting for a lost son. He collected pictures from
nature: the lilies of the field and the birds of the air are cared
for by God. He invested himself in the lives of individuals:
Zacchaeus the tax collector and Mary of Magdalene. He
borrowed from traditional wisdom and renewed its meaning:
"You have heard it said . . . but I say to you." He felt deeply
about life: he wept at the death of Lazarus and was angry with
the moneychangers in the temple.

When Jesus spoke, people listened. Mark 1:22 says, "The
people were amazed at his teaching, because he taught them
as one who had authority, not as the teachers of the law." The
word *authority* here is from the Greek *exousia*. *Ex* means "out
of" and *ousia* means "essence" or "inner reality." Jesus spoke

out of his inner reality.[15] His message was self-validating and authentic. Jesus never wrote anything that exists today, but his spoken words collected in the New Testament indicate a man who was alive at the center. He had imagination, wit, strong emotions, tender love, powerful language abilities, and an inviting personality. He is the model for Christians in general and for Christian writers in particular.

When all is said and done, what is Christian writing? Like all other writing, it strives for excellence. Christian writing communicates its vital message with metaphors. Its words are bouillon cubes which melt in the mind of the reader to provide concentrated nourishing sustenance. Its sentences are springs, coiled, compressed, and ready to spring loose in the reader's mind to produce surprise and effect. Its paragraphs are lozenges to dissolve slowly on the mental tongue to soothe and heal. Its pages are Jalapeno peppers that look harmless enough but after one bite the reader will know he has chomped down on something significant.

Like all writing, Christian writing strives to spin its tales to keep the reader's attention. We are like Scheherazade who told stories to a caliph who married many brides successively and had them beheaded the next day. Scheherazade told him such an enthralling and suspenseful story that the sultan stayed the execution a day so he could hear the end of the story. That went on night after night. Sheer interest in the story kept Scheherazade alive. Today readers can execute a writer with a yawn.

Christian writing aims to produce a "Rice Krispies" effect. We want our message to go "snap, crackle, and pop" in the minds of our readers. A writer succeeds when a reader says, "Hmm, I've never thought of it that way before," or "Well, I didn't know that," or even "I don't agree with this at all!" To jump-start the reader's brain is a worthy goal. Empty words will not do that. As Ecclesiastes 6:11 says, "The more the words, the less the meaning, and how does that profit anyone?"

Christian writing uses similes to hang pictures on the gallery of the mind. A writer is like a midwife struggling to assist in the birth of a new manner of conveying the Word. Or, the Christian writer is like a circus clown bringing joy, laughter, and humanity to a theater of absolute skills and death-defying stunts. Or again, the writer is like the sculptor Michelangelo who could look at a block of granite and see an angel. The writer can look at a blank page and see a story wanting to take shape and life.

The Christian writer is like a carpenter who crafts his structure piece-by-piece. The care and commitment to excellence is evident by the finished product. The Christian writer is like a star thrower. Anthropologist Loren Eisley was once walking along a beach where he saw people gathering shells. One man was collecting starfish that had washed up on the beach that night. Whenever he found one still alive the man would throw it back into the water. Eisley began to throw the starfish back, too. He said, "It was like sowing, the sowing of life." This is a picture of Christian writers: enablers of life rather than cataloguers of death. They offer hope, truth, and life rather than tragedy and destruction.

Christian writing is oxymoronic. An oxymoron is a figure of speech where an effect is created by a paradoxical coupling of terms. The world literally means "sharp fool." Christian writing is a romantic disenchantment. The imagined romantic life of a writer jetting off to exotic locations, working in a lavish office with the latest equipment, and living off fat royalty checks is tempered with the disenchantment of the reality. Writers would live far below the poverty line if we depended on royalties alone. We might take the bus across town if we can find the right change. Our office might be an ironing board in a corner of the pantry equipped with a #2 pencil and a Big Chief school tablet.

Christian writing is a boring challenge. We crank an 8-1/2 X 11-inch battle zone into the IBM Selectric or boot up

Microsoft Word on the Macintosh or scratch a Bic pen on loose leaf paper. Any of those actions creates anxiety and excitement. The writer knows that communicating by this medium can be challenging and boring at the same time. Writing is work and work can be drudgery. It can also be exhilarating as we discover things about ourselves and our world we never before imagined.

Christian writing is a contemporary anachronism. It seems out of date and out of sequence in time. Who talks of God anymore? Yet the question of God is never far from most people, even the outwardly nonreligious. The Christian writer poses the God question in many different ways, sometimes obliquely, sometimes overtly. It may be done like Max Lucado does it or like Walker Percy did it. But whatever the approach, the question of ultimate reality forms and informs our work.

Christian writing is a joyful tyranny. To be a writer is to be possessed by some inner need to write. This need can be tyrannical. Do "normal" people spend a fortune on writing equipment and resources? Do "normal" people stay up at all hours of the night punching the keyboard in the slight hope that someone may actually read their work? To be a writer can be a terrible joy. It holds terrors with one arm and lilting joy with the other. We writers are hugged with both arms at the same time. No wonder we can be a bit eccentric!

... In Him Was Life, And That Life Was the Light of Men. ...

Again, this chapter is not meant to construct a systematic theology of Christian writing. Rather, the idea was to take this diamond and turn it a bit to allow different facets of light to emerge. The basic conviction of Christianity is that Jesus is the light of the world. As light he forces out darkness and keeps the terrors of the night at bay. We who write are mere candles to this sun. But light is light, whether much or little.

To make our light shine we must overcome several attitudes and situations that strangle our writing. One attitude is a false stress on humility. There is an attitude among some Christians that goes something like this: "Jesus said to deny ourselves. But if I seek publication in my writing then I am promoting myself and thereby sinning." My answer to that? Hogwash! Any writer who thinks like this has some inner fantasy about becoming famous and then losing zeal for Christ. You can forget it. There is an almost infinitesimal chance you will become famous as a writer, so you can escape from this false humility. Even if you did, a Christian writer is a servant of the Word with words. But a servant is still a servant and there is no room for "stars" or "celebrities" among us. The recent televangelist scandals taught us this fact.

Another situation that hurts our writing is the non-connectional nature of our lives. Christian writers are not like Nashville songwriters. We do not gather in taverns to guzzle beer, swap stories, argue, posture, and write songs. We are not suggesting that we do so. We have churches and maybe even writers' clubs, but most writers work in isolation. Proverbs 27:17 says, "As iron sharpens iron, so one man sharpens another." I often wish for closer contact with others who share my interest in writing. My editor friends are greatly valued, but I see them irregularly. A good writers' conference is useful in breaking the sense of isolation and sharpening us.

Some writers are simply lazy. They will not hustle, sweat, study, write and re-write, pay the price of being a writer. Writing is not a dainty pastime. It is real work with real demands and rewards. We have friends who tell us they envy our work. But they could write also if they were willing to pay the price in time and energy. They want "to have written" and enjoy the finished product. They do not want to write and put up with the anxiety and sweat involved in the process.

Another attitude that affects some Christian writers is presumption. This comes from the person who says, "God will give me the message and write it for me." That is pure presumption. God gave us minds with which to think and bodies with which to write. God inspires and energizes us through his Spirit, but the work is left up to us. The late Red Smith once correctly said, "Sure, writing is easy. All you have to do is sit down and open a vein."

A narrow understanding of holiness holds back some Christian writers, and this is another attitude that strangles our writing. James 1:27 tells us to "keep oneself from being polluted by the world." We want to heed that warning, but what does it mean? Some Christians seem to think that they can avoid worldly pollution by simply being ignorant of life around them. If that is the case, what do they have to offer people? The trick is to be in the world but not of the world, to be aware of life and issues but not to be dragged down by attitudes and actions apart from God.

Playing loose with facts is another attitude that hurts Christian writers. One editor speaks of some Christians who speak and write "evangelastically."[16] Truth is not elastic and will not stretch. We are not referring here simply to making mistakes. Everyone does that. The point is that some writers feel free to disregard facts or to spin them in their favor. Others will not bother to check the accuracy of so-called facts before acting on them. One case in point is the supposed petition from Madeline Murray O'Hair to have religious broadcasting banned. For over a decade and a half, the Federal Communication Commission has received millions of letters protesting this atheistic intrusion. The only problem is that there is no such thing as the O'Hair petition. It never existed. It got started as a rumor and took on a life of its own. The Christian writer, of all people, must be accurate with facts and check things out. We can be creative and imaginative in our writing but we cannot invent truth or imagine facts.

Fear of failure holds back many Christian writers. They do not like rejection. If they never send out manuscripts they will never be rejected. But failing to try is a worse failure than trying and being turned down. Besides, we are in good company if our manuscripts seem like boomerangs that keep coming back. Successful people in all walks of life face rejection. Actor Dustin Hoffman was rejected four times from the Actors Studio before he finally made it through. Sidney Poitier was once thrown out of a theater group for black actors. Watercolorist Dong Kingman did not make it at The Oakland School of Painting, yet at a recent auction one of his watercolors outbid a Picasso. Sometimes writers face their own personal rejection. Anthony Burgess said he might revise a single page as many as twenty times before he gets it right. Ronald Dahl, the short story writer, said that by the time he nears the end of a story, the first part will have been reread and corrected as many as 150 times. Ernest Hemingway said that he rewrote the final chapter of *A Farewell to Arms* 39 times. One of your authors can speak to this matter from personal experience, for he once had a book manuscript turned down by 87 publishers. The 88th published it and it became a main co-selection by the Religious Book Club. Mark Twain was quite right when he said that "Writing is easy. All you have to do is cross out the wrong words." Accept rejection as a temporary setback but never quit.

So go ahead. Write. Seek publication. Be salt and light in this dark and decaying world. You will not get rich and famous (but if you do, remember us in your will). Give to others what Christ has given to you. The blessing is in the doing. Write. Right now.

ENDNOTES

[1]Theodore W. Jennings, Jr., *Introduction To Theology* (Philadelphia: Fortress Press, 1976), 6.

[2]Ibid., 7.

[3]This humorous list was published in *Parables*, (May 1990), 3.

[4]Carl F. H. Henry, quoted in a special mini-report, "Trends In The Church," from "National and International Religion Report," no date given.

[5]John Warwick Montgomery, "The Emperor's Clothes," in *Moody Monthly*, (April 1987), 10.

[6]"Doublespeak Tries to Sneak By," a Scripps Howard New Service story in *The Commercial Appeal*, (Memphis, July 4, 1988), A2.

[7]John Wesley, quoted in W. E. Sangster, *Power In Preaching* (London: The Epworth Press, 1958), 68.

[8]Don M. Aycock, *Walking Straight In A Crooked World* (Nashville: Broadman Press, 1986.)

[9]Coauthored by Don M. Aycock and Leonard George Goss. (Grand Rapids: Baker Book House, 1984).

[10]Sherwood Anderson, quoted by Charles L. Wallis, editor, *Speakers' Illustrations for Special Days* (New York: Abingdon Press, 1956), 55. The original source is Howard Mumford Jones, editor, *Letters of Sherwood Anderson* (Boston: Little, Brown & Company, n.d.).

[11]This tale of the Baal Shem Tov is told in many places. This one came from Martin E. Marty, *By Way of Response* (Nashville: Abingdon Press, 1981).

[12]J. B. Priestley, *Rain upon Godshill* (New York: Harper & Bros., 1939), 164.

[13]Robert Frost, in a letter to Louis Untermeyer, January 1, 1916, quoted in Stanley Burnshaw, *Robert Frost Himself* (New York: George Braziller, Inc., 1986), 282.

[14]Fred Craddock, *As One Without Authority*, revised edition (Enid, Okla.: The Phillips University Press, 1974), 82.

[15]If you are interested in reading more about this, consult chapter three in Don Aycock's *Eight Days That Changed The World* (Nashville: Broadman Press, 1990).

[16]Chip Bailey, "Editor's Notebook," *Remnant Christian Magazine*, (September 1990), 19.

2

THE CHALLENGE OF WRITING

Congratulations?

So you wish to write a book. We're not entirely sure whether to offer congratulations or condolences. Estimates are that should your book be published, it will compete against 60,000 titles and new editions published in the same year. Think of it—sixty thousand! Imagine how many manuscripts are submitted to publishers that never see the light of day. It boggles the mind.

But we writers are a strange breed. You are thinking, "Yea, I know the competition is stiff, but verily, mine won't be one of the rejected manuscripts. Surely mine *will* make it." We applaud your courage, tenacity, and slight craziness. (Anybody who wants to write a book is probably slightly crazy.) We have put this book together to help you realize that dream of seeing your book in print.

The Authors' Assumptions

We assume several things about you, the reader of this book. We assume first that you have something vital you want to say in the book you contemplate writing. Because yours is a religious book (or else why would you be reading this guide?), it can help people live more fulfilled, complete lives. Not long ago, religious books were seen as "fluff books"—usually dramatic conversions, celebrities' accounts of their "faith," or over-simplified approaches to difficult problems.

This situation is changing. Now do not get us wrong. We are not against all stories of celebrity conversions and so forth, even those which are badly written. It is just that the reading public's tastes are changing. They are demanding the cookies be put on higher shelves, in more quality books with sounder themes to help one think through issues and find real solutions. They want material with more substance and less fluff. You can deliver such books to publishers ready to develop, produce, and market them. The next section of this chapter expands this idea a little more.

A second assumption about you is that you want to share your vital message in a full book-length manuscript. You are willing to spend the hours of seemingly endless toil necessary for good writing. You are willing to give up watching your favorite television show, including Sunday afternoon football games, and put up with comments from family and friends like, "Aw, he's *only* writing a book." We devote little space in this guide trying to pique your interest in writing. If you lack interest, then do not waste your time reading this book for inspiration.

Our third notion about you is that you know the rudiments of English grammar, spelling, syntax, and all the other bits and pieces of information your high school English teacher kept saying you would need to know someday. That someday is now. If you need to refresh yourself, as we all occasionally do, go to a local library or bookstore and read one or two good primers on grammar. Writing styles are as individual as fingerprints, but certain guidelines do exist. Be sure to check out Chapter 10 of this book, for many very helpful titles appear in our selective bibliography under the "Grammar, Style, and Usage" section. You need to know the basic principles.

A fourth assumption about you is that you are interested in writing a nonfiction religious book. If you plan to work on the great American novel, or an Erma Bombeck-like book of humor, or "Ninety-Six Ways to Cure Hangnails," or books of other distinct genres, we are afraid this book will not be of much help to you. Obviously some overlap on pertinent writing clues can be found in all books on writing. Chapters on editors and contracts, for examples, would be helpful to others, and much of the other material besides, but the real focus here is on nonfiction religious books.

What About Religious Books?

The tastes and demands of a reading public change. The time was when books on religious themes were looked at with suspicion, both by many readers and by the publishing industry. More than one person suggested that subsidy publishers (or vanity presses—you pay them to publish your book) made money on books with religious subjects because so few in publishing would touch them. Referring to this type of publisher, one observer noted, "They offer a bland steady flow of essays that God is love, Nature is true, and in the long run, the Spirit triumphs."

This was mostly true, especially years ago. But times certainly change and even general publishers have found a reading public for religious books. Today, many religious books outsell non-religious titles. We are not referring to the poorly written banal tomes in which some subsidy publishers specialize. Well-written books with vital themes in religion have proven they have a place in the publishing world. Many larger commercial houses now have religious departments as part of their publishing programs. These lines of books are extremely successful. And dozens of highly professional firms specialize in publishing religious titles.

Sherwood E. Wirt, founding editor of *Decision* magazine, offers several resolutions for the would-be writer of religious material.[1] His suggestions would apply, of course, to any writer:

1. I will not write corn—banal, sentimental, obvious stuffy tripe.

2. I will either seek to write imaginatively, or I will not write.

3. I will not waste my time on insignificant material.

4. I will write to change lives, if I can.

5. I will politely ignore those who would flatter me.

6. I will write in quantity but strive for quality.

7. I will thankfully give whatever glory comes to God, who alone imparts all gifts, including this gift.

If we all adopted these resolutions, we would certainly improve on the writing of our books and avoid the common faults of book manuscripts. What are some of the faults? Consider these: The manuscript has no focus, no special reader in mind—it is directed at no one in particular; the manuscript is sloppy, showing a disrespect for writing, for the editor, and for the entire publishing process; the manuscript is sent to the wrong publishing house, showing a total lack of proper market research on the part of the writer; the manuscript does not cohere and is not logical; the idea of the manuscript is not timely; the apparatus (footnotes, etc.) is incomplete and inaccurate; the manuscript lacks a table of contents; and, an agent has not been helpful but has merely duplicated the work already done by the author.

At least knowing what faults to avoid will help get us started in the right direction. But now let us consider the actual process of writing religious books.

Writing: The Process

You have a great idea for a book. But you are asking yourself, "How do I get started?" and "Am I really sure I can do this?" Almost all writers ask these questions, so you are in good company.

Let us consider the counsel of several well-known and highly respected authors of nonfiction religious books. If we learn from their experiences we might be able to avoid some of the traps and pitfalls most writers face. There are other writers currently more popular than these listed here, and certainly of a more evangelical persuasion, but these writers have been chosen because of their fame while they were living, as well as the fact that their work has stood the test of time.

William Barclay

One of the best known religious authors of our time was the late William Barclay, a Scottish professor of divinity. Barclay wrote scores of important books during his career as teacher and writer. His books have sold into the millions, and they are still selling well among pastors and divinity students all over the world. Barclay's philosophy of writing was deceptively obvious. He said, "I can and do work."[2] In other words, he was willing to pay the price for writing. He quoted Collin Brooks who defined this process as follows: "The art of writing is the art of applying the seat of the pants to the seat of the chair." And he was not talking about the chair at the dinner table!

Barclay said he was influenced by his fellow Britisher, Winston Churchill. Churchill was a writer of incredible discipline. His multiple-volume history of the second world war attests to this fact. At his birthplace outside Oxford, England, Blenheim Palace, Churchill had an elaborate library and study. One can tell immediately that he took his writing seriously.

27

First-time authors sometimes do not take their writing seriously. But they can be assured that if they do not, no one else will. These writers are tempted to "wait for inspiration" before beginning. Perhaps they have never heard the dictum, "Good writing is ten percent inspiration and ninety percent perspiration." Someone once asked Churchill about inspiration, distractions, and other things that thwart an author's effort. His answer was typically pointed and slightly gruff:

> You've got to get over that. If you sit waiting for inspiration, you will sit waiting until you are an old man. Writing is like any other job—like marching an army, for instance. If you sit down and wait until the weather is fine, you won't get far with your troops. Kick yourself; irritate yourself; but write; it's the only way.

William Barclay learned his lesson well from his mentor. He worked hard at "applying the seat of the pants to the seat of the chair." Barclay's students well knew his work habits. Whenever he was not busy teaching classes or talking with his students about academic matters, he could be found at all times pounding on his typewriter. But, and his former students underscored this point, Barclay always had time for his students. As much as he worked at it, writing was not his god.

Other than tenacity, Barclay denied having any special gift for writing. In fact, he claimed never to have had an original thought in his life. He called himself a "pipeline" or a "theological middleman." He felt he could take the large bills of theology and philosophy and break them down into small change so average persons could understand. Of course, the ability to do this takes uncommon skill and superior talent and intellect. Because he was willing to do so, millions of people have benefited from the labor of William Barclay.

This brings us to a point that must be emphasized and re-emphasized—the person who wants to write must work extremely hard. One of the authors once queried an editor about a book he wanted to do. The editor answered immediately and said he was interested. He wanted to see three chapters, but they were not ready. When the author beat around the bush about them, that editor wrote a short, never-to-be-forgotten note. It said, "The only way to learn to write is to write. Well?"

Phillip J. Gearing and Evelyn V. Brunson have written a good book entitled *Breaking Into Print*. Their advice on the process of getting the words from your mind onto paper is worth considering:

> Writing demands self-discipline, so establish a daily routine that includes at least two hours to be applied to the material you are trying to produce. Many times you will sit down at the typewriter or with pen in hand thinking that you have nothing to put on paper today. But, as you sit in that writing attitude, you find yourself putting words on your paper, words you would have missed had you not kept to your routine.[3]

Norman Vincent Peale

Another well-known author of religious books was the late Norman Vincent Peale, former pastor of the Marble Collegiate Church in New York City. Like most successful authors, Peale had established a routine for his writing.

> I can do much better in the morning. I'm fresher. I can stick at it for a longer period of time, and my energies seem to be at a maximum. So, what I like to do when I'm writing a book, is to get out of bed at six o'clock, get dressed, have breakfast, and get everything out of the way so I can start working at seven o'clock.
>
> I write in longhand. In fact, I write every single word myself with a pencil. I use plain white paper and have perhaps a couple dozen pencils lined up, all sharpened. I

write with one until it is worn down and then throw it aside and write with another, and finally I pick them all up, sharpen them again, and then start wearing them down again. I sharpen them myself with an electric sharpener.

After I've written two to three thousand words I go through the penciled copy and mark it up. Sometimes it looks pretty terrible. Then, when I can't read it any more myself, because it is so marked up, I have it typed. I then go over the typed copy once; I may take out some material or put more in. The copy turns out to be fairly clean after the first typing, as a rule, because the major revision has been in the penciled work.[4]

Peale offered this advice to would-be authors:

I get manuscripts or several chapters from people who want to write books. In many cases, they just do not know how to go about it. They do not put it together properly. They do not build an orderly outline. They seem lacking in the ability of getting the interest of the reader with the opening paragraphs, the attention getters and so forth.

They do not dramatize their material. You've got to make it so it attracts and holds the reader's interest. Sustained interest is a hard thing to achieve. Even the brightest person in the world can't hold to the same subject for too long a time.

Peale further advised aspiring authors to forget striving for literary effect. Say what you have to say in the simplest and most interesting way and then end. Avoid wordiness.

Dr. Peale learned his writing style by serving as a newspaper reporter before becoming a minister. He thus learned the art of working at a steady pace, putting people into his material, and being concise. Apparently he learned his lesson well. Besides selling in the millions, his books have been responsible for helping countless readers live through crises and find fulfillment in their lives.

Harry Emerson Fosdick

The name Harry Emerson Fosdick is recognized by tens of thousands as one of the most theologically creative ministers of the twentieth century. But Fosdick was also a prolific author, and like those already mentioned, he worked with a steady routine. He discussed the process of writing one of his bestsellers, *The Meaning of Prayer*:

> It started with a series of sermons, went on to a series of midweek discussions where I could get the questions, objections and difficulties of the people, and then in an abandoned cottage on the Maine coast, near our summer home, I sat down daily for two months at a rickety kitchen table in a bare room and wrote the book. When I sent the manuscript to the publishers, I told them that a book on prayer could not expect a large sale and that I thought two thousand copies would be adequate. I guessed wrong that time.[5]

Fosdick was a master at understatement. That book he wrote at the rickety kitchen table sold over a million copies and has been translated into seventeen languages. He learned discipline early in his career, and this discipline paid off during his many busy years as Senior Minister of the Riverside Church in New York City.

Elton Trueblood

Another author will help us understand, at least partially, the process of getting started on the right foot and of working steadily. That author is the late Elton Trueblood. Like the other men mentioned above, Trueblood wrote extensively. Besides once serving as editor of a religious journal, Dr. Trueblood also wrote thirty-one books. Many of these are still in print.

In his autobiography, *While It Is Day*, Trueblood tells of his writing program and habits. As with the previous authors, we will allow him to describe his own work:

> In my case all is done longhand with a fountain pen, with ink that flows effortlessly. By this method I avoid the mechanics of the typewriter, and the speed of the pen seems to match the speed of my mind. Writing all morning in this fashion, I can without strain produce two thousand five hundred words. Because unbroken speed helps to create smoothness of style, I make only a minimum of corrections as I produce the first draft. Later, of course, especially after the chapters are typed, I substitute, delete, and add to my hearts content. But it is the original writing which is both exhilarating and energy-consuming![6]

Many authors like "to have written," that is, to be finished with the project, see their name in print, and to get the royalty check. Trueblood, however, enjoyed the actual writing process and described it as follows:

> I should like to convey to my readers something of the joy of writing which I regularly experience. The very act of writing can be remarkably creative. When I sit down with paper in front of me, I know in general what I want to say, but I seldom know the details. As the ideas are expressed in written form, however, they begin to grow and to develop by their own inherent logic. Always I am a bit surprised by what has been written, for I have become in some sense an instrument.

Trueblood was a morning person, at his mental energy peak early in the day. Thus he did his writing in the mornings only and used the afternoons and evenings for editing and re-writing. This is not to say he never wrote in the afternoons. As he put it, ". . . the author who takes his profession seriously will expect to be invaded by ideas at all times. . . . The important thing, then, is never to be without pen and paper, for the ideas are as fugitive as they are precious."

We must remember that Trueblood was also a busy professor at Earlham College in Richmond, Indiana, at the same time he was doing most of his writing. How did he handle the responsibilities? Again, his counsel from his own words:

> A public man, though he is necessarily available at many times, must learn to hide. If he is always available, he is not worth enough when he *is* available. I once wrote a chapter in the Cincinnati Union Station, but that was itself a form of hiding because nobody knew who the man with the writing pad was. Consequently nobody approached me during five wonderful hours until the departure of the next train for Richmond. We must use the time which we have because even at best there is never enough.

Consensus

When we take the experiences of William Barclay, Norman Vincent Peale, Harry Emerson Fosdick, and Elton Trueblood, and then add them together factoring in their advice to new writers, what do we get?

First, if you are serious about writing, you must write. This sounds absurdly obvious, but many people miss it. The only way to get experience is to get experience.

Second, you need a quiet, private place where you can write. Not everyone has the luxury of owning a lavish private office or cabin by the beach. But almost everyone can find some space to call his or her own, at least for an hour or two. Your family will understand and, if requested, learn to leave you alone for awhile.

Third, develop a routine that is right for you. You may not even feel awake until noon. If so, then trying to write in the mornings will be frustrating and futile. Find what time of day or night is best for you and work creatively. Line up the tools that best suit your needs. For example, can you write better with a typewriter or a computer, or, like Peale and Trueblood, do you need to write everything in longhand? Perhaps you can do both. Most books on writing suggest the use of a typewriter or computer because it is faster than writing with a pencil.

Fourth, be willing to revise and edit your own work. It can always be better. Your words can be expanded, rearranged, or even deleted without the universe suffering irreparable damage. Too many religious writers have the notion that inspired writing is writing *directly* inspired by God, and therefore requires no editing. God *does* inspire writers with the divine creative nudge. But this does not negate the necessity to edit and rewrite serious work. If your work actually has been inspired, if you want it to count for something, then you must handle it as a sacred trust and polish it to a fine edge.

By now you see really how hard writing books can be. At the same time, you should also see what joy writing can add to your life.

Writing For Quantity

Let us give you some statistics that might possibly shock you, but we hope they will also inspire you when you think about cranking out a book or two.[7]

Charles Hamilton, alias Frank Richards, creator of "Billy Bunter," averaged writing 80,000 words a week. This is about 320 pages per week, or sixty-four pages daily.

Georges Simenon, a Belgian writer and creator of "Inspector Maigret," wrote a 200-page novel in eight days. From 1919 to 1973 he wrote 214 novels under his own name and 300 others under nineteen other pen names. His books, including many translations, sold 300 million copies.

John Creasey wrote 564 books in his lifetime. Once, he wrote two books in six and a half days.

Earle Stanley Gardner had 140 titles of his books published. Over 170 million copies sold.

Ursula Bloom published 468 full-length books from 1922 to 1972. That is an average of more than nine per year.

Walter Gibson, creator of "The Shadow," wrote 283 "Shadow" novels. He did it in seven consecutive years, writing one novel every two weeks. That equals about 120 finished pages each week.

Agatha Christie wrote 85 books, 17 plays, 15 films, and over 100 short stories.

Michael Avallone wrote 184 novels from 1953 to 1980, with over 40 million copies being in print. He once finished a novel in one and a half days.

If you feel more depressed than inspired by such statistics, do not feel alone. Most writers will feel the same way until they reassess their own writing goals. We are not necessarily to produce a plethora of novels and short stories. At least some of us are concerned for nonfiction that takes research and planning. Many writers would rather produce a few quality titles than a glut of mediocre books. Not much polish and revision goes into a book that is written in a day and a half.

The purpose for our giving these statistics is only to point out that you can write a book if you really want to. We know. The kids are crying; the phone is ringing; the relatives are coming for a visit; your stack of work from the office is piled up nearly to the sky. . . . The list is endless. But think about it this way. If you produce just one worthy typewritten page per day for two hundred days, then you will have a two-hundred page book in about six and a half months. Put that way, that doesn't sound so hard, does it?

ENDNOTES

[1]Sherwood E. Wirt, with Ruth McKinney, *You Can Tell The World*, (Minneapolis: Augsburg Publishing House, 1975), 22.

[2]William Barclay, *William Barclay: A Spiritual Autobiography* (Grand Rapids: William E. Eerdmans, 1975), 28.

[3]Philip H. Gearing and Evelyn V. Brunson, *Breaking Into Print* (Englewood Cliffs, N.J.: Prentice-Hall, 1977), 49.

[4]Norman Vincent Peale, in Ralph Daigh, *Maybe You Should Write A Book* (Englewood Cliffs, N.J.: Prentice-Hall, 1977), 157ff.

[5]Harry Emerson Fosdick, *The Living Of These Days* (New York: Harper & Row, 1956), 91.

[6]Elton Trueblood, *While It Is Day: An Autobiography* (New York: Harper & Row, 1974), 64.

[7]These statistics were compiled by A. "Doc" Shepherd in *The Christian's Writing and Self-Publishing Newsletter*, Vol. 1, No. 1, 4.

3

HOW TO GET AND PRESERVE IDEAS

Mark Twain once wrote to a friend, "Take your mind out and dance on it. It's getting all caked up." Unfortunately, that terrible malady was not limited to Twain's time. We all get crusted up on occasion and must take the necessary time and effort to clear up our minds. Without doing so, we will be like ocean-going ships that get slowed down by the accretions of barnacles on their hulls. There, too, periodic scraping is in order.

Boredom and tedium are two barnacles of the mind slowing the flow of ideas and curtailing creativity. The writer must want to clear them away in order to produce the best writing possible. You, the reader, want to produce a book. You may already have an idea about want you want to say, but that idea might not be at all clear and sharply focused. In this chapter we wish to assist you in getting ideas, working creatively with those ideas, and preserving them for your writing.

Use Your Imagination

To say "use your imagination" to a writer is like saying "Don't worry" to a neurotic. The obvious question is "Yes, but how?" Being creative and imaginative is no easy task for most of us. We are taught to think in certain patterns and forms. Education often teaches us what to think, but not always how to think. We can be like racing horses, fitted with blinders to see only straight ahead. Certainly the mind can be thus fitted. What we want to do, then, is remove those blinders and loose our imaginations. We want to "uncake" them.

A correct assessment from David Campbell is that "creativity demands commitment. To change one's life even in a small way requires energy, participation, and enthusiasm. You cannot be creative while inert. You have to get involved."[1] One's first reaction might be to say, "But I don't have any creativity." That is not so, for we all do. We use our creativity whenever we write anything. Some use the facility obviously more than others, but we all have it. The trick is to learn how to use it.

Understanding Creativity

What is the creative imagination? This question fascinates researchers and philosophers alike. We know the answer when we see it; we know a creative person when we see one. But even then, getting a handle on that elusive quality of creativity is difficult. The famed psychologist Rollo May devoted much attention to this issue in a book no writer should be without, even religious writers. Entitled *The Courage To Create*, this celebrated book explores creativity and how to use it. In that book May defines creativity as "the encounter of the intensively conscious human being with his or her world."[2] The creative person's will, passion, and commitment to his or her subject is part of this encounter. While we may not be able to will creativity, May assures us that "we can will to give ourselves to the encounter with intensity of dedication and commitment. The deeper aspects of awareness are activated to the extent that the person is committed to the encounter" (p. 46). In other words, you are far more likely to be creative if you are absorbed by, enthralled, and caught up in your writing than if you merely dabble with a topic of marginal interest.

May teaches that when persons are creative, they are representing the highest degree of emotional health. They are therefore "actualizing" themselves. The writer, for example, faces the wilderness of a blank sheet of paper. He accepts the challenge to conquer it; he throws all of himself into the task. Mind, will, imagination, and reason all join forces to slay the dragon of the blank page. The writer tames chaos to make cosmos, that is, order, form, and reason. May speaks of this process in his own writing:

> I prefer, therefore, to endure the chaos, to face "complexity and perplexity" as Barron puts it. Then I am impelled by this chaos to seek order, to struggle with it until I can find a deeper, underlying form. I believe I am then engaged in what MacLeish describes as a struggling with the meaninglessness and silence of the world until I can force it to mean, until I can make the silence answer and the non-being be (p. 108).

We do not suggest, in quoting May, that he wrote from any traditional religious perspective. But we are talking about imagination, a subject on which May can inform any writer. To write like this, using one's imagination, calls for more strength and determination than is popularly supposed. It requires, as May puts it, actual courage. He defines courage as "the capacity to move ahead in spite of despair" (p. 3). He places it in context as follows: "Courage is not a virtue or value among other personal values like love and fidelity. It is the foundation that underlies and gives reality to all other virtues and personal values. Without courage our love pales into mere dependency. Without courage our fidelity becomes conformism" (p. 4).

You, as a writer, must have the courage to create, to bring something significant from nothing. You must throw yourself into writing with verve and force. You must use language to express your very soul. W. H. Auden once remarked, "The poet marries the language, and out of this marriage the poem is born." Isn't this the way *all* good writing finds life?

Cultivating Imagination

The ability to use the imagination in your writing, like any other ability, can be strengthened and improved. Listed below are fifteen ideas and techniques you can use to great advantage in improving your imaginative capabilities:

1. Commune with God's nature. Spend some time outdoors, even if it is only in a park during your lunch break. Watch carefully the sights, paying attention to color, texture, movement, and dimension. Listen to the cacophony of sounds. Try to feel the many things which interest you.

2. Read the best books available. Good reading always stimulates the imagination and teaches techniques for using it. Do not read in only one area and certainly avoid only contemporary works. Meet the great writers face to face. Spread out and read the classics.[3]

3. Develop devout contemplation. Learn to take time simply to think about things. Set aside designated periods of each day to listen to the inner dialogue going on inside you.

4. Remember to keep within the limit of fact. Do not allow your imagination to supply factual information. We know of one graduate student who made up a scholar to

corroborate his research. This is going far beyond the realm of cultivating a healthy imagination.

5. Be perceptive at all times. You will have to work on this one. Specified contemplative times are great, but if you keep your eyes and ears open you will be aware of all sorts of ideas and impressions continually flooding your senses.

6. Study suitable literature dealing with those specific subjects on which you work. The goal here is to feed the mind factual data and to suggest ideas for working with your subject. There will be times when you will subconsciously incorporate much of what you read. It will then emerge in new and different forms from your subconscious imagination. It will then be uniquely yours.

7. Take sufficient time to work through the material so it can be incorporated into your subconscious mind. Researchers who study the phenomenon of the imagination say that one must feed the mind but then allow time for "incubation" as the material matures. This may take days, or even years.

8. Have an abundance of your subject material on hand. This will save your frustration in having to hunt it down when you begin to get ideas and start to work.

9. Have a sufficiently difficult problem, one which challenges the intellect. If you are going to spend a large amount of time writing a book, shouldn't you be supremely interested in working with a challenging topic?

10. Try to remain optimistic about your subject. The imagination thrives on optimism.

11. Keep a sense of humor. This helps avoid the frustration that thwarts creativity.

12. Endeavor to keep your motivation high. Without it, creative imagination will wane.

13. Be patient. Remember, you get the chicken by hatching, not smashing the egg.

14. Try to maintain your peace of mind. Your imagination cannot function well if your mind is filled with all sorts of worries. Remember Mark Twain's reflection: "I've had many troubles in my life, but most of them never happened." No words offer greater counsel against worry than Matthew 6:25-34. Read and reread them.

15. Keep physically fit. A lazy body produces a lazy mind.

These ideas will help you begin developing your imagination. You simply *must* do it. W. MacNeile Dixon reminded us a half century ago that the human mind is not a debating hall but a picture gallery. Today's writers must hang pictures on the walls of that gallery. Imagination is the paint and creativity is the brush for our work.[4]

The Imagination in Writing

A little poem speaks to a function of the imagination in writing:

> Biting my truant pen,
>> Beating myself for spite,
> Fool, said my muse to me,
>> Look in thy heart and write.

Our imaginations help us look into the heart. We can get inside ourselves, and, through imaginative thought, into the mind and heart of someone else. One author sketched this process of introspection as follows:

> Writing, like life itself, is a voyage of discovery. The adventure is a metaphysical one: it is a way of approaching life indirectly, of acquiring a total rather than partial view of the universe. The writer lives between the upper and lower worlds: he takes the path in order eventually to become the path himself.
>
> I began in absolute chaos and darkness, in a bog or swamp of ideas and emotions and experiences. Even now I do not consider myself a writer, in the ordinary sense of the word. I am a man telling the story of his life, a process which appears more and more inexhaustible as I go on.[5]

This chapter is about ideas. What we are saying is that our imaginations and creative interactions with ourselves and our world are the best sources of ideas for our writing. As Virginia Wolf once observed, "Odd how the creative power at once brings the whole universe to order." As writers we seek this wholeness, both in ourselves and in our external worlds.

The wise writer will therefore tap the energy of the creative imagination and make an ally of his subconscious mind. Stuart Cloete described the benefits of this latter task:

> The front of your mind is continually drifting about—prying into what your intentions are toward unpaid bills, and deciding whether you're hungry or not hungry, and thinking up clever little lines to answer the argument that was ended last night. Meanwhile your subconscious is slogging along trying to complete the job that your conscious mind is hindering.[6]

Playwright J. B. Priestley spoke of this as his being able to "tap a reservoir of creative energy and skill, which reservoir is really the source of all so-called inspiration.'"[7] To tap this reservoir, the writer must toil like a miner under a landslide, as someone put it.

You might be thinking that creative work can be done only under "ideal" conditions, with everything approaching perfection. Listen to H. V. Morton's ideas as he described such a place.

> What a haven of rest! It is the place which women friends instantly declare the perfect spot for any writer of their acquaintance to "settle in" and produce a book. As I looked at the veranda, the eucalyptus trees and the sunlight, and as I listened, hearing only a mule going past on the road and a bird singing in the tree, I could imagine the sound of those decisive, ringing tones that have plagued many a man's souls: "What a lovely place to settle down and write—so quiet, so peaceful, nothing to distract you. . . ." And, flinging myself into the basket chair, I apostrophized the misunderstanding shade: "Madam," I said, "it has been proved time and again that the perfect place for a writer is in the hideous roar of a city, with men making a new road under his window in competition with a barrel organ, and on the mat a man writing for the rent."[8]

You will find rewards concomitant with the exercising of your imagination in writing. Some of these rewards include your gaining a new sense of creation. You also gain a new sense of freedom, along with a sense of self-worth and identity. When you write creatively, you simply know that you have peeled the veneer off reality, studied its contents, and described it for your readers.

We have been referring to the fact that creative writing is better for you, the author. It is also better for your readers. You can move the person reading your words when those words are imaginatively written far more than you can with pedestrian writing. Consider the two examples of writing styles given below and see which one stirs your own imagination and engages your will.

Example 1:

Everybody can agree that poverty is a blight on the American consciousness. "How," we collectively ask ourselves, "can we call ourselves a land of plenty and of caring, and yet allow people to live on such meager incomes?"

This question is not unique nor is it new. As far back as the eighteenth century we can find traces of various organizations whose *raison d'etre* was to alleviate the suffering of the unfortunate denizens of urban ghettos and rural slums.

Example 2:

What is poverty?

Let us be very specific and precise. It is of the senses.

Poverty is a smell. It is the cooking smell of old grease used and re-used, saturated into clothes and hair and rotting upholstery; the sleeping smell of beds crowded with ill-nourished bodies, and threadbare blankets soaked with odors of sickness and staleness.

Poverty is a sound. It is the sound of perpetual crying: an infant mewling, a mother mourning, an old man moaning. The sound is of shrieks in the night, noise the day long. Shuffling feet, hacking coughs, rustling vermin, insistent leaks and drips and crackings.

Poverty is a sight. It is the sight of slumped shoulders, useless hands stuffed into empty pockets, averted eyes. The scene is of land ill-used—barren, blasted, junk-strewn wasteland—or of streets that are blighted wilderness of asphalt, brick, steel, and random-blowing trash.

Poverty is a feeling—through the pores. . . on the feet. Cold so sharp it burns and heat so sweltering and oppressive it chills with a clammy sweat. The feeling of poverty is dull aches, twinges, pangs, brief satisfactions, creeping numbness. Pain.

Poverty is a taste. It is the taste of hot saliva boiling into the mouth before nausea, or dried beans and chicken gizzards and hog skins and too many starches and too few fruits. Stale bread and spoiling vegetables, cheap coffee and the sweet momentary fizz of soft drinks that allay but do not alleviate hunger pangs.

But poverty is more than the sum of its physical parts. It is not only hunger today but fear of tomorrow. Not only present chill but future freeze. Not only daily discomfort but accumulations of illness. It is fear, but fear made impotent by the enormity of today's demands and an insufficiency of energy to forestall tomorrow's defeats.[9]

Is there any doubt about which piece is the more creative and moving?

Write From Experience

We have been thinking about the imagination as a source of ideas for writing. Your own experience is also an excellent source. This does not rule out the creative use of those experiences. You might think that your experiences are not unique or in any way exciting. You have never been to Paris, do not have a Ph.D. degree, nor have you had a life-threatening illness. Understand that these or similar situations are not necessary ingredients for experiential writing. What is necessary are unique individual experiences, and being true to those experiences.

Helen Hull believes that the universality of our common experiences makes excellent material for writing. She couched her argument as follows.

The writer may refuse to see and to accept the limitations and the scope of his imagination. He finds his own material commonplace and thinks to escape its dullness by flights into more romantic, farther fields, taking passage on what he calls imagination. He does not trust his own experience, he does not value it; he does not know that within that experience, provided he can penetrate deeply enough, he possesses on the one hand all that he can achieve of originality in creative work, and on the other all he can know of universality.[10]

Did you catch that phrase, "He does not trust his own experience"? That is a problem many "average" writers have. We feel that if we could just do something special or travel to some exotic spot, then we could really write. But consider one more author's opinion about the uniqueness and trustworthiness of our individual experiences.

To have learned through enthusiasms and sorrow what things are within and without the self that make for more life or less, for fruitfulness or sterility; to hold to the one and eschew the other; to seek, to persuade, to reveal, and convince; to be ready to readjust one's values at the summons of a new truth that is known and felt; to be unweary in learning to discriminate more sharply between the false and the true, the trivial and significant, in life and in men and in works; to be prepared to take a risk for the finer and the better things,—that is perhaps all we can do. Yet somehow as I write, the words "perhaps all we can do" seem a very meager phrase. The endeavor to be true to experience strikes me at this moment as the most precious privilege of all.[11]

"The endeavor to be true to experience"—there it is again. Experience is the key to good writing. This is true especially of religious books. Religion is as much a matter of the heart as of the head. One's total life experience is involved. Let us give you some personal examples.

Seminary students usually find little devotional material designed for the unique needs of budding theologians. One of the authors and his wife began writing prayers/poems for themselves. In them they tried to express their feelings and hopes, along with their frustrations. Even the slightly tongue-in-cheek title of the collection was chosen to reflect that experience, *Not Quite Heaven*.[12] Consider some of the following thoughts:

GRADES
2 Thessalonians 3:5

A "B-"?!
But it can't be!
    I worked so hard and studied so long.
    The grader is crazy.
    The professor is nuts.
But any idiot can clearly see that this is an "A" exam.
I know that I forgot to include the dates, but that's not important.
Did I really spell "religious" wrong?

Sometimes I feel that I'm flunking the real test—life.
    You're a real hard grader, Lord.
And there is never a chance for a makeup. It's a strange fact though:
somehow we all pass.

LAUNDRY
Numbers 16:9

"It toileth not, neither doth it spin."
Read the sign on the broken washing machine.

Seems life here is many times like the laundry—
    Hot
    Wrinkled
    Waiting for a chance for a washer or dryer.
Eureka! At last!
    —darn, no change.
Decisions, decisions—do you dump out someone's clothes, or do you exercise patience?
Lord,
Help us love the person who uses the dryer for two hours for three towels. Amen.

The lesson here is that anyone can write from their personal circumstances, whatever they are. That same author got great mileage out of his studies for a professional degree. After completing the required thesis, he published it, and then compiled an anthology for publication of the materials from his thesis study.[13] Since he was a pastor at the time, he often saw people who were apathetic about church membership and involvement. He sought literature designed to tell him how to help these people, but found very little. As a result, he called several professor friends and said, "Let's do a book together on this subject." Several long sessions of brainstorming and critiquing each other's work produced a book.[14]

Other examples are when the same author preached a series of sermons on Jesus' use of concrete items and situations to teach spiritual lessons. This was later expanded into essays which produced another book for publication. Two other series on Lent and Holy Week were produced in book form and also published.[15] This book itself is the result of our experiences in writing and publishing. We have learned a good deal about the technical side of writing, editing, and publishing. We are just using our experience as a source for our writing. If we did not trust our own experiences, we would have little to say.[16]

We have already mentioned Harry Emerson Fosdick. He drew from his own experiences to produce many of his books. He wanted to know more about immortality, so he put all his questions and observations into an orderly arrangement, and then announced to his church that he would begin preaching evening sermons on the subject. He turned these sermons into one of his most popular books, *The Assurance of Immortality*. As a counselor, Fosdick was also well-known. He used his counseling experiences as grist for his mill. The essence of his experience in the counseling field, including the stories of human need that he personally experienced, was published as *On Being a Real Person*.

Harry Neal provides another example. He said he once happened to see a street meeting of the Salvation Army in New York City. He began to wonder what made these people tick. He wanted to know who they really were, so he began to interview members of the Army and to do research into their origins and goals. The result was a captivating history of the movement, *The Hallelujah Army*.

Many people have an interest in trying to write a book. Call it creative impulse or whatever you like, but everyone seems to say at one time or another, "You know, I think I'd like to write something one of these days." How strange and even frightening the publishing business can appear to would-be writers, as though publishers and those who work for them are like monsters in the entrance of a cave. But people who work in publishing are not as fearsome as all that, and they are always looking for new writers. One thing we have learned is that if a first-time writer can write reasonably well and has something to say that is said intelligibly, there is no reason that writer cannot be published.

If you keep your eyes open and your mind in gear, you will have plenty of experiences suggesting ideas for books. Using your creative imagination and personal experience are essential, but do not rule out two other equal essentials: interest and research. You may simply have a strong interest in language study, for example. That might help you master Greek and Hebrew, which could help you write in the area of biblical exposition. You may enjoy getting to know famous persons, so your area might be interviewing. You can extensively research whatever area of interest you have, and become an "expert." Chapter 8 has more information about research methodology.

Preserving Ideas

Some unpublished writers wonder how to keep up with the various ideas they might get for books. If you ask ten different experienced authors how they do it, you will without doubt get ten different ideas. Some authors jot everything down in notebooks. If they are weeding a garden, for instance, and an idea strikes them, they lay down the hoe and immediately record the idea. These people always carry a pen and pad. The memory is often faulty and an idea once forgotten is usually gone forever.

You must choose a method that works for you. The authors of this book almost always carry pens and pocketsize notebooks. Anything that seems unique gets recorded. One might overhear a conversation illustrating a problem common to many people. A particularly strange or in some way unique event may occur. Perhaps a quotation or other thought worthy of keeping leaps out. When they get back to their individual studies, they rewrite the event or comment or observation on a 8-1/2 x 11 piece of paper and file it for future reference.

Since both of the authors speak or preach regularly, this has forced them to be alert for any possibilities for sermons or speaking illustrations. In this regard they have developed their separate filing systems which are simple and efficient. Each writer needs to develop a system that will work for them. One way to file is to have a folder for every topic. For example, someone using this kind of system might have a file on "family," one on "the future," and so on. This is all right, but it can get rather bulky.

Many use a central index on 3 x 5 cards. Whenever there is a newspaper clipping or anything else to file, one simply goes to the file index, makes a note of the clipping under the appropriate category, and then marks a file number on the clipping and drops it in a file folder. This filing system uses a continuous numbering system. The first folder is numbered 1-25. The contents may hold twenty-five different subjects. The second folder is 26-50, and so on. The key to the system is the index box. Everything going into a folder is assigned a number. If, for example, you have an article on infant care, go to the folder presently in use. You might see that the last item there has the number GF 213. This indicates general file 213. Get a 3 x 5 card under the heading "BABY" and make a notation of what the article is about, and then assign it a number. Since the last item filed was 213, this new article is 214. Then write that number on the upper left corner of the article and drop it into the file.

In preparing the writing of this particular chapter, index cards were consulted to see what was under the topic "imagination." On the card was GF 12, GF 64, GF 72, GF 101, and several references to books previously read on the subject along with new ones to consult. The files were pulled and the books were examined or reexamined. A large amount of material was at hand, material that had been cross-indexed under "creativity."

This system is not by any means new. You can read about it in various books.[17] Anything is better then keeping clippings in a shoe box! This system will serve you well, and allow you to constantly expand your files with good, fresh material on many topics. On the other hand you may find this method of filing and keeping your notes organized totally inappropriate for your needs. Find whatever works for you and use it. Filing takes time, but in the long run it saves time.

Christopher Morely once wrote, "It was a good day to fly a kite. I didn't have a kite so I went out and flew my mind." That is really remarkable advice for the creative writer. Dance on your mind, fly it as a kite, unfold it on regular intervals just as skydivers do with their parachutes. Ideas will roll forth like water over Niagara.

ENDNOTES

[1]David Campbell, *Take The Road to Creativity And Get Off Your Dead End* (Niles, Ill.: Argus Communications, 1977), 7.

[2] Rollo May, *The Courage To Create* (New York: Bantam Books, 1976), 56.

[3]The mistaken preference for the more modern books is brilliantly addressed by C. S. Lewis in his "Introduction" to Sister Penelope Lawson's translation of *St. Athanasius On The Incarnation* (New York: Macmillan Publishing Company, 1981).

[4]The relationship between theology and imagination has been the subject of much scholarly research over the past decade. For an introduction to the subject, see the Th.D. dissertation by Don M. Aycock, *Religious Imagination in 20th-Century American Theology: A Study of Four Representative Figures* (New Orleans: New Orleans Baptist Theological Seminary, 1986).

[5]Henry Miller, quoted in *The Choice is Always Ours* (Wheaton, Ill.: Quest Books, 1975), 342.

[6]Stuart Cloete, quoted in *In the Minister's Workshop,* by Halford E. Luccock (Nashville: Abingdon Press, 1944), 205.

[7]Priestly quoted in *In the Minister's Workshop*, 206.

[8]Morton quoted in *In the Minister's Workshop*, 211.

[9]Wilma Dykeman, *Prophet of Plenty* (Knoxville: The University of Tennessee Press, 1966), 1-4.

[10]Helen Hull, *The Writer's Book*, (New York: Barnes & Noble, Inc., 1956), 40.

[11]John Middleton Murry, quoted in *The Choice Is Always Ours*, 393.

[12]Don and Carla Aycock, *Not Quite Heaven* (Lima, Ohio: C.S.S. Publishing Company, 1981), 8, 14.

[13]Don M. Aycock, *The E. Y. Mullins Lectures On Preaching* (Washington, D.C.: University Press of America, 1980). And, Don M. Aycock, ed. *Preaching With Purpose and Power: Selected Mullins Lectures* (Macon, Ga.: Mercer University Press, 1982).

[14]*Apathy In The Pew: Ministering To The Uninvolved* (North Brunswick, NJ: Bridge-Logos Publishers, 1990).

[15]Don M. Aycock, *Symbols of Salvation* (Nashville: Broadman Press, 1982); *Eight Days That Changed the World* (Nashville: Broadman Press, 1990); and, *God's Most Unmistakable Message* (Lima, Ohio: C.S.S. Publishing Company, 1994).

[16]Another book that is the result of our experiences in writing and publishing is Leonard George Goss and Don M. Aycock, *Inside Religious Publishing: A Look Behind the Scenes* (Grand Rapids: Zondervan Publishing House, 1991). Yet another is Don M. Aycock and Leonard George Goss, *Writing Religiously: A Guide to Writing Nonfiction Religious Books* (Grand Rapids: Baker Book House, 1984).

[17]The book that explained this system to the authors is Paul Gericke, *The Minister's Filing System* (Grand Rapids: Baker Book House, 1971.)

4

GETTING IT ALL ON PAPER

An editor at a well-known publishing house once advised his authors to "Work hard, type neatly, consult the dictionary, pay heed to grammar, and don't write in the hope of making money or becoming famous, but because you are compelled to write."[1] Being compelled to write by some inner drive is laudable, but even a writer so compelled still faces the mundane question, "How do I get it all on paper?" No one can offer an exact formula for "getting it all on paper." But we can suggest some guidelines to follow and traps to avoid so you do not have to preface your works as Edward Gibbon (1737-1794) once did: "Unprovided with original learning, unformed in the habits of thinking, unskilled in the arts of composition, I resolved to write a book.'"[2]

Mechanics

Writing is not nearly so mysterious as it is mechanical. Logic and form lie behind the presentation of ideas via words. Your task, as an author, is to find that logic and form and to use them as vehicles for your thoughts. How is this done? Of course you have to have a central idea first. Most nonfiction books center around a theme or a topic. Many inexperienced writers forget this fact and put down on paper virtually any ideas that come to them, seemingly in a random fashion. They then call the end result a book. But it is much too loose and unorganized to be considered a unified piece of writing.

Sherman R. Hanson, longtime editor of the former Bethany Press, has said that "the major problem with most beginning religion writers is their assumption that if their work has a pious sound, it is publishable. To do worthwhile writing in this field people must study and think critically; their writing must show evidence of responsible work in ecclesiological and theological disciplines."[3]

The beginning writer's tendency simply to write whatever comes naturally without putting it in a logical order results sometimes in an author getting a muddled idea of what his topic and who his intended audience is. James E. Ruark, Senior Editor at Zondervan Publishing House, says, "Some religious books will appeal to a wide range of Christian readers because of the subject matter; others really have a targeted audience. It is important for the writer to keep the audience in mind. For example, sometimes a book dealing with counseling problems will try to address both the counselor and the counselee; but this does not make sense. The writer might decide whether the book is one which the counselor should use or the person who needs the counseling. In the case of the latter, a book addressed to the counselee might prove to be one that a counselor will give to the client, and therefore it still has a market in both audiences—but is addressed to one."

The counsel of one other editor will be helpful here. Leslie H. Stobbe, of SP Publications, realizes that many writers tackling their first book-length project tend to put ideas on paper somewhat randomly as the ideas occur to them. "When done, they send a manuscript off to a publisher. They often do not have a clear idea of who their market is, so they do not target the book for a specific market. They do not have a clear outline, revealing what they want to have happen in the mind/life of the reader. They are more concerned with the information they feel they 'must share,' rather than with meeting a 'felt need' in the market."

Having really a clear idea of exactly what you are trying to say, and to whom you wish to say it, is essential in writing a nonfiction religious book. But once that central idea is firmly and coherently in mind, the ways of expanding and exploring it are legion.

Brainstorm

One helpful way to begin is to ask yourself questions like, "What do I already know about this subject? Why does this topic intrigue me? What have my experiences been?" Brainstorm it. Use your memory. As you do so, write down every idea that occurs to you. At this point pay no attention to how the thoughts flow or how your notes look. You can rearrange and tidy these up later. For the present, simply let your mind produce everything it has on your subject. That subject might be, for example, how God works with people in times of crisis. As you think about it for awhile, you may recall a time when your Aunt Jane nearly died, and how her church prayed and God brought her safely through the crisis. You might remember personal situations where you felt God was truly present and working (or perhaps that He seemed absent).

Then use your imagination. What can you imagine about your subject? How can you envision things being different? We are not suggesting you "invent" experiences, but merely see things from different perspectives, which is what using the imagination is all about.

Outline and Research

Probably you will not get too far before you exhaust your own reservoir of knowledge on any subject. Your next move will be to begin to research the topic at hand. Go to a local library and look through the card catalog for other books on your general topic. You will want to do this before you get too far along with your project, because someone else may have recently written a book on the exact topic you have in mind. If so, you will want to give some serious thought about working on another topic, or at least shifting the focus of your work. Remember that you want your book to fill an actual need in the market that no other book fills.

Read everything you can get your hands on related to your subject. Make careful notes as you go along. If you quote someone, double-check that you have done so correctly. Be sure to get the full bibliographical information from the book, because you will need it later to identify your source. The purpose of this research is not to rehash what someone else has already said, but to lay the backdrop for what you are going to say. Someone once snidely commented that the art of writing history books is the art of taking bits and pieces out of books that no one has read and putting them into a book that no one will read! This is not what you want to do.

Reading as background study will give you an overall perspective and "bird's eye" view of the field. It will furnish you a body of knowledge about your subject on which to draw and, if necessary, refute and revise.

Finding suitable material in a general library, especially in the field of religion, might be a problem. Try to locate the library of a local college with a religion department, or a theological seminary/divinity school or Bible college. If you do not have access to any such institution, you might consider using the services of a lending library. An excellent one is the

Congregational Library, located at 14 Beacon Street, Boston, Massachusetts, 02108. This is a non-sectarian library that is well-stocked and gladly lends books, journals, and periodicals to anyone asking for them. The best thing about it is that the services are free (although they do accept donations). If you write to this library, someone will put you on a mailing list to receive regular notices listing new accessions. Their Bulletin is published quarterly with a modest annual subscription fee. Another library service is the Kesler Circulating Library, Vanderbilt Divinity School of Vanderbilt University, Nashville, Tennessee, 37203.

After reading books and articles on your subject, begin working on a plan of writing. In other words, develop an outline. Any good handbook on grammar will give you detailed instructions on outlining your writing. You may not care to go into great detail, but you will need to break up your topic into small, manageable portions. That is the purpose of the outline. After all, you can eat an elephant if you take it one bite at a time.

Let's consider the outline for this book. First, we have both read many books on the subject of writing. Most of these were read, by the way, for pure edification. We simply enjoyed reading them, but as we read we realized that not a single book, so far as we could tell, was devoted to the matter of writing nonfiction religious books. That is why this book has been written. Work on the outline began by jotting down areas and ideas that a book like this should cover. This outline was reworked and changed several times until it reached the present form. Initially, it was felt that after the first chapter, which is a theological look at writing, we should discuss briefly in Chapter 2 the challenge and the process of writing and attempt to justify the book. At first we thought this chapter should be very involved, talking about the technicalities of writing and that sort of thing. This idea was changed, however, to focus on more of a "how to" approach.

We felt that chapter 3 should center in on ideas from which to write. How does a writer get his or her ideas? Where do they come from? How are they preserved? And so on.

Getting your ideas on paper is usually a difficult process, so we thought the fourth chapter on mechanics would be necessary and helpful.

Most new writers admit they are scared or intimidated by editors, so chapters five and six attempt to "demythologize" these ivory tower types. We contacted dozens of editors and publishing executives known to one or both of us either personally or through correspondence and asked them to give us their views and counsel for beginning writers. They were very helpful, giving much more information than we could possibly use.

Since beginning writers so often are confused by book contracts, we felt that if we could explain some contract samples in detail in chapter 7 that would alleviate most of the confusion.

Novice writers need to know the basic research tools, so chapter 8 is devoted to explaining what these tools are. Chapter 9 is dedicated to what every beginning author really wants to know—the book markets. We include some of the better religious book markets here, along with the names of the editors to contact.

We felt the final materials in the book should be devoted to offering the beginning writer further help. For this reason, we included an annotated bibliography in the tenth chapter. Finally, since new as well as established writers alike constantly ask publishers for style manuals, we wanted to include a sample manual in chapter 11. (The one we included is, for the most part, the style manual used by the editors at Crossway Books in Wheaton, Illinois, so the reader will have a fairly standard manual for reference.)

You can see from all this that the process of developing an outline is not secret or mysterious. Rather, it is logical and developmental. Besides that, it is plain hard work.

Flesh out the outline

Once you have done sufficient research on your subject and have established a working outline, the time has come for applying the seat of the pants to the seat of the chair. It is time to begin writing.

This is not only the point that is the most difficult to describe, but it is also the most tricky on which to advise. Writing has to do with the individual expression of your unique ideas. It is personal, and as such, no one can tell you exactly how to write. However, some general advice on style might be helpful.

Margaret K. McElderry, former editor of Harcourt, Brace, and World, offers this instruction: "Don't try to tailor your writing to any specific 'market.' First, have something you really want to write about, whether it's fiction or nonfiction. Then write to the best of your ability, to please yourself."[4] Every editor we know would tell you to think for yourself, and to write honestly what you think.

The temptation to try to make your writing *sound* like "religious" writing is especially strong. To think that by using the language of Zion your book will be helpful or saleable is a mistake. King James language was perfect for people who lived in the sixteenth century, but it is not sharp or effective today. All the sharp edges are worn smooth from years of use. Sherman R. Hanson notes that "writers must master the craft of writing. Sweetness and piosity just will not make up for sloppy literary styling." Leslie H. Stobbe also mentioned that writers must learn to express themselves with uniqueness and clarity, since, he noted, "many beginners do not have the writing skills to produce a unique, eminently readable product." James Hoover of InterVarsity Press wrote that some beginning writers seem to prefer flair without substance or substance without flair. The key is to find the right combination.

The issue here is individual writing style. But for a writing style to be truly "personal," one must continually work at it. Wishing and dreaming about being a writer won't help. Many editors will tell you that most writers simply have not written enough of anything to find their own styles. One editor says he gets at least one manuscript each week on the end times by some "scholar" who thinks he or she has it all figured out. (These are never actual academicians, but laypeople who have chosen the end times as their pet area.) But that editor realizes that these aspiring authors understand neither eschatology (the theological doctrine of final things) nor do they understand much about writing, for the writing styles on most of these manuscripts are all but rescuable.

It is really a very simple matter. If you want to write, you must write. Write a journal for yourself. Write short articles for magazines. Work on some book reviews for a local newspaper. Write pieces for your church newsletter or bulletin. Learn how to use words and to express yourself in sharp, unique ways. The thing is to systematically get your thoughts down on paper. When you can take a sharply focused idea and expand the idea into 30,000 words, then you are ready to write a book. In fact, it is a book. The only tools you need are the common ones: words, paper, a typewriter, or word processor. But you must want to keep at it, for writing is a demanding taskmistress.

Just as you outline the book as a whole, outline each chapter in the same way. This will facilitate your flow of thoughts as you move through the actual work of putting the words on paper. If your chapter is to be twelve pages long, for example, you might have six subdivisions or points on your outline for that chapter. If each is worthy of equal treatment, then you may attempt to write two pages on each point. Most writers will find it much easier to work this way, knowing that they do not have to simply fill up twelve blank pages, but that two or three pages can be completed before moving on to expand another aspect of the main idea.

Revising

Once you have finished the book, do not immediately celebrate or ship it off to a publisher. Invariably, it is not ready. You still need to revise it. This, like the writing itself, is difficult work and is done according to individual preference. Some writers work on a few pages and then revise them. Others finish the entire manuscript and then revise the complete work. Rewriting or revising is one of the author's bloodiest disciplines, and no one much cares for it. But remember this epigram: most people can write, but only writers can rewrite.

It is in fact revision that separates the amateurs from the pros. Donald Murray describes this difference: "When the beginning writer completes his first draft, he usually reads it through to correct typographical errors and considers the job of writing done. When the professional writer completes his first draft, he usually feels he is at the start of the writing process. Now that he has a draft, he can begin writing."[5]

Elton Trueblood described his method of revising his writing: "I can support Dr. [Samuel] Johnson's famous words, 'The production of something where nothing was before, is an act of greater energy than the expansion or decoration of the thing produced.' The perennial advice, therefore, is 'Invent first and embellish later.' I find that my scissors are among the most used of the literary tools on my desk because, after a chapter is in typescript, it becomes obvious to me that certain lines will fit better in some place other than that in which they were originally located. Accordingly, on the second typing, one page may be made up of a number of small parts clipped together."[6] A writer with a computer and powerful word processing program can do this easily.

Leave the material you want to revise for awhile. Let it get "cold" in your thinking. This way it will seem fresh when you read it later. Knowing it less intimately after leaving it for a time, you will also be able to view it more objectively.

Read your work aloud for mistakes of all sorts—grammar errors, misspelled words, misplaced modifiers, continuity, and pace. Cut out non-essential words, and remember that today's market demands an economy of words. Do not develop the habit of writing exceedingly elaborate and overly elegant sentences all the time. Cut out a few good words to make room for even better ones. Smooth out and tighten sentences and make transitions logical and natural.

Once you have the material in what you consider "final" form, you might have a friend read it to see if he or she can spot errors of thought or style that escaped your attention. Choose this reader with care, however. You would not want a less than careful reader to proof your material. Find a thoughtful reviewer who will try to save you from walking the plank with embarrassing mistakes.

Typing/Printing

Type out or print your final manuscript version with great care. Edd Rowell, Jr. of Mercer University Press says that many beginning writers err at this point and seriously hurt their chances of having a publisher accept their manuscript. When the material is forwarded to the publisher, he says, "the manuscripts should be typed, double-spaced on the page (this includes footnotes, bibliography, and all other manuscript contents), with adequate margins on the page. Of course, double-spacing requires twice the amount of paper, but it increases efficiency tenfold."

Some writers will try to grab the editor's attention by using peculiar materials—like buff paper and green type. But look at your manuscript from the editor's viewpoint—would you really give serious attention to such a manuscript? Use good quality, standard white 8-1/2 x 11 bond paper, and use a pica or elite type, always with a black ribbon. If you hurt the editor's eyes, or otherwise make it difficult to peruse your typescript, you don't have much of a chance to sell your book.

(Don't forget to look at the "Preparation of the Manuscript" section in the sample style guide included in chapter 11 of this book.)

Recap

Remember that the mechanics of getting your ideas onto paper can be the most frustrating part of the writing process, but if you keep a few simple guidelines in mind, you can get through this difficult period.

Focus the major theme of your book sharply. Answer these questions in your own mind: Exactly what am I trying to say in this book? Why am I trying to say it? Who will read it? Why would anyone read my book instead of someone else's? What makes my book unique, significant, important? What contribution will it make? Is there a real need for this book? Will the book help people to have a deeper understanding of their faith, or help them to live more effectively as Christians? Is my book consistent with what Scripture teaches, or does it stand in conflict with it in some way? Does my thinking stand within the stream of historic Christian truth?

Refine and shape your ideas carefully. Do not yield to the temptation simply to dump them onto the paper as they occur to you.

Brainstorm your topic. Call to mind what you already know about your subject. Draw up a tentative outline based on your research. After you have finished researching, revise the outline if necessary and write your first draft. Try to develop your own style of writing. Revise the manuscript. Read it over several times to make sure that your ideas are logical and clear and your sentences smooth. Correct spelling and grammar errors. Read the manuscript aloud to check for continuity and pace. Revise again and again, if necessary.

Use a good quality typewriter or print the material out on a high quality printer. Use good 8-1/2 x 11 paper.

When you have done all of this, you are certainly ready to begin contacting publishers about your work, if you have not done so by now. Many experienced writers contact publishers before a book is finished. Opinions on this practice vary for book writers who have not published much work. Inexperienced writers might want to try approaching publishing houses before their work is entirely finished, but remember that some publishers want to see a significant amount of the writing sample, or even the complete manuscript, before making a final publishing decision. In any case, the next three chapters will help you contact and negotiate with book editors of publishing firms.

ENDNOTES

[1]Dan Wickenden, quoted by David Raffclock, *Writing For the Markets* (New York: Funk and Wagnalls, 1969), 79.

[2]Edward Gibbon, in Laurence J. Peter, *Peter's Quotations* (New York: Bantam Books, 1979), 544.

[3]Unless otherwise noted, all information from publishing personnel is from personal correspondence.

[4]Margaret K. McElderry, in *Writing For the Markets*, 84.

[5]Donald M. Murray, "The Maker's Eye: Revising Your Own Manuscripts," *The Writer* (October 1973), 14.

[6]Elton Trueblood, *While It Is Day* (New York: Harper and Row, 1974), 64.

5

CONTACTING EDITORS

When you have finished your book, or at least an expanded outline with a couple of sample chapters, you face a crucial juncture: whom to contact in order to get the book published. Which publisher should see your material? How does a beginning writer contact an editor? What should he or she say? What material should accompany the initial contact? This chapter will answer these and similar questions.

Some writers feel they must finish a manuscript in its entirety before they then ship it willy-nilly to any publisher they can find. This only rarely works, and there is a much more logical and methodical way to approach it. You, as a writer, obviously need to learn the art of writing. But you also need to learn the art of selling your writing. Study the kinds of books various publishers issue. Browse religious bookstores to check out recent publications. Read the catalogs and bulletins of the publishers; many will send these to you free of charge. Almost every publisher with any sort of an active publishing program will have authors' guidelines that can also be had without cost. These guidelines will tell you what are the requirements for submission and what you should send along with your book proposal. Some editors want to see samples of your writing, or samples from the actual manuscript you will be submitting. The guidelines will tell you what to send. Study them carefully, for they will give you specific instructions as to submission requirements and any special slant that a publisher wants. Check with the publisher you are interested in to see what is available.

By all means, consult the books published by the various houses. Get acquainted with a publisher's tone or style of publishing. When you do, you will know that a firm like Crossway Books or Tyndale House Publishers would be more likely to issue a thoroughgoing evangelical book than would Westminster Press/John Knox Press or Doubleday. Harvest House, Fleming H. Revell, or Zondervan, for examples, would be less likely to publish serious, scholarly titles than would, say, Wm. B. Eerdmans Company, Fortress Press, or Oxford University Press. Knowing the publisher after studying their book line, you would probably not want to send an issues-oriented book written from a liberal perspective to Moody Press—but you might want to try HarperSanFrancisco.

Query

Once you have decided upon a publisher, send a query letter to the appropriate editor. Most publishers appreciate the query approach, and do not wish to receive unsolicited manuscripts in the mail. You can find the editors in periodically updated guides to the religious book markets. For example, in most good libraries you can find volumes such as *The Writer's Market* and the *Literary Market Place*. These volumes and others like them will show you what kinds of books a given publisher specializes in. They also list requirements for submission and will most likely include an address and phone number of the house—along with the names of the acquisition editors in most cases. You should study these books closely and determine which publishers you think would be interested in your writing project. (By the way, these guides will also give you the names and locations of agents who work with religious books as a specialty.) You need to show your editor that you have done as thorough a job of research on their publishing company before you contact them. You can also find in many Christian bookstores some volumes that will give you the same kind of information on specifically *Christian* publishers. There is, for one example, *The Christian Writer's Market Guide*. Also available is *The Guide to Religious and Inspirational Markets*. Chapters 8 and 9 will have much more information on these publications and markets.

In your query letter, introduce yourself to the editor. Tell the person who you are and what your qualifications are for writing on your topic. Give the editor a brief description of the contents of your book, mention how it differs from other books on the subject, and gauge the readership for which the manuscript was written. Be sure to mention your interpretation of the importance of the book. Send a sample chapter or two, along with the outline, if that is the initial material that a given editor wants to see. Again, follow the specific instructions given in the publishers' guidelines. Remember that an editor does not usually need to read an entire manuscript in order to know if the book fits in with their list, or whether the material is actually publishable.

Always enclose with any material a self-addressed, stamped envelope. This will facilitate the response of the editor and/or the return of your material. After you do this, wait! Depending on their schedules and work loads, editors may need up to three months to reply to your query, although most do so within a few weeks.

From the Editor's Viewpoint

The best way to find out what editors need to see from an aspiring author is simply to ask them. The responses below are helpful comments from various editors and are taken from personal correspondence to the authors.

Roland Seboldt of Augsburg Fortress had these comments for writers: "All letters should be clearly written and typed to gain the attention of the editor with a minimum amount of time expended. Publishing houses such as ours receive 5000 manuscripts and queries per year. This means that the ones clearly expressing their purpose and market target will get the most immediate attention."

Edd Rowell, Jr. of Mercer University Press notes that "the most important thing in insuring that an editor will read a manuscript is that the author has chosen a timely subject and then has dealt with it carefully in the way the subject has been researched and written. Secondly, a clean and well prepared manuscript . . . is the best insurance that it will be read."

Editor Sherman R. Hanson offered a warning to writers on the matter of queries: "They [beginning writers] can't expect their work to be seriously read by an editor if their thinking is fuzzy and their writing inane."

Another editor, Jack Gargiulo, advises writers to give only a brief summary of their work along with an outline. He also urges authors to point out how the book project developed. In other words, was it experiential? Was it developed in the classroom, or through research?

Daniel Van't Kerkhoff, acquisitions editor at Baker Books, cautions that while the submission of ideas can be done via the query letter alone, authors really should include a couple of sample chapters so the editor can see their writing style, the idea development, and so on.

Zondervan's James E. Ruark offers very substantial advice on the topic of submissions: "Being honest, specific, and courteous goes a long way. Honest: Perhaps the writer feels 'the Lord inspired me to write this book and send it to you,' but subjective guidance has limitations; every manuscript must stand on its merits when it is evaluated. Specific: Tell the editor why this book is different and why it merits consideration. If a writer is doing a book about marriage, what makes it different in content or approach from half a zillion other books already in the bookstore? There are different approaches or specific problems that are publishable; make sure you have one. Courteous: Don't impugn the publisher's integrity; be neat and tactful in your presentation. Also, should you get a rejection letter that is obviously a standard form, try to understand that although the publisher might like to offer specific criticisms, it is not usually possible to do so. Any specific criticism should be taken as an encouraging sign that the proposal had enough merit to warrant a little extra attention; but publishers who accept unsolicited manuscripts simply cannot respond to each one with an individualized letter."

Leslie H. Stobbe wisely advises authors to include in their proposals a two-page selling synopsis which describes the target market along with the "felt need" they are meeting.

InterVarsity Press editor James Hoover notes that "a cleanly-typed, well-written letter is much more persuasive than one that is sloppy and poorly-written. An editor cannot help making some judgment of an author's writing ability based on his or her letter of inquiry. A letter of inquiry should give some indication of the author's qualifications as well as the reasons for writing about the proposed topic. I find a low-key approach that nevertheless convinces me of the value of the author's ideas much more persuasive than a snow job concerning the author's anticipated sales for the book."

The late Association Press editor Robert W. Hill told authors to be careful to define their work in a short, to-the-point letter. Tell, as clearly as possible, exactly what your book is. And echoing a similar sentiment is Regal Books' Donald E. Pugh, who likes to see query letters which answer these questions: Why another book? Why this particular book? What makes this book deserve a place in the market? What qualifies the author to write about this subject? What would make someone pick it up?

Joe S. Johnson, former editor of the line of inspirational books at Broadman & Holman Publishers, had this advice to offer: "There is nothing in particular the writer can do to insure that an editor will read his/her idea or manuscript, carefully or uncarefully. The best means of egging the editor into reading the manuscript is to make it so rare and so unique that the editor, for his sanity, will have to read it. . . . The best means of assuring that an editor will read and read your material carefully is that your material be prepared convincingly and attractively—well-typed, no misspellings, no punctuation errors, no sloppiness. And by all means attach a synopsis and/or outline of your material."

The Continuum Publishing Group's Frank Oveis reminds authors to "study the various religious publishers. Follow their ads and reviews in the religious media as well as in professional journals such as *The Christian Bookseller* and *Bookstore Journal*. Then determine which publishers are likely to be interested in your manuscript. In my experience, many writers haven't the foggiest idea what sort of religious books we do."

Martha Perry, at Liguori Publications, notes an interesting predicament into which many beginning writers fall: "Some of the major problems beginning writers seem to have in writing nonfiction religious books are opposite extremes. Many writers present their subject in such an erudite manner that the normal 'lay' person is completely at a loss in understanding the points presented. At the other side of the pole, other authors belabor a point until the reader is made to feel rather dense. The primary view of the author should be to communicate—be concise, not clever. Most editors are not looking for another Andrew Greeley nor another Erma Bombeck." Along with many other editors who communicated with the authors, Perry also notes this: "To insure that your material will be read, **it must be neat.** If an editor has to read through coffee stains, smudges, and crossed out words, he will soon give up."

Editors usually urge writers to use pica font because script or elite type is hard reading for eyes that may be tired from wading through similar material.

She continues with more good advice, "Another point to remember when presenting your material or query letter is to use a professional approach. State your intention, give some personal background concerning yourself and your proposed project, and rest your case. Avoid wordiness, as most editors are too busy to read page after page of chattiness."

Keith M. Bailey pointed out that beginning writers often forget to seek creativity. "They are rehashing old themes on which considerable work has been done in the past, or they are writing in areas where they are not well qualified. Therefore, the material lacks substance and credibility." When contacting an editor, the writer should take care with his or her query letter: "It should not be a mimeographed sheet, such as I often find coming to my desk. It should have attached to it at least a two-page resume of the book, table of contents, and sample chapter, so that the editor has some idea of the nature of the book."

Since Harvest House Publishers produces books for the more popular Christian reading audience, Robert H. Hawkins is concerned that many beginning writers do not know how to write in a simple style that will interest "the average person on the street." A book will have trouble selling if it is not in "lay language" or interesting enough for the mass of people.

When an editor at Moody Press, Philip Rawley noted that "many beginning writers fail to research the market carefully and as a result offer a publisher a book on a subject that has already been saturated with books. Along with this, new writers often fail to research their *subject* well, resulting in a work that is shallow and doesn't deal adequately with the data available on the particular topic. . . . A new author can help himself with a publisher by asking what that publisher needs, and tailoring his query to those needs." He further agrees that most editors like to receive a query letter as opposed to a full manuscript.

73

Editor John Sloan of Zondervan pointed out some of the weaknesses beginning authors must work to overcome. These include "a lack of in-depth vocabulary resources—and sometimes a lack of adequate research to back up the material that is being written. If the research is adequate, many times the writer will face another problem: the writing of material that sounds too stilted or academic. . . . The ability to submit a well-written query with paragraph summaries of each chapter and an overall synopsis of the book is a must. This will get your idea quickly before the editor's eyes and into his thought patterns as to whether this book will fit into the publishing schedule and philosophy of that particular house."

Betty Fuhrman responded from the Nazarene Publishing House that "basically there are too many inexperienced authors who are writing in areas beyond their ability. Many send in poorly written queries which turn off potential publishers at the start. There are also too many with below average ideas who try to write because they want to help somebody profit from their experience. This is a good motive but unfortunately does not insure a quality manuscript."

Thomas Nelson's former managing editor, Bruce Nygren, thinks that inadequate research determining existing books on a particular subject is often a problem for a novice author. Another problem is generally poor writing skills. He feels sure, however, that editors will pay attention to book ideas that are fresh and creative.

Consensus

By now you have realized that various items have been mentioned repeatedly. These include the following:

Neatness—make all correspondence, manuscripts, and outlines as neat and attractive as possible. Remember, if you are competing with roughly 5,000 queries in a year, you need to have an edge. Neatness is that edge.

Clarity—have in your mind exactly what you want to write about, with a very clear idea of who will read your book and why. Express yourself as clearly as possible.

Timely subject—be aware of what people are reading; do not rehash subjects that have been done *ad nauseum.*

Outline and/or summary—never send a finished manuscript until asked to do so; editors would rather read a two- or three-page abstract and detailed outline than a 200-page manuscript.

Honesty—do not try to "snow" editors about your work; a little humility about its value goes a long way.

Courtesy—editors, despite popular opinion, are people, too; treat them as such.

Creativity—write in such a way as to make sure your editor, and ultimately your reading public, will have to read the book.

Awareness—know who publishes what type of material. Do not waste your time sending a query letter and additional material to a publisher who will not view your project as consistent with his or her acquisition goals.

Discouragement

As you begin fleshing out your ideas and searching for a suitable publisher for your material, you will no doubt often be told, "Sorry, but we're unable to express a publishing interest." Rejection slips or letters can injure a writer's pride almost quicker than anything else. Writers must develop thick skins! Some editors reject an idea or manuscript with form letters, most often because they simply can't respond to each individual inquiry. Others will write nice letters and perhaps explain exactly why the idea was turned down. Some will even offer advice as to revision or other possible publishers you should contact.

No writer who has ever written much has ever survived without receiving rejection letters. You will not escape either. But remember this—do not get discouraged! If your idea truly is worthy and your execution of it is done in an excellent way, someone will eventually express a publishing interest in your book project. We speak as experts on rejection slips. Don Aycock has received almost as many rejection slips as Len Goss has sent! Both have had manuscripts turned down many times. All authors will experience ups and downs; the key is to keep writing and sending out your material. Don't give up. Someone will bite.

6

WHAT DO EDITORS WANT?

In the preceding chapter, we offered some of the comments and ideas religious book editors related on submitting synopses and manuscripts. We will now expand on this and pass along other general comments and opinions editors have on writing. As before, the editors will speak for themselves. We think that you will find their advice both illuminating and practical.

As writers open themselves to the call of God in our time and place, we must remember, according to Celia Hahn, Editor in Chief of the Alban Institute Book Publishing Program, that "congregations have always been shaped by men and women who knew God as companion in their history and a presence with them now in their visions and hopes for the future. We must be willing to be grounded in our holy history, yet open to bold new visions. Rather than becoming depressed about this post-Christendom world, we will be open to new opportunities, to looking at our mission in a way that is different than ever before."

Roland Seboldt of Augsburg Fortress had this to say on writing nonfiction religious books: "Books which speak to the needs and aspirations of people will always have value. Books that help people solve problems, grow in faith, and see a new perspective in life need to be written in every generation to apply the old truths of Scripture and the Christian tradition to the world in which we live." In addition to giving advice on what kinds of books need to be written, Seboldt also noted, "My first suggestion [to beginning writers] is always to get started by writing articles, short pieces, letters to the editor, newspaper columns, items for the parish paper of the congregation. Generally, writers do not start by writing books first. First writers do short pieces in other media and then gradually develop their skills for book publishing."

We asked editors what kinds of religious books they thought would be selling in the near future. Edd Rowell, Jr., of the Mercer University Press, mentioned that, "the areas of interest in nonfiction religious books is so broad that it is difficult to say in a few words what are the most interesting subjects today. In general, however, I would say that those books of most interest are the ones which deal with timely subjects in a readable and authoritative way. Personally, I would like to see some good scholarly treatments of evangelism, religious conversion, and the whole spectrum of the new right movement. Of course, well-researched treatments of biblical studies and church history are of perennial interest."

Roy M. Carlisle, an agent in San Francisco, had this to say: "What am I looking for today? People. People who are experiencing the heights and depths of life. People who are willing to be in touch with their own passions and concerns. People who connect with the deeper currents of life in general and, more particularly, life in the Spirit. All of us are drawn to these types of people. And when they combine this passion for life, this sensitivity to God's call to 'come further up and further in,' with the habits of constant reading, reflection, and writing they are on the way to becoming an insightful and thoughtful writer. They have also discovered that creativity grows out of the soils of these disciplines. I find myself depending upon these people to tell me what should be written; and they rely on me to encourage them in their writing, to work

78

with them to develop and express their ideas in publishable form. My prayer is that many will be called and many chosen."

Sherman R. Hansen, formerly of The Bethany Press, reminds beginning writers that, "Books that help readers think responsibly about the church's life and mission, and others that show 'how to' get at things like evangelism and stewardship will always attract readers." Further, "Aspiring authors, like aspiring architects, engineers, and astronomers, just have to work. They have to study, learn, grow, and become able to check their 'notions' against 'realities' and 'truths'. If they are to fulfill their promise they must labor patiently and persistently, over an extended period of time."

Several editors wrote us that they feel authors who write in areas of prayer, spirituality, and Scripture will probably be on target as far as having an audience. Bo Hoskins, President of Roper Press, reminds writers that, "in Bible studies and Bible stories, start with the text, and *then* apply. Imagination in how to apply is exciting as long as it does not replace the message of the book. Integration of Christian principles is essential. 'Tacked on' pithy thoughts will find a cool reception."

Editors also remind aspiring authors never to give up. Seek various publishers. "Cannibalize" your book and try to get it published in pieces in magazines if nothing else works out.

Baker Book House's acquisition editor Dan Van't Kerkhoff notes, "It is difficult to define what type of nonfiction books sell well. There are many categories. Basically, the author as well as the publisher should take a hard look at the marketing potential. This means that he must connect with a broad general need among his designated readership. Autobiographies are hardly worthwhile. The author should be familiar with the religious bookstore through talking with bookstore managers. He should also scan the latest catalogs by the largest religious publishers. Scanning book advertising in such magazines as *Moody* will also indicate the subject areas that are being published successfully."

Robert T. Heller, Associate Publisher of The Crossroad Publishing Company, offers these cautions: "The standard remains the same regardless of subject—you have to have something to say; content is more important than style. Too many nonfiction books are published today that are simply expanded magazine articles which are ephemeral in nature, outdated at publication. The value that a book offers to a buyer is a full treatment of a subject from an author who, at the least, is qualified to write on said subject and who, better yet, has achieved a certain notoriety in his or her chosen field. Clever titles help, good clear organization and felicitous use of language make the reading experience more enjoyable, but without a subject worthy of serious treatment, it is all a pencil with a broken point. It's apparent to me that, particularly in that segment of the religious market labeled Evangelical, we are in a period of asking deeper questions about faith and life. There is always a place for inspiration, but, for the moment, information questions take precedence. The important task for the nonfiction religious book is to take unchanging truth and integrate it with our changing lives—a worthy challenge."

The concerns of the scholarly publishing community are varied, of course, but can be represented by the comments of Jon Pott, Vice-President and Editor in Chief of Wm. B. Eerdmans Publishing Company: "War and peace will continue as a major issue, especially now that one needn't be a bearded or braless placard-carrying peacenik to be worried about it. The literature will probably be somewhat less rhetorical now and more reflective, sophisticated, and nuanced.

"Geopolitical concerns will also, I should think, remain big, perhaps eclipsing concerns for domestic hunger, poverty, and injustice. Racism doesn't seem a vital area to be writing in now unless one is able to do a compelling post-civil-rights analysis that really lays bare the deeper levels of racism that, many would argue, remain entrenched.

"As in the case of war and peace, much of the rhetoric on the women's issue and the church may also be spent. The next stage will be one of more subdued reflection and analysis, and also of proposing strategies for implementation.

"Another area I will be watching with considerable interest is that of medical ethics. Abortion will remain an issue, but lots of other questions relating to life and death will also be game for discussion.

"On the more strictly theological front, I should think that ecumenical matters will be important in many sectors— especially given a document like Baptism, Eucharist, and Ministry. The more fundamentalist churches, of course, won't be much interested, but I think that interest will grow appreciably among a number of more ecumenically open evangelicals. In this connection, of course, any new books on the Lord's Supper may be relevant, as will books having to do with liturgy. I might say that I think the theological world is also probably ripe for a solid study in ecclesiology; not much has been done here that I can think of.

"I don't know where 'spirituality' is these days, except that it seems to be post-charismatic. My hunch is that the spiritual tradition associated with the Catholic and Episcopal traditions will be appropriated by more of the Protestant sector. Think of Henri Nouwen, to name perhaps the most visible symbol, and in a sense Richard Foster.

"Well, I've probably gone on far too long about what is far too obvious. Let me mention one more thing that is more general and possibly a bit less apparent. Given the conservative swing in this country, I wouldn't be surprised if even among liberals there won't be a growing appreciation for the virtues of responsibility and commitment. The modern family seems to be making something of a comeback; women's magazines seem not quite so glib about the joys of extra-marital affairs (more talk about lasting relationships); there seems in the air even among the chic a bit more sense that what feels good may in the long run be related to being disciplined and fulfilling obligations. A good sophisticated book about commitment would interest me."

Some editors find defining exactly what type of book sells well a bit difficult. James E. Ruark, Senior Editor at Zondervan, is one such editor. Speaking specifically about his own company, he says, ". . . our publishing program is broad enough that no single kind of book dominates our list; also, we are not a 'fad' publisher, although we of course are responsive to trends. Our backlist is very strong, and most of the books we publish are likely to have a pretty good life. . . . Another reason why this question (about what types of books sell well) is so difficult is that by the time I were to suggest a topic, we would probably have three manuscripts here for evaluation already. A look at our catalog would quickly reveal several main interests that we have, but there are many variations within these categories: Bible study, popular psychology, personal stories, and more professional and academic books including biblical language aids. I am more interested in knowing what an aspiring writer feels qualified to write about and what ideas he or she has."

Ruark also has advice on other topics of interest to beginning writers. "First, do your homework. Not only on your subject but in regards to the religious book marketplace in general. Establish your credibility. We receive many, many commentaries on the Book of Revelation or biblical prophecy that are subjective, redundant, and logically inadequate—and written by laypersons who have no qualifications, professionally speaking, to be writing on the subject.

"Second, plan to work hard. You don't find time to write a book, you make time. You can plan on more perspiration than inspiration, as Thomas Edison suggested. And as John Irving says, three ingredients necessary to be a writer are 'stamina, patience, and passion.'

"Third, don't look to writing as an easy way to make money. Established writers can gain a steady income from writing, but most religious book writers do it as an avocation even after they've achieved some success. The financial rewards are gratifying and important, but they are not the only reward; and often the amount of work necessary to achieve success involves a price. Most often the money doesn't come quickly; in writing books, there is a waiting time before the book is off the press, and royalties may not be paid for up to a year after the book is published (your contract will give specifics on this).

"Fourth, keep trying. If rejection slips start piling up, reconsider what you are doing wrong or failing to do. Be open to constructive criticism from qualified critics. Your friends may like your work, but there's no risk in their telling you they like it; there is risk in their trying to critique it, and their evaluation may not really be qualified. If you have talent and take adequate steps to develop it, you will meet with success in time. Nothing makes a publisher happier than to receive a highly publishable work from an unknown writer. That is one of the best rewards and challenges of religious book publishing. We like to hear from you."

Leslie H. Stobbe at SP Publications has this thoughtful advice for new writers: "Every book that meets a broadly felt need will sell if written reasonably well. It's up to the author to be well enough read in daily newspapers, weekly or monthly magazines, and in frequent enough touch with people where they really live, to come up with 'trends'. A visit to a local Christian as well as secular bookseller is most helpful." Stobbe also has this reminder: "Write to meet a genuine need, not to merely express yourself."

InterVarsity Press managing editor James Hoover echoes this advice: "Don't write to write. Write to say something. Write clearly, write personally, and avoid jargon." Further, books of substance that capture the reading public's imagination will have a book-buying public. Also those which are "well-written, well-illustrated from a personal experience and well-thought-through from a biblical perspective."

Kenneth Guentert, Editor at Resource Publication, writes that, "we look for 'authors' who see a book as an aid to their 'work' rather than 'writers' who think their 'work' is done once they've sold a book to a publisher."

Victor Books' former executive editor, James Adair, had this to share. "In regard to what beginning authors should consider writing in the area of nonfiction: If I were a beginning author, a person able to put words together like a good word carpenter, I think I'd leave my Ivory Tower and come down to earth. I'd look for a good story to tell and work with someone who has the story to make it into a good book. I'd not only assume the job of writing the manuscript but would become the agent in contacting publishers with a proposal and finally negotiating contracts for the project.

"The beginning author, in my opinion, has little chance of having his nonfiction published, as good as it may be, if he writes independently—unless he is an expert on the subject. Even experienced authors don't do well with books they write from research. I recall one well-known author who wrote a book on crucial issues relating to science that affect us. He interviewed a number of scientists but the book didn't do well at all. Now, if he had written the book for someone with a name, someone people respected for his/her expertise, the book likely would have done much better. I don't mean to say beginning writers should give up on doing nonfiction of their own. But I would encourage them to think of creating books for those with expertise on subjects, people who are too busy to write or not gifted as word carpenters. Often a royalty split of some sort can be worked out, with an advance to help put bread on the table while the project is under way.

"But the beginning writer should probably not tackle a book until he/she has successfully written many newspaper and magazine articles. Serve an apprenticeship first. As for topics for books for the future, science, family, money, survival. Plus many subjects relating to living the Christian life, that help Christians solve problems that confront them."

Some books released from the Christian presses are "crossover" titles—written from a Christian perspective but their main audience is the general reader. These titles, when done well, can be quite successful in the marketplace. For example, the goal at Lion Books "is to publish books that meet the needs of readers who may not consider themselves Christians. We look for subjects of interest to ordinary people (not just Christians). The Christian content must be natural and unforced, growing out of the topic." Writing honest crossover material is extremely difficult for most Christian writers: "He or she will be committed to the often-difficult task of writing as a Christian for those who may not share their faith." Doing this kind of book is certainly one way of leaving the Ivory Tower and coming down to earth. But the writer has to be informed and shaped by biblical faith, and be prepared to work very hard and to get things right. One way to get things right, according to Lloyd B. Hildebrand, the Managing Editor of Victory House, is to "develop fresh approaches that incorporate show-don't-tell techniques that create vivid images for the reader. Keep the writing simple and direct—aimed at the needs of people. Cultivate empathy for the reader and his/her needs. And avoid preachiness."

The late Chief Editor of Association Press, Robert W. Hill, believed that books with some degree of inspiration would always sell fairly well. He also said, "My advice to any author is to think out clearly and present on paper the skeleton of the work. Then flesh out this bare outline with detailed major considerations. Write clearly and to the point. The chips will then fall where they may."

Writers are always interested in *how* an editor goes about making publishing decisions. Asked to comment on what kinds of religious books will be selling in the near future, Wendell Hawley, Senior Vice President of Editorial at Tyndale House Publishers, shared his thoughts. "Like anyone else in the predicting business, one would like to have a foolproof crystal ball which would give infallible information. Since such an invaluable tool is not in my possession, I will launch out with a few guesstimations. On many different occasions I have found it very worthwhile in trying to assess a current situation or a future possibility, to take a long look back. This, I find, often clears our perspective, as we try to visualize the possibilities of the future. Looking back over past best-seller lists, I find that various books fall into different categories. I try to analyze the books of yesteryear by saying, 'What proved to be a fad, and what proved to have sustained readership appeal?' Viewing the best-seller list over a number of years, I try to see if there is a pattern of sales with various topics. I ask myself, 'What seems to sell "on its own" and what requires much author visibility to sell the book?' Looking for answers to these questions often gives me insight as to the kind of manuscript or book I will be looking for at some point in the future. For instance, in the last fifty years we have had several cycles of interest in prophetic books. I believe that we are on the verge of yet another upswing in readership interest on prophecy.

"As I look at the present list of books, I asked myself a number of questions, such as, 'What is the outstanding book in any given subject area, and what makes that book unique, and, if the book has weaknesses, can we find a writer who can improve on the subject matter?' I try to watch for areas which seem to already have too many books on that given topic. Sometimes I receive a manuscript from a writer saying that they researched the area and couldn't find anything on this given topic, so they decided to write a book on the subject. Many times I could give the writer the names of a dozen books selling quite well in the bookstore on that very subject. Which leads me to the next question I am always asking myself. 'What areas seem to always absorb another book?' And I find at least two areas which seem to always allow for yet another book on the subject. That is books on motivation, and books on the family. Both subject areas, of course, will need to be written on by authorities in the field.

"In the religious area, I think two things are evolving. One, there is a spirit of contemplation and deeper devotional living than what seemed to be apparent in recent years. I believe there will be an interest in books on holy living, walking with God, fellowship with God, the 'deeper life' appeal. There also seems to me to be a realistic spirit of ecumenicity as it relates to various religious groups within the Christian framework. Books which relate to Christians getting along together as believers, I believe, will sell better than polemic books arguing the superiority of one doctrinal persuasion over another.

"In summary, then, I look to see an increase in prophetic books, a continued strong interest in books on the family, motivational books, devotional books, and good wholesome books which may be termed diversionary reading."

Many book editors who work in nonfiction advise beginning writers to take it one step at a time. Get in print in magazines first. Often a publisher will contact the writer of an article to have it expanded into a book. Do your homework. Put your best foot forward. You never have a second chance to make a first impression.

Many potential authors think that what a publishing house wants to see from them is the actual manuscript on which they are working. That is almost never true. What most editors *do* want to see is a well-done book proposal. At Baker, Revell, and Chosen Books, the editors *insist* on seeing a proposal before examining a finished manuscript. "There are good reasons for you to develop a proposal before writing most of the manuscript. This enables you to obtain from us the guidelines for the project, which increases the likelihood that we will accept it for publication." This is also true at Pelican Publishing Company: "We must turn down 99% of all submissions to us, so none of us has time for in-depth exchanges with potential authors until we respond [to a proposal] with a solicitation."

At Moody Press as well, "we ask authors to write concerning their manuscripts before sending them to us. Your letter should describe your idea and explain why you wrote the material, who the specific audience is, how readers will benefit from the book, and how this work differs from what is already in the bookstore. Then tell us a little about your own spiritual journey, so that we may know you better. You may include a sample chapter, and please enclose a stamped, self-addressed envelope."

More good advice was sent to us by Carole Johnson, the Editorial Manager at Tyndale House Publishers. Many writers submit manuscripts and proposals, hoping someone will rescue them from the slush pile: it hardly ever happens. "The main reason is that we simply don't have the staff to read the proposals we get. Another reason is that few first-time, unagented, unrecommended authors submit professional-looking proposals. Whether you are submitting a proposal to us, to another publisher, or to an agent, inform yourself about how it's done. Read the current *Writer's Market* (Writer's Digest books), your number-one source of information. Other excellent reference books include *Children's Writer's and Illustrator's Market* (Writer's Digest), *Elements of Style* (White), *Edit Yourself* (Ross-Larsen), *On Writing Well* (Zinsser), *The Children's Picture Book* (Roberts), and *Nonfiction for Children* (Roberts)."

One of the secrets to catching an editor's attention, according to Vicki Crumpton, Acquisitions and Development Editor at Broadman & Holman Publishers, is helping them to see the marketability of your idea. "The following questions are commonly asked by our editorial, sales, and marketing staffs as we consider products: What other books or articles have you published? Have you read other books in your subject category? What makes your idea unique? What features or reader benefits have you included to make your book attractive to potential customers? Is you topic timely? How can you help market your book? Do you lead conferences or speak frequently in public? Do you have access to radio or television? Are you a recognized authority in your field? Are there prominent people who could give endorsements for this book?"

Ellen Hake, the Editorial Director at Starburst Publishers, also sees one's own salability as important, especially to smaller Christian houses that have no direct sales representatives in the general marketplace. She advises writers to "write on an issue that slots you on talk shows and thus establish your name as an expert and writer."

Deborah Grahame-Smith, Senior Editor at Morehouse Publishing, agrees that seeing the marketability of your book project is of utmost importance. She says, "Christians, like everyone else, are reading more for information and personal (spiritual) growth than for escape or entertainment. The religious market is also increasingly competitive, therefore writers need to have some market sensibilities and do their homework. What evidence is there to indicate a real need for your book? Who will use it? How will your book compliment or compete with ones already on the shelves?" And Beth Feia, Editor at Servant Publications, adds this: "We appreciate authors who can succinctly and convincingly articulate why their book is unique and *needed*. We appreciate authors who have a clear sense of the needs their book will meet and how it improves upon what is already on the market (this takes market research)."

Frank Oveis of The Continuum Publishing Group muses that, especially for newer writers, "Fads and modes are easy enough to spot. The problem isn't types and genres, it's quality."

Broadman & Holman's former editor Joe Johnson offers some very helpful general advice for beginners on the substance of books and other matters:

> (1) Keep on writing, whether or not you are published. Real writers write and write and write, even if it is only

for their personal edification. (2) Refine what you submit. Shame on you if you write an editor: 'This is just a rough draft. This is not my best.' I don't want to waste my time on rough drafts. I want good stuff, not junk. (3) Spell out the facts about your manuscript-purpose for writing, intended market, possible uses of the book, selling points, promotion, and advertising ideas. (4) Introduce yourself, if you're a new writer. Send a well-written biographical sketch. List your writing credits, if any. I appreciate honesty. 'I have written only one article for publication,' one lady wrote. I appreciated her candor. (5) Be kind and polite. Editors are human, too. Yes, they're at the mercy of authors in this business, believe it or not. Going around an editor to his superiors is not going to help matters. Intimidation is not going to work. After all, if an editor recommends your book, and it launches you into a successful career—and opens up new vistas for you—the editor is one of the best friends you'll ever have. Treat him like a friend. (6) Keep an idea file or notebook. Never throw away your notes. Who knows when one of those ideas written on the back of a napkin will become a tremendous book? (7) Write every day. Write something. Force creativity. That's right. Waiting on 'inspiration' is bad business and a cop-out. Write a diary, if nothing else, or a commentary on your daily devotions. (8) Pray for enablement. Yes, pray, if you're going to write for a religious market. Ask God for divine insight.

Johnson also says:

"(9) Make sure that you request permission for all material not covered by fair usage. The standard rule in copyright circles is that fair use covers quotations of fifty words or less provided there is sufficient publication information listed. For poems that are not in public domain (including song poems) it is always best to gain written permission from the person or firm which owns the copyright. For extensive uses of prose from the same source, the writer should seek written permission from the owner of the copyright. This will save horrible headaches for the editorial team in the event the book is published. (10) Read widely. I've had fledgling authors explain to me that they seldom read. That's a mistake. Reading widens your horizons, gives you insight, and helps your vocabulary. It doesn't mean that you copy another author's style, either. I'm a combination of all the people I've read. I pride myself on being a consummate author. No ego intended. I'm also a cognate of Charles Allen, Art Buchwald, Erma Bombeck, Eric Hoffer . . . Arthur Miller, Frank Baum, and James Baldwin. I owe a debt to all of them—and to thousands of others."

Martha Perry of Liguori Publications notes that some publishers, Liguori included, do very well with self-help books. She said, "We have seen an upsurge in inspirational books based on true-life experiences. Overcoming a handicap against great odds makes for exciting and interesting reading, as long as the writer avoids the tone of maudlin sentimentality. Heroes and heroines are not cloying, sickeningly sweet people; and they become larger than life through their handling of difficult situations.

Another form of publication that will always have an audience would be the presentation of down-to-earth ideas and suggestions of how to cope with some of life's problems. Human nature being what it is, these annoying little (or large) bugaboos will continue to plague us. Everyone gains some measure of satisfaction from hearing their problem is not insurmountable and that there just might be a very practical solution that they have not thought of or tried."

Perry encourages beginning writers to keep trying to come up with significant ideas and manuscripts. "The main thought an aspiring writer should keep in mind is to persevere. Just because one publisher does not like or cannot market the author's material is no basis for assuming that the material is unpublishable. Any constructive criticism offered by various editors should be weighed and implemented if possible; this is a good learning experience. Readers enjoy a well-written, interesting story—just because the story is true (and religious or spiritual) it need not be dry and dull. Write with enthusiasm and it will come over in the writing."

Many editors will remind writers that the most popular kind of nonfiction religious book today is the "how-to-do-it" book dealing with practical aspects of the Christian life, family life, life style, or that category of books that deal with the how-to-do-it of ministry in the local church—evangelism, discipleship, and other forms of outreach ministry. There is still a good market for well-written devotional material.

Keith M. Bailey, formerly of Christian Publications, offers beginning authors the following general advice concerning topics and writing methods in the how-to genre: "First, they should give careful attention to their research. Make sure their material is credible, and, if they are quoting, that it is well documented. They should carefully proof their manuscripts discovering errors in grammar and punctuation. They should do at least three revisions and rewrites before submitting it to any publisher. Many beginning authors in their anxiety to publish, submit material before it is really polished and has the attractiveness it should have to appeal to an editor."

He further notes that "new authors should not attempt to invent new styles, but should work hard at becoming true craftsmen in the writing trade. There may be a few born geniuses among writers, but most good writers are the product of diligent and hard work in writing and rewriting. A new writer should make a goal to learn to be precise in stating material. One glaring weakness of many new writers is the lack of precision and consistency in the language used. Terms change meaning from chapter to chapter, leading the reader to utter confusion."

Harvest House President, Robert H. Hawkins, agrees that "how-to" books are some of the best selling books for

Christian publishers. Unfortunately, "human interest stories are generally not the type of books that sell unless the author is speaking to 1,000 or more people every week. The book that is on a subject that is of vital interest to masses of people is the one that really sells."

Philip Rawley, a freelance editor living in Dallas, urges new writers to read both widely and well: "Reading good writing is great training for writing well."

Zondervan's John Sloan advises aspiring authors to attend as many writers' conferences as possible. He also suggests that anyone wanting to write should read widely, both to help in his illustrative use of material in writing and in building vocabulary skills. Sloan suggests further that writers begin by working on magazine pieces before venturing into the book field.

One of Thomas Nelson's trade editors notes that "any well-written, creative book on almost any subject will always draw attention and may sell well." Included in this list are books on the home and family, prophecy, Bible exegesis linked meaningfully to everyday life, high-interest biography, and one-of-a-kind specialities. As far as general advice: "Don't shortcut study and practice in the mechanics of effective writing. Become a 'good writer' first, then go on to becoming a 'good Christian writer'."

Wrap Up

As you can see from the comments of the editors above, each is different. Each represents a different style and philosophy of publishing religious books. From these words of advice, you, as an aspiring author, should realize that you really have your work cut out for you. However, do not be intimidated. You can, through study and discipline, write and get published. John Van Diest, President of Vision House Publishing, was no doubt correct when he said, "I believe the best books are yet to be written!"

Whatever you do, don't forget to pray about your submission and do your best to present as perfect a manuscript as possible to the publishers. As you "flesh out" your outline, and deal with the actual heart of your book, keep the comments of these experienced editors in mind. You might avoid having your work turned down by one of them.

7

A GUIDED TOUR OF THE
PUBLISHING CONTRACT

You have written your sample chapters, contacted a publisher, and are camping out by your mailbox. One day the postman brings a strange looking document entitled "Letter of Agreement." Only after you read the thing four times do you realize it's a contract from the editor offering to publish your book. But now what?

The first thing not to do is run out and buy a Cadillac. Yes, you will probably make some money from your book, but not enough for a new car. At least not right away. Support your writing habit until it supports you. Franz Kafka supported himself and his writing as an insurance salesman. Wallace Stevens did this as a lawyer. T. S. Eliot was a book editor, and Zane Grey a dentist. Walt Whitman worked as a secretary for the Department of the Interior. Kurt Vonnegut did PR work for General Electric. John Steinbeck was a journalist. Dorothy Parker and Aldous Huxley worked as copywriters, and O. Henry was a bank cashier before fleeing to South America after being charged with embezzlement![1] The message is, don't quit your day job.

Religious book sales in the United States reach well beyond $2 billion. You want your share of that total, but in all probability your share will be fairly small. Your rewards for writing will be something higher than just money. As Harry Emerson Fosdick once said, "Across the years one of the most gratifying rewards of my ministry has been the stream of letters, often from out-of-the-way places all over the world, bearing messages of appreciation for help received from those earlier books of mine."[2] This is an all-important perspective to keep on your writing ministry. After all, anyone can make money, but not everyone can make a positive, lasting contribution to another's life.

Back to contracts. What you must do, instead of planning to spend your future earnings at this point, is to try to understand the nature of the publishing contract. It is simply the written record of an agreement—a memorial or reminder of an original agreement—agreed to and signed by the author and the publishing company. Contracts deal with future uncertainty by "providing advance solutions for different, predictable eventualities. They say, 'Here's what I'll do, and here's what you'll do, if your book needs revising, or sells 1,000,000 copies, or someone sues us, or any number of other events occur'."[3] There is no assurance that even when a publisher commits time and money to a publishing project that there will ever be a return of investment. Writing and publishing a book is always a "gamble" for both the author and especially the publisher. Therefore, one way to look at the publishing contract is as an imperfect attempt at a fair division of the cost of losing and the rewards of winning.[4]

If a religious publisher offers to publish your book, the contract offered you will no doubt agree to have the publisher pay all printing and production costs, and to pay you specified royalties, among certain other standard matters. But remember, not every contract is alike. In this chapter we want to alert you to those areas on which you should concentrate. If you are offered a contract, the first thing to do is to read it especially carefully. Talk to a lawyer knowledgeable in literary law about it if you have any reservation. Some literary agents can also help.[5]

We are not lawyers, nor experts on contracts, but we have seen our share of publishing agreements. Book publishing follows predictable patterns, and most of the publishing contracts you will come across will be fairly standard. (An example of one standard publishing agreement can be seen later in this chapter in Sample B.) This is not to say that even standard contracts can't be modified. They can. Most publishers are very used to making changes in the contract. As the author, you should be aware of the more typical contract provisions as well as some of the variations that can be used. What we want to do here is to show you two actual contracts, one rather simple and the other more complex, and to give you a "guided tour" through the more complicated one.

One last word before we begin looking at the sample contracts. The purpose of the publishing contract is not to put something over on anyone. This is not an adversarial process. Authors and publishers must protect themselves—but they should also be equitable.

Now, *please refer to the sample contracts at the end of this chapter.*

The Simple Letter of Agreement

The first contract is a letter of agreement, like the one shown in Sample A at the end of the chapter. It is simple, easy to understand, and short. The author's name goes in the blank line on #1, and the name of the manuscript goes in the second line. #2 has to do with royalty payments. If a straight fee is agreed upon for the work under contract, then the line 2a is marked out and the fee is stipulated in 2b. Most publishers pay a royalty based on the net price received (i.e., a percentage of the actual amount of money invoiced and received by the publisher for sales of the work), but they sometimes buy a manuscript outright with a "flat fee" or "straight fee." This type of form is popular when publishers negotiate such a straight fee payment.

Numbers 3, 4, 5, and 6 of this agreement specify clearly who is responsible for what. The author simply signs the contract and returns it to the publisher. You will not see many agreements in publishing that take this form. We will spend more time on the more typical publishing contract.

The Standard Publishing Contract

The second contract we will examine is a much more complicated document. (Consult Sample B.)

#1 is a standard grant clause. The grant of rights clause allows the author to transfer some or all of the ownership of a work to a publisher, giving the publisher permission to publish the manuscript. This clause tells you all the things your publisher can do with the work once it is bought. It will define whether the grant of rights to the publisher is complete and exclusive, or is limited in one way or another. Many religious publishers will ask for the "sole and exclusive right to print, publish and sell" their edition of your book in the English language in North America.

From the publisher's point of view, the basic starting point for the grant of rights is *all rights*. (The reason for this is easy to understand: the publisher finds it difficult to administer minor exceptions.) However, this is often unrealistic. Authors are seldom willing to grant such sweeping rights, and that is why most contracts define carefully exactly what rights are being assigned to the publisher and what rights are being reserved by the author. The "primary right" that an author grants to a publisher is the right to print the work in book form—and even the primary right can be limited according to the terms of the contract.

Publishers and authors both should be reasonable and not try to get more than they need in this clause. If a publisher has an active subsidiary rights department and is able effectively to get more income through rights sales, why not let the publisher have them? On the other hand, if the publishing house is not active in the sale of such rights, why do they need to ask for all rights?

Another matter of concern for writers of today is the question of electronic media. Be sure to have this spelled out in your contract in the grant of rights clause. Remember, if you have no protection, you have no rights.

#2 allows the publisher to copyright the book in the author's name. You are just as likely to find contract language that gives the publisher the right to take out the copyright in its own name. But since all a publisher needs is the legal right to publish, and not necessarily ownership of the copyright itself, most do not mind if authors insist on having their books copyrighted in their names and not that of the publishing house. This is sometimes an area of negotiation between an author and a publisher. If the copyright is to be kept in the author's name (where the author's name appears on the copyright page), the license to publish the book is then transferred to the publisher. If the publisher copyrights the book in its own name, then certain provisions are usually made in the contract for the copyright to revert to the author after certain things occur, such as the book going out-of-print.

Publishers normally take responsibility for handling the formalities of copyright. Keep in mind that the whole reason for the publishing contract is to transfer rights from author to publisher, allowing the latter to publish the material owned by the former. If the author in fact grants all rights to the publisher, most publishing houses will as a legal matter copyright the work in their own name.

Clause #4 is a warranties and indemnities clause which is actually a protection used by publishers to indemnify them against possible lawsuits. The author certifies that the work is original and not plagiarized. The author further promises the publisher that he or she has every legal right to enter into a publishing agreement, and in so doing they are not interfering with anyone else's rights. Should these promises be breached, the author agrees to pay the publisher for any loss (cf. #26).

In the fifth clause the author agrees not to try to publish another book which would compete with the sale or impair sales of the work referred to in the contract. If the contracted work anthologized sermons, for example, the author could not offer a condensed version of the anthology to another publisher.

The author agrees to secure any necessary grants of permission to quote copyrighted works in #6. The general rule is that permission must be granted for all material still under copyright (unless it falls under the "fair use" doctrine of the Copyright Act, which permits a small amount of copying of a protected work without obtaining permission of the copyright owner). Since it is the author who knows what he or she has borrowed, it is sensible that the permissions responsibility should rest with the author and not the publisher.

#7 stipulates that the author will read the galley proofs of the manuscript and return them promptly to the publisher. It also stipulates that the author will not try to make major changes in the manuscript at that time. The reason for this is that once the material is set in type in galley proof form, it is expensive to make such corrections. Galleys, by the way, are the tentative layout of the material in page form, the proofs being drawn from uncorrected copy set in a single column, on which an author proofreads and marks any errors in the margins. The typesetter then goes back and makes any necessary corrections prior to page makeup.

The eighth clause spells out the deadline for delivery of the final copy of the manuscript to the publisher. (The original meaning of the word *deadline* meant the boundary around a prison beyond which no prisoner could go safely. If one stepped over the line, they were dead!) Many publishers are not that rigorous about the manuscript delivery date. If an author has a legitimate reason for being late, usually all that is required is keeping the publishing house properly informed. But don't count on this in all cases. The delivery date is very important because the publisher can terminate the contract if an author fails to get the manuscript to the editor in time. And if any advance money has been paid, the publisher can demand that it be returned. Authors should realize that publishers themselves operate under strict deadlines, and the late delivery of manuscripts can cause problems with work schedules, the printing of catalogs, and promotional pieces for the books, and with sales more generally. Most writers will admit that the deadline is a wonderful discipline, and they are thankful to get one.

The ninth clause is directly related to the preceding one. It gives the publisher the right to terminate the contract should the author fail to deliver the manuscript within a specified period of time from the stated delivery date.

The author agrees in #10 to provide an index if the publisher wants one. This is often a matter of negotiation, too. The publisher can provide an index as easily as the author.

#11 gives the publisher the right to edit the work. This is extremely important since it indicates who has the last say about what appears in the book. It is entirely standard for a publisher's contract to insist on the house's right to change the written material to fit its own editorial style. If you as the author wish final editorial control of everything in your book, you must be very sure to amend the contract to say so. Such a position is highly impractical for all but a few well established writers, however. It is best that you require of your editor that he or she consult with you regarding all changes, including the change of title. This also can be added to the contract.

The twelfth clause tells the author when to expect publication of the book once the manuscript is delivered in satisfactory condition. Usually an author can expect the finished book within twelve or eighteen months after the manuscript has been approved, depending of course on the publisher's schedule and on what sort of editing, typesetting method, graphics, and printing technology are to be used by the publisher on the particular book project.

#13 is *the* crucial paragraph for many authors. A royalty is a payment made to the author in exchange for granting the publisher the right to publish and sell your book. Sometimes a publisher will offer an author a one-time payment for a work, and in this case there is no continuing royalty payment. But most book publishing operates with a continuing royalty arrangement calculated as a percentage of the publisher's income from the sale of the book. The royalty is calculated in different ways, and it is of utmost importance to understand what this portion of your contract says.

Most publishing contracts stipulate a royalty rate of a certain percentage on the net sales of the book (usually twelve to fifteen percent of net sales on a trade book). This means that the royalty will be figured on what the publisher receives from bookstores, libraries, distributors, book clubs, and other places where the book is sold. Let's say a book retails for $15.95. The royalty rate is not based on that figure, however. It is based on the price given to outlets. A discount of 40 percent is common. This means that the author would receive a ten percent royalty on $9.57 instead of the $15.95 list price. In other words, the author is given ten percent or fifteen percent (or whatever the contract calls for) of whatever the publisher receives for the sale of the book. This is a very fair and clean arrangement, and it is easy to police. In this way, the available royalty money is figured on the basis of what the publisher actually *receives* from the sale of the book to all the various sales channels the publisher uses.

A few publishers offer a basic royalty rate based on the suggested *retail* price of a book, with rates for paperbacks commonly a bit lower than for hardcovers. While it may seem that this arrangement favors the author more than the one based on the net price (the royalty payment being based on the retail price of the book which is higher than the net price), the fact is that publishers almost never sell books at the retail or list price. Consequently, this system of royalty payment is irregular anymore. It is better to figure the available royalty money on the basis of what the publisher actually *receives* from the sale of the book.

Letters "a" through "m" of #13 in the sample contract spell out in detail what royalties will be paid under certain conditions. These stipulations are often found in standard contracts. Authors should pay far more attention to these adjustment provisions than they normally do. Remember, the matter of royalty percentage payment is as open to negotiation as anything else in a publishing contract. Remember also that some advance money is often paid to the author either at the time of contract signing, or when the final manuscript is submitted (or a combination of both)—but the advance money is always debited against future royalty earnings.

#14 stipulates what subsidiary rights belong to the publisher. This section of the contract could be called "Subsidiary Rights" or "Rights Conveyed" or "Grant of Rights." It is here that your contract will detail exactly what subsidiary rights belong to the publisher, and which belong to you as the author. As we mentioned in the Standard Grant Clause (#1), publisher's like to begin by seeking all rights. If you find this unrealistic because you might want to keep, say, television or movie or audio/video rights, this should be spelled out.

These rights are called "subsidiary rights" or "sub rights" because they are usually subsidiary in importance—less important than the primary right you give the publisher to initially publish and sell your book. However, as you can see from the sample contract under section 14, the area of sub rights includes a wide variety of media, some of which could actually prove more valuable than the right to publish the book in traditional form. In most cases, you will not be too concerned about your religious book being made into a movie!

Clauses fifteen through eighteen explain in greater detail other matters related to royalties and payments. Most contracts in book publishing provide for royalty accounts to be computed annually or semi-annually, with payments figured "less returns." Returns are those books a bookseller returns to the publisher for credit because they failed to sell. Returns certainly affect royalty payments to authors because a publisher does not want to pay royalty based on a large number of books originally shipped if a significant portion of unsold books will be returned a few months later. So some publishers have a "reserve against returns" clause, with the sort of wording you will see in #15. This allows the publisher to withhold part of the author's royalties for a specified period of time (since publishers only allow bookstores to return books for a specified period of time). A "reasonable reserve" in these matters is usually based on a return rate of twenty to twenty-five percent of the books shipped. Be sure you get this spelled out.

Clause #19 in the sample contract does not include any type of insurance on the part of the author. But things are changing. Many publishers now buy defamation and liability insurance for themselves, and a growing number are now providing similar protection for their authors. This arrangement is a fairly recent addition to some publishing agreements.[6]

Number 22 is the "termination" or "remainder and out-of-print clause." This language gives the publisher the prerogative of declaring the book out-of-print when the demand for the work "shall not . . . be sufficient to render its publication profitable." When a publisher declares a book out-of-print, due to the demand for the book dropping to the point the publisher cannot justify reprinting it and keeping it in the marketplace, the rights in most cases go back to the author. There should always be a written document to verify that the transfer of rights has been given. Since the publisher will declare a title out-of-print usually when a book has failed to sell a specified number of copies within a stated period of time, authors are wise if they can get this number and period of time stated in their contract. The author should ask the publisher to be specific in this area.

In virtually all publishing agreements, the author has the right to buy unsold copies of the book, usually at a deep discount, before it is remaindered, along with the plates and negatives in some cases, if the author wishes. With this option, the author can then sell the book to another publisher, or even self-publish it. Therefore, the author may be able to purchase remaindered copies as well as to recover the copyright or publication license at the same time.

"Remaindering" is a way the publisher can sell remaining copies of a book from the publisher's inventory at a fraction of the actual cost or worth. Put another way, reserve the right to discontinue publication and to dispose of unsold copies at a very low ("remainder") price. This is almost always a last-ditch effort for the publisher, since books are remaindered only after the publisher has determined they can be sold no other way. The publisher is usually required to notify the author if they determine that the book must be remaindered. Many publishers will allow an author to require that the book not be remaindered for a designated period of time after its publication. But all published books are subject to remaindering if in the long run they do not continue to sell.

In paragraph 23, the contract states how many complimentary copies of the finished book the author gets for personal use. Most contracts contain such a clause. The important thing here, though, is not the number of free copies the author is allowed (it's usually anywhere from five to twenty-five), but the price at which the author can purchase additional copies of the book from the publisher. This "buy-back" option is important for many writers who lecture or otherwise offer their own books for sale to the public through their appearances. Usually the publisher will insist on paying a more limited royalty on buy-backs if the author wishes a more generous discount on the books bought back for resale. Again, the discount is a matter for negotiation.

While the language in our sample contract does not suggest this, in many contracts this clause would prohibit authors from reselling their author's copies. If an author makes personal appearances, or speaks on the lecture circuit, or has other opportunities to make direct sales of their books, they should ask to have such prohibition against resale language dropped. Most publishers are open to permitting resale so long as the initial sale of copies to the author is royalty-free. In this way, the author is not earning a royalty why buying copies of their own book—but they are allowed to resell the book and keep the difference between the wholesale and retail prices.

#24 is another key clause. It is understandable that a publisher who takes a chance on one book project by an author wants to tie that author to the house for a possible future project. The publisher naturally enough wants to participate in an author's success by gaining the right to publish the author's subsequent book and reaping the benefit of a developing readership waiting for the next publication. This the publisher can do through two contract clauses, "the option clause" and "the right of first refusal clause."

The option clause is certainly the most forceful clause from the publisher's point of view. It requires the author to sell his or her next book to the same publisher on the same terms of the present contract. Under the option clause, the author may not submit any future book to another publisher until after the original publisher has made a publishing decision. Most authors will wish to vigorously negotiate this type of clause, thinking of it in the nature of indentured servitude.

Perhaps a more reasonable clause, at least from the author's point of view, is the right of first refusal clause. In this type of agreement, the author has to allow the original publisher the "first chance" at the author's next book project. Sometimes the publisher asks that it also be given a second chance—to match a better deal given the author by another publishing firm. A third variant of the option clause is the "capping rights" or the "right of last refusal." This gives the publisher one last chance to make a deal with the author by taking into account all other publishers' offers and trying to top them. The terms of these rights to first, second and last refusals, including the response time a publisher has to make a decision, are open to negotiation. Negotiation is not normally possible under an option clause.

As an author, you would be better off either to negotiate the removal of these clauses altogether, if you can, or to sign a right of first refusal clause with a short publisher's response time. We have heard of some writers who purposely keep a "terrible" manuscript around for the sole purpose of living up to the letter of the law in such a right of first refusal clause. They say they know it is so bad that no publisher could possibly want it. After offering the "terrible" manuscript to the original publisher upon the publication of a first book, they can then turn to other houses to negotiate other projects as they wish. Of course this rarely happens in religious publishing!

The assignment clause in #25 is contained in all publishing contracts. It protects both the publisher and the author should either wish to transfer the contract rights to another party, which transfer of rights has to be in writing. Assignments can occur when an author designates that the income from a book be paid to a creditor, for example, or when a publishing company sells its book list to another publisher, or when the company itself goes out of business. Usually a publisher keeps the right to make assignments unilaterally, but when the author wishes to assign rights or royalties to a third party the publisher typically reserves the right to agree with the assignment for it to be valid.

#26 is related to #4. Both have to do with copyright infringements and possible legal action taken against the author or the publisher. Generally, a copyright infringement suit is brought in the name of the person owning or controlling the rights that have been infringed against the person thought to be infringing the rights. What is important in this section is to see if it is the author or the publisher, or both equally, who takes the financial burden if someone makes a claim of infringement of copyright on the work. As the author, you should ask for an infringement provision in your contract that limits your financial liability to claims considered by a court. Otherwise, you could be held liable by the publisher for legal costs involved in claims that are bogus. Often, a publisher will withhold royalty payments pending the outcome of a lawsuit. You need to know how much of the entire royalty is to be withheld, and for how long. Also, find out if you are liable for any agreed-upon amount in the event that a judgement is made for the claimant.

A promotion clause, such as in #28 in the sample contract, is typical of publishing contracts—the right to use an author's name virtually is implied in the other terms and conditions of the contract—though what is included in this section depends on the size and kind of publisher you deal with. Many larger, mostly general houses, commit to large sums of money for publicity and advertising campaigns, including author tours, media appearances, and bookstore signing parties. This happens also in religious publishing, especially in the larger houses, but not nearly so regularly. However, all houses, large and small, will want to promote an author's work by using the author's name, photo, and biographical summary. The typical publishing contract will give the publisher this right.

The author bestows on the publisher the "right of publicity" when they sign a book contract, giving the publisher the right to decide how and when to use the author's name in the promotion of the book.

Some publishers wish to require the author to assist in certain promotions. In that case, the contract should clearly state whatever obligation in this regard is required, and which party bears the expenses. If there are some things you definitely would or would not do in the publicity and promotion of your book, these should be spelled out in this section of the contract.

The "Law Applicable" or "Governing Law" clause of #29 can be a headache for an author who lives in one state while his or her publisher's office is in another state. This clause simply specifies what body of law will apply in a legal dispute between the publisher and the author. It means that the author must agree to tackle whatever legal hassles ensue from the book in the publisher's state. The author cannot be sued in his or her own state since through this clause they agree that jurisdiction over disputes will always be in the publisher's home state. Many lawyers who practice literary law prefer the law of the state of New York, as much of the case law concerning the publishing industry has been decided in New York courts.

Remember that this "choice of law" clause does not determine where a lawsuit must be filed. The venue and jurisdiction of a suit usually cannot be chosen by the parties to a publishing contract, for a number of other factors determine these things.

This sample contract has a provision for other stipulations, which is what clause #32 is about. It is added to the existing agreements already given and allows either party by mutual consent to add other matters that they wish to specify. Normally, all changes in the contract terms are to be in writing (oral agreements are not effective) and signed by the party against whom the new terms are to be enforced. Authors should always have a confirming letter signed by the publisher.

For Further Assistance

For additional help in knowing what to look for in a contract, the periodical *The Writer* will send you an article by Irwin Karp entitled, "What the Writer Should Look For in His First Book Contract." The address of *The Writer* is listed in the next chapter. Another resource is a quarterly briefing service newsletter on the latest developments in print, audio and electronic publishing law entitled *Kirsch's Publishing Law Update*. See footnote five at the end of this chapter for the address. Most large city bar associations have committees of specialists in literary law and intellectual property law. These committees often are willing to offer inexpensive legal work, sometimes even pro bono work, for authors unable to pay much for legal services. For referrals, you can call the bar association and ask for the name of the chairperson of the appropriate committee.[7]

Any contract you sign with a publisher is an important, formidable document which could have a serious impact on your future. Be careful. Read it carefully and, if necessary, check it out with someone who knows publishing or literary law. While it pays to be cautious, remember that reputable publishers have no desire to "rip you off" or to create bad feelings between themselves and you. Publishers live off the output of writers, so the relationship between the publisher and the author must be a symbiotic one. Most publishers want to cultivate a good working relationship with an author because if that writer's books sell, the publisher will want more of them.

We hope you and your publisher come to a meeting of the minds with a contract accommodating the needs and expectations of both parties, and that your first contract is signed, sealed, and delivered very soon.

Sample A

LETTER OF AGREEMENT

Mailing Address_____

City, State, Zip_____

Social Security Number_____

This agreement between_____
(Name of Author)
party of the first part, and Black Hole Publishers, Inc. of Wheaton, Illinois, organized and doing business under the laws of the State of Illinois, party of the second part, witnesseth:

1.   That, whereas,_____, is authorized to assign publication rights of the manuscript entitled _____and the
(Name of Manuscript)
distribution rights during the full term of copyright and all renewals thereof to the Black Hole Publishing Company.

2.   Royalties:

    a.   _____percent (_____%) royalty will be paid on the gross sale of all books sold.

    b. $_____shall be paid at the time of publication for the rights to publish the author's manuscript.

    c.   The author will receive a 40% discount on all books purchased from Black Hole Publishers, Inc. on all orders for five (5) or more copies.

        d.   No royalty shall be paid on books sold to the author at the 40% discount schedule.

        e.   One hundred and fifty copies are royalty exempt for review and gift purposes. Also, no royalty shall be paid on any additional copies given away for the purpose of review or promotion or on copies damaged by fire or water, or on copies sold as "remainders" or at below cost.

        3.   Black Hole Publishers, Inc. will furnish five (5) copies of the book to the author without charge.

        4.   If at any time the sale does not warrant the continuation of the title, Black Hole Publishers, Inc. shall have the right to "remainder" the remaining stock, royalty exempt. However, the author shall be given the right to purchase the balance of the stock at production costs.

        5.   Black Hole Publishers, Inc. will handle all the typesetting, layout, design, and printing of said publication in its catalogues, through bookstore promotions, in its periodicals as long as it seems feasible and practical.

        6.   Black Hole Publishers, Inc. understands that the manuscript is original and free of any copyright infringements. (The author should request a release for reprinting any long quotations from a copyrighted source.)

_____   _____

(Signature of Author)   (Date)

_____   _____

(Representative of B. H.)   (Date)

Sample B

PUBLISHING AGREEMENT

Frumious Bandersnatch, Inc., Publishers

Grant

1. In consideration of the stipulations and covenants of the respective parties hereto, the AUTHOR hereby grants to the PUBLISHER its successors and assigns, the sole and exclusive right to publish and sell, or license the publication and sale of the above work in book form throughout the world during the full term of copyright and all renewals and extensions thereof, including the subsidiary rights hereinafter specified.

Copyright

2. The PUBLISHER, at its discretion, will register copyright to the WORK within three (3) months of publication in the name of the AUTHOR in accordance with the requirements of the copyright law of the United States. The PUBLISHER will take reasonable care to affix the proper copyright notice to each copy of the WORK.

Amendment of Law

3. All references to copyright made in this agreement are subject to such amendment and change as may be enacted by the Congress of the United States of America or by any other legal authority with regard to the present Copyright Act or by the adoption of any new Copyright Act.

Author's Guarantee

4. The AUTHOR certifies to the PUBLISHER that he is the sole author and proprietor of said work; that the work is original and does not infringe upon the statutory copyright or upon any common law right, proprietary right, or any other right whatsoever; that it contains nothing of an objectionable or libelous character; that the work is not in violation of any right of privacy; and that he and/or his legal representative shall and will hold harmless and keep indemnified the PUBLISHER from all suits and all manner of claims, proceedings, and expenses, including attorney's fees, which may be taken or incurred on the ground that said work is such a violation, or contains something objectionable or libelous or otherwise unlawful. The AUTHOR undertakes for himself, his heirs and assigns, to execute at any time, on request of the PUBLISHER, any document or documents to confirm or continue any of the rights defined herein. AUTHOR guarantees that WORK has not heretofore been published; that he is the sole and exclusive owner of the rights herein granted to the PUBLISHER; and that he has not heretofore assigned, pledged, or otherwise encumbered the same.

Competing Edition

5. The AUTHOR shall not, without the consent of the PUBLISHER, publish any abridged or other edition of said work or any book of similar or competing character tending to interfere with the sale of the work covered by this agreement.

Permissions

6. If copyright material from other sources is included in the work, the AUTHOR shall, at his own expense, obtain from the copyright owners or their representatives written permission for use of such material, and shall deliver such permissions at the time of delivery of the final manuscript.

Author Proofs

7. The AUTHOR agrees to read and correct the galley and page proofs and return them to the PUBLISHER in such time and manner as will not delay the printer, and to pay, as a charge against royalties, or, at the option of the PUBLISHER, in cash, the expense of any alterations or additions authorized by the AUTHOR (other than those due to printer's errors) in the proof in excess of ten percent (10%) of the cost of composition of the said work as originally supplied by the AUTHOR, but in no case shall the PUBLISHER's share of this cost exceed fifty dollars ($50.00), except by mutual and express consent.

Delivery of Final Manuscript

8. The AUTHOR agrees to deliver into the hands of the PUBLISHER on or before the day of _____ 19__ a final revised copy of the manuscript, legibly typewritten and satisfactory to the PUBLISHER in content and form and ready to print from, including all charts, drawings, designs, photographs, and illustrations which are referred to in the text and intended to be a part thereof suitable for use by the PUBLISHER in preparing copies for reproduction. In the event the AUTHOR chooses not to deliver such charts, drawings, designs, photographs, and illustrations, the PUBLISHER may supply them, charging the cost thereof against and deducting it from any or all monies accruing to the AUTHOR under this and/or other agreements between the AUTHOR and the PUBLISHER.

The PUBLISHER may with the consent of the AUTHOR, supply charts, drawings, designs, photographs, and illustrations which in their opinion are necessary to the content, promotion, and distribution of said work, charging the cost thereof against and deducting it from any or all monies accruing to the AUTHOR under this and/or other agreements between the AUTHOR and the PUBLISHER, except the cost of engraving and printing.

The length of the manuscript shall be approximately _____ words, and shall contain the following kind and approximate number of illustrations: _____.

Time Limit for Publication

9. If, within the time specified in paragraph 8, such manuscript and support material is not delivered, the PUBLISHER shall not be bound by the time limit of publication hereinafter provided for, and in the event the manuscript is not delivered within three (3) months after delivery date specified in Paragraph 8, the PUBLISHER shall have the right of election to continue this agreement in effect or to terminate it and to receive back from the AUTHOR any monies paid or expended hereunder.

Index

10. If the PUBLISHER requests, the AUTHOR agrees to supply within 15 days after final page proof of the text has been submitted by the PUBLISHER, an index in proper content and form and ready to set type therefrom. If the AUTHOR fails to do so the PUBLISHER may have one prepared and charge the cost thereof to the AUTHOR.

Editing

11. The text and illustrations of said WORK shall be subject to editing and revision by the PUBLISHER prior to first publication, or to any subsequent printing; provided, however, that such editing or revision shall not materially change the meaning, or materially alter the text of said WORK without the AUTHOR'S consent. Editing to correct infelicities of expression, misstatements of fact, misquotations, errors in grammar, sentence structure, and spelling, and editing to make the WORK conform to the PUBLISHER'S style of punctuation, capitalization, and like details, shall not be considered as material changes.

Publisher's Agreement to Publish

12. The PUBLISHER agrees to publish said WORK at its own expense, not later than eighteen (18) months from the date of receipt of satisfactory manuscript, unless specified otherwise in this agreement in such style, and at such price as the PUBLISHER shall determine as best suited to its success (including special prepublication price, if any). It is understood that advertising, number and destination of free copies, and all details of manufacture and publication shall be in the exclusive control of the PUBLISHER, and the stock of plates and books shall be the property of the PUBLISHER.

Royalty

13. The PUBLISHER shall pay to the AUTHOR royalty as follows:

(a)   Ten percent (10%) of the net sales on all copies of the regular trade edition (except as noted hereinafter) sold by the PUBLISHER within the United States of America (by net sales is meant gross receipts less discounts to the trade);

(b)   Five percent (5%) of net sales of the paperback edition sold by the PUBLISHER within the United States of America (by net sales is meant gross receipts less discounts to the trade).

(c)   When in its judgment it is necessary or advisable, the PUBLISHER is authorized to sell copies of the WORK at a discount of fifty percent (50%) or more. When copies are sold at discounts of fifty percent (50%) or more, a royalty of five percent (5%) of net sales shall be paid to the AUTHOR.

(d)   When copies are sold by the PUBLISHER through mail order, coupon advertising, or radio or television advertising, the royalty shall be five percent (5%) of the amount received therefrom, excluding postage and other handling charges.

(e)   For the purpose of keeping the WORK in print and in circulation as long as possible, the AUTHOR agrees that, after two (2) years from the date of first publication of the regular trade edition, if in any twelve (12)-month period the sales do not exceed two hundred and fifty (250) copies, the royalty shall be one-half of the prevailing rate.

(f)   The PUBLISHER shall have the right to arrange for foreign editions of said work, paying the AUTHOR fifty percent (50%) of the net payments received by the PUBLISHER.

(g)   The PUBLISHER shall have the right to make arrangements for sales of American edition copies of the WORK outside the continental limits of the United States and its dependencies, paying the AUTHOR on such sales a royalty of ten percent (10%) of the amount actually received by the PUBLISHER.

(h)   On copies of any cheap edition published by another firm, for which the PUBLISHER shall have the exclusive right to arrange, the AUTHOR shall receive fifty percent (50%) of the amount received by the PUBLISHER. Royalties on any cheap edition issued by the PUBLISHER shall be fixed by agreement between the AUTHOR and the PUBLISHER.

(i)   On copies of a textbook edition at a reduced suggested retail selling price issued for sale to educational institutions, a royalty of five percent (5%) of the textbook suggested retail selling price shall be paid to the AUTHOR.

(j)   On bound copies sold from PUBLISHER'S stock to or through recognized book clubs, a royalty of five percent (5%) of the suggested retail selling price shall be paid to the AUTHOR, provided, however, in the case of copies sold through the PUBLISHER's recognized book clubs for use as one of two or more books offered as a main selection, the royalty shall be one-half of the aforementioned royalty; and provided, further, in the case of copies used as bonus or introductory offers in the PUBLISHER's recognized book clubs, no royalty shall be paid.

(k)   The PUBLISHER shall have the exclusive right to make arrangements with recognized book clubs granting them permission to print special editions of the WORK. Compensation for such rights shall be divided equally between AUTHOR and PUBLISHER.

(l)   On the sale of sheet stock from the American edition sold to a foreign publisher, the AUTHOR shall be compensated at the rate of ten percent (10%) of the net amount received by the PUBLISHER.

(m)   No royalties shall be paid upon copies given to the AUTHOR, salesmen's samples, damaged copies, returned copies, copies given away to publicize the WORK or to promote sales, or copies sold at or below manufacturing costs as determined by the PUBLISHER.

Subsidiary Rights

14. The following shall be considered as subsidiary rights, for the sale of which the PUBLISHER shall be solely responsible; serial rights before and after book publication; dramatic, public reading, and other nondramatic performing rights; motion picture rights; translations, digests, abridgements, selections, and anthologies; also mechanical, visual such as microfilm and micropoint (other than motion picture), sound reproducing, and recording rights (including but not limited to television and broadcasting, phonographic, wire, tape, video, and electro video recordings other than motion pictures); lyric rights and adaptions of said WORK for commercial use. The division of receipts from the sales of subsidiary rights shall be as follows:

(a)   Except as provided in (c) and (d) of section 13, fifty percent (50%) to the AUTHOR and fifty percent (50%) to the PUBLISHER.

(b)   Dramatic and/or motion picture, television and broadcasting rights, and adaptations for commercial use: seventy-five percent (75%) to the AUTHOR and twenty-five percent (25%) to the PUBLISHER of the amount received by the PUBLISHER.

(c)   The PUBLISHER is authorized to grant permission, at no charge and without paying royalty, for use of the work, or selections therefrom, by recognized organizations for the physically disabled.

Royalty Payments

15. Royalty accounts shall be computed annually to the first (1) day of April of each year, and statements thereof shall be rendered and the amount shown due thereby paid on or before the thirtieth (30) day of the following June. However, if in the opinion

of the PUBLISHER, there is a risk of booksellers returning for credit a substantial quantity of unsold copies of the WORK the PUBLISHER may withhold a reasonable reserve with which to compensate for such returns.

First Royalty Statement

16. If the WORK shall have been on sale for a period of time shorter than three months as of April 1 of a given year, the first statement shall be postponed until the next succeeding April 1 for computation.

Accounts Due Publisher

17. The AUTHOR agrees that any account, bills, advances, or amounts of any nature that may be due the PUBLISHER by the AUTHOR, whether under this agreement or not, shall be chargeable against and may be deducted from any or all monies accruing to the AUTHOR under this and/or other agreements between the AUTHOR and the PUBLISHER.

Taxes on Royalties

18. It is mutually agreed that any taxes, domestic or foreign, which are or may be levied on the AUTHOR'S royalties, when paid by the PUBLISHER are proper charges against the royalty earnings due under this agreement, and may be withheld by the PUBLISHER.

Insurance

19. No insurance whatever need be effected by the PUB-LISHER for the AUTHOR.

Properly Spacing Author's Books

20. For the purpose of orderly and systematically promoting the AUTHOR'S reputation and acceptance as a writer, the

PUBLISHER agrees not to publish this WORK until six months shall have elapsed since publication of the AUTHOR's next preceding book, whether the next preceding book was published by the PUBLISHER or not, and the AUTHOR agrees that he will not permit his succeeding book to be published until six months shall have elapsed after publication of this WORK, whether the next succeeding book be published by the PUBLISHER or not.

Unavoidable Delay

21. It is mutually agreed that neither the AUTHOR nor the PUBLISHER shall be held responsible for any delays which may be due to abnormal conditions existing in manufacturing, publishing, and distribution of books, including shortages in manufacturing facilities, personnel, and materials.

Termination

22. If at any time during the continuance of this agreement the demand for the WORK shall not, in the opinion of the PUBLISHER, be sufficient to render its publication profitable and it wishes to discontinue permanently the publication of said WORK, the AUTHOR shall have the right to buy from the PUBLISHER as an entirety all copies on hand at the cost of the manufacture and the stamps, electrotype plates and engravings of illustrations (if in existence) at actual cost to the PUBLISHER, including the composition. If the AUTHOR fails to exercise this option by paying for the same in cash within thirty (30) days after notice has been mailed to him by the PUBLISHER to his latest known address by registered mail, the PUBLISHER may destroy or dispose of the same as it sees fit without commission or percentage, and this agreement shall forthwith cease and terminate.

Author Copies

23. The PUBLISHER will furnish six (6) copies of the published WORK to the AUTHOR at no charge. Should the

AUTHOR desire additional copies for personal use, they shall be supplied at forty percent (40%) discount from the suggested retail selling price, carriage additional.

Right of First Refusal

24. The AUTHOR grants the PUBLISHER the right of first refusal on his next work. The AUTHOR shall not offer the same to someone else on more favorable terms without first offering the same to PUBLISHER on the same terms. Such option shall be exercised within ninety (90) days after the receipt by the PUBLISHER of the complete and final manuscript; provided, however, that in no case shall the PUBLISHER be obligated to accept or decline such manuscript earlier than ninety (90) days after the publication of the WORK covered by this agreement. Should the PUBLISHER decline the first manuscript so offered under the option, the AUTHOR is relieved of obligation for further submission.

Assignment

25. This agreement may be assigned but only in its entirety and shall be binding upon and inure to the benefit of the personal representatives and assigns of the AUTHOR and upon and to the successors and assigns of the PUBLISHER. No assignment shall be valid, as against the PUBLISHER, unless a copy or duplicate original of the same shall have been filed with the PUBLISHER.

Suits for Infringement of Copyright

26. If the copyright of the WORK is infringed, and if the parties proceed jointly, the expenses and recoveries, if any, shall be shared equally and if they do not proceed jointly, either party shall have the right to prosecute such action, and such party shall bear all the expenses thereof, and any recoveries shall belong to such party; and if such party shall not hold the record title of the copyright, the other party shall permit the action to be brought in his or its name.

Sums Due and Owing

27. Any sums due and owing from the AUTHOR to the PUBLISHER, whether or not arising out of this agreement, may be deducted from any sum due, or that may become due from the PUBLISHER to the AUTHOR pursuant to this agreement.

Author's Name, Likeness, etc.

28. In connection with the publication, advertising, and marketing of the WORK, PUBLISHER shall, without restriction, have the right to use, and allow others to use, AUTHOR's name, signature, and likeness, and biographic material concerning AUTHOR.

Law Applicable

29. This agreement shall be interpreted according to the law of the State of _____ regardless of the places of its physical execution.

Modification

30. This agreement constitutes the complete understanding of the parties. No modification or waiver of any provision shall be valid unless in writing and signed by both parties. The waiver of a breach of any of the terms hereof or any default hereunder shall not be deemed a waiver of any subsequent breach or default, whether of the same or similar nature, and shall not in any way affect the other terms hereof.

Limitation of Agreement

31. This agreement shall not be binding upon either the PUBLISHER or the AUTHOR unless it is signed by all and delivered to the PUBLISHER within a period of forty-five (45) days from the date of this agreement.

Amendments

32. This contract contains a memorandum of all the agreements, expressed or implied, between the parties hereto, but may be amended at any time by mutual consent of the parties hereto, but only in writing, signed by both parties and affixed to this contract and made a part thereof.

The changes, alterations, interlineations, and deletions made in Paragraphs _____ of this contract, and the additional typed clauses numbered _____ were made and added before the execution hereof.

Notice provision: Any notice to be given hereunder shall be sent by registered or certified mail, return receipt requested, addressed to the parties at their respective addresses above given. Either party may designate a different address by notice so given.

IN WITNESS WHEREOF the parties have duly executed this agreement the day and year first above written.

_____   _____
Author's Signature   Publisher's Signature

_____   _____
Date   Date

ENDNOTES

[1]Gregg Levoy, *This Business of Writing* (Cincinnati, Ohio: Writer's Digest Books, 1992), 9-10.

[2]Harry Emerson Fosdick, *The Living of These Days* (New York: Harper & Row, 1956), 135.

[3]Brad Bunnin and Peter Beren, *Author Law & Strategies* (Berkeley, Calif.: Nolo Press, 1983), 6. The publishing contract (or at least an implied contract) is also the only legal remedy for the misappropriation of ideas. For a good discussion of idea protection, with very interesting examples, see Jonathan Kirsch, *Kirsch's Handbook of Publishing Law* (Los Angeles: Acrobat Books, 1995), 7-20; for more guidance on the actual publishing contract, see *Kirsch's Handbook,* 59-135 and Linda F. Pinkerton, *The Writer's Law Primer* (New York: Lyons & Burford, Publishers, 1990), 35-43.

[4]Bunnin and Beren, *Author Law & Strategies,* 6.

[5]Helpful guides for the working writer on the publishing contract are Ted Crawford, *The Writers Legal Guide* (New York: Hawthorne Books, 1977), Kirk Poking and Leonard S. Meranus, editors, *Law and the Writer* (Cincinnati, Ohio: Writer's Digest Books, 1978), Brad Bunnin and Peter Beren, *Author Law & Strategies* (Berkeley, Calif.: Nolo Press, 1983), Richard Balkin, *A Writer's Guide to Contract Negotiations* (Cincinnati, Ohio: Writer's Digest Books, 1985), Linda F. Pinkerton, *The Writer's Law Primer* (New York: Lyons & Burford, Publishers, 1990), and Jonathan Kirsch, *Kirsch's Handbook of Publishing Law* (Los Angeles: Acrobat Books, 1995).

For a newsletter on the latest developments in print, audio and electronic publishing law (including copyright, contracts, libel, and invasion of privacy, idea protection, etc.), writers and editors may subscribe to *Kirsch's Publishing Law Update,* a quarterly briefing service, at P.O. Box 34962, Los Angeles, California, 90034.

[6]For example, Stuart Speiser looked at publisher's liability insurance when it was rare in "Insuring Authors: A New Proposal,'' in *Publishers Weekly,* May 7, 1982, 26.

[7]Some helpful names and addresses are in Linda F. Pinkerton, *The Writer's Law Primer,* 82-5.

8

TOOLS OF THE TRADE

One writer likened the reading of religious literature to being stoned to death with popcorn. That is an interesting image. Popcorn is light, fluffy, and not very substantial. Religious literature probably got this reputation because some writers of such material thought all they had to do was to sit down and pound out whatever sounded sweet—things about the brotherhood of man and the Fatherhood of God, we suppose. There may be a small place for such writing, but that place is not in most religious books or articles, especially not the good ones.

How do you keep from serving up theological popcorn? You do it by researching your topic. Regardless of what you are writing about, you do not know all there is to know about it, nor will you ever know all there is to know about it, and you will benefit from doing a little homework. Research will add substance and perspective to your work. Remember, you are not a spider, spinning your web of words from only your own insides. A writer is more like a honey bee, taking a bit of pollen from this flower and then that one, and putting it all together to make its honey.

Publishers want to see that you have done your homework. When you submit a manuscript or a manuscript idea to a publisher, you need to determine what category you think your book falls into. Is it biography or business? It is church life or Christian living? Are you writing a novel? Are you writing a book for Christian education or counseling? Is your book about evangelism or divorce? Are you writing on the cults, or on family devotions, or on church history, or on humor? Is your book a text that could be used in a college course on apologetics or a seminary course on hermeneutics? And so on. You have to figure out in your own mind just what it is that you are doing. Then, you need to find reference material in a good library that will help you locate publishers that publish the kinds of books that you are writing. This basically is market research, and you need to do it so that you are sending your proposal only to publishers whose list matches the kind of book you are writing. What kind of reference material can you find? You can find periodically updated guides to the religious book markets. For example, in most good libraries you can find volumes such as the ones we introduce below. These volumes and others like them will show you what kinds of books a given publisher specializes in. They also list requirements for submission and will most likely include an address and phone number of the house—along with the names of the acquisition editors in many cases. You should study these books closely and determine which publishers you think would be interested in your writing project. (By the way, these guides will also give you the names and locations of agents who work with religious books as a specialty.) You need to show your editor that you have done a thorough job of research on the publishing company before you contacted them. With these kinds of tools in hand, you will know, for example, what Thomas Nelson wants to publish, and what Tyndale House wants to publish, and what Harvest House includes in their publishing program. You will know not to send to Crossway

Books any biblical fiction; but if you are writing in the area of contemporary critical issues, they may be interested in what you are doing. If you don't show that you have done your research, your material will come back to you in very rapid fashion.

Writer's Market Books

Although most valuable reference books can be consulted in a good library, there are some you will no doubt wish to own and use as tools in your writing profession. Let us introduce you to four of them. They are gold mines of information and marketing tips. They will not be resources for research into your various topics of interest (except that the fourth one we recommend does have some material on that), but are instead resources for the writing process and the selling of your writing.

The Writer's Handbook: This is a must for the beginning writer. The volume is published by The Writer, Inc., the people who also publish the monthly magazine *The Writer*. They are located in Boston, Massachusetts. The book is updated annually so the current market information can be included. The latest edition is edited by Sylvia K. Burack. Within its covers are most of the things you need to know about the writing and selling of short stories, novels, short novels, articles, nonfiction books, confessionals, poetry, plays, material for juveniles, science fiction, book reviews, and much more—in all, more than 2,500 markets for manuscript sales.

The *Handbook* is divided into different sections: "Background for Writers," "How to Write" (including writing techniques for general fiction, specialized fiction, articles and books, poetry, juvenile and young adult material, and playwriting), and "Where to Sell" (including the article markets, fiction markets, poetry markets, greeting card markets, the college, literary and little magazine markets, humor, fillers, and short-item markets, juvenile, teen, and young adult magazines, the drama market, and the book publishers). There are 100 or so contributions on a variety of topics by highly-regarded authors like Sidney Sheldon, Stephen King, Ken Follett, John Jakes, Phyllis A. Whitney, Neil Simon, and Joyce Carol Oates. Then there are many chapters of practical advice and instruction on writing techniques, literary agents, editors, copyright, manuscript preparation, and so on.

The first section has chapters on matters pertaining to pre-writing themes. For example, some of the topics covered include agents, a writer's education, the ABC's of copyright, journal keeping, the myths that haunt writers, and how to develop a writer's eye. All of the articles are helpful to the novice who may be asking, "Do I really want to be a writer?"

The second section is for those who answer this latter question affirmatively. It deals with techniques for writing. Sample topics in one of the latest editions are "What makes a fiction writer?," "How to write a novel," "Leaving the reader satisfied," "Finding the right shape for your story," "Writing from research," "Four tests for a paragraph," "Titles that talk," "Checklist for a salable article," "Writing for the teenage market," "Writing for the inspirational and religious market," and "Writing a television play."

Section three has chapters on markets and business issues, along with some important things that writers should beware of—like literary prize offers, syndicates, writers colonies, writers conferences, organizations for authors, and listings of literary agents and markets. On the markets for your work, the lists include such places as popular magazines of general interest, specialized magazines using such genres as detective and mystery fiction, science fiction, and romance magazines. Poetry markets are included, as are organs to sell fillers and humor, religious materials, juvenile and young adult writing. A good selection of book publishers is offered as well. Virtually all writers have a keen interest in market lists.

In the list of book publishers provided in *The Writer's Handbook*, you will find the entries presented as shown in the following examples from a recent edition:

ABINGDON PRESS—201 Eighth Avenue South, Nashville, TN 37202. Mary Catherine Dean, Ed. Religious books: mainline, social issues. Religious books, juveniles, general nonfiction. Query with outline and one or two sample chapters. Guidelines.

BAKER BOOK HOUSE—P.O. Box 6287, Grand Rapids, MI 49516-6287. Religious nonfiction. Dan Van't Kerkhoff, Ed., general trade and professional books. Allan Fisher, Ed., academic and reference books. Royalty.

The entries give you the "who, what, and where" of the publishing trade. The book is a massive paperback volume. All in all, it is well worth the money you will spend for it. Study it and mark it up, for this is a tool you will want to keep sharp.

Writer's Market: This is published annually by Writer's Digest Books in Cincinnati, Ohio. These are the people who publish the monthly magazine *Writer's Digest. Writer's Market* differs from *The Writer's Handbook* in that the *Writer's Market* is almost exclusively market information. There are 4,000+ buyers of freelance writing, giving names, addresses, pay rates, editorial needs, plus a new section of computer software publishers looking for freelance material. Less than ten percent of the book is devoted to matters related to writing. That is because this reference specializes in the selling of writing—of all sorts of writing, including articles, short stories, books, scripts, fillers, gags, photos, verse, plays, and fiction. Indeed, the subtitle of the book is "Where To Sell What You Write."

This reference aid also includes advice from experienced freelancers that will spark new ideas, tips on record keeping and what to charge, a section on agents and syndicates, and a manuscript submission chart to help writers keep track of their work. The up-to-date contact information and market listings under Book Publishing in *Writer's Market* contain fuller entries than those in *The Writer's Handbook*. More information is given that helps writers better judge the market potential for their particular project. The two examples cited above appear as follows in a recent edition of *Writer's Market*:

ABINGDON PRESS—201 8th Avenue, South, Box 801, Nashville, TN 37202. (615) 749-6403. Editor Trade Books: Mary Catherine Dean. Senior Editor Reference/Academic: Davis Perkins. Senior Editor Church Resources: Ronald P. Patterson. Editor Professional Books: Greg Michael. Publishes paperback originals and reprints; church supplies. Receives approximately 2,500 submissions annually. Published 100 titles last year. Few books from first-time authors; 90-95% of books from unagented writers. Average print order for a writer's first book is 4,000-5,000. Pays royalty. Publishes book an average of 18 months after acceptance. Query for electronic submissions. Computer printout submissions acceptable; prefers letter-quality. Ms guidance for SASE. Reports in 2 months. Nonfiction: Religious-lay and professional, children's religious books and academic texts. Length: 32-300 pages. Query with outline and samples only. Reviews artwork/photos. Recent nonfiction title: *Mixed Blessings*, by William and Barbara Christopher. Fiction: Juveniles/religious (12 and up). Recent fiction title: *God's Love Is for Sharing*, by Helen Caswell.

BAKER BOOK HOUSE COMPANY—P.O. Box 6287, Grand Rapids, MI 49516-6287. (616) 676-9185. FAX (616) 676-9573. Editor, trade books: Dan Van't Kerkhoff. Editor, academic books: Allan Fisher. Publishes hardcover and trade paperback originals and reprints. Averages 120 titles/year. 25%

of books from first-time authors; 85% of books from unagented writers. Subsidy publishes 1% of books. Pays 10% royalty. Publishes book within 1 year after acceptance. Simultaneous and photocopied submissions OK. Computer printout submissions OK; prefers letter-quality. Reports in 3 weeks on queries; 6 weeks on ms. Book catalog for 9 X 12 SASE and $1.20 postage. Manuscript guidelines for #10 SASE. Nonfiction: Biography, juvenile, humor, reference, self-help, gift books, Bible study, Bible commentaries and textbooks. Subjects include child guidance/parenting, language/literature, philosophy, psychology, religion, sociology, women's issues/studies. "We're looking for books from a religious perspective—devotional, Bible study, self-help, textbooks for Christian colleges and seminaries, counseling and humorous books." Query or submit outline/synopsis and sample chapters. Recent nonfiction title: *Your Hidden Half*, by Mark R. McMinn. Tips: "Our books are sold through Christian bookstores to customers with religious background."

As you can see, the market listings for book publishers in this market digest are fuller and more complete than the previous one. You know, among other things, what publishers handle in their publishing programs, what materials they want to see, and to whom manuscripts should be sent.

The Christian Writers' Market Guide: This book is revised and updated each year by Sally E. Stuart. It is published by Harold Shaw Publishers of Wheaton, Illinois. As a tool for writers interested primarily in religious publishing, this one is far more valuable than the previous two. The guide makes the job of marketing your writing much easier because it helps you to focus on targeted publishers who publish the kinds of things you are writing. It includes a listing of nearly 900 Christian publishing houses, the parameters of their publishing programs, their publishing guidelines, how many books the house produces each year, what to submit, and how to submit materials to them. Also included is information on periodicals according to circulation and publishing topics, a listing of editorial services and literary agents, information on writer's conferences, fellowship and critique groups and clubs across the country, and extensive suggestions on how to use the market resources in the book.

In the book publisher market listings in *The Christian Writers' Market Guide* you will find the following extremely useful information in this format:

1. Name of publisher.
2. Address, phone and fax numbers.
3. Denomination or affiliation.
4. Name of editor(s) to whom submission should be sent.
5. Sometimes a missions statement or a statement of the publisher's purpose.
6. A list of imprint names.
7. Number of inspirational/religious titles published per year.
8. Number of submissions received annually.
9. Percentage of books from first-time authors.
10. Whether or not they will accept books through agents. ("Accepts ms through agents" means they are open to that, not that they require it.)
11. The percentage of books from freelance authors they subsidy publish (if any).
12. Whether they reprint out-of-print books from other publishers.
13. Preferred manuscript length in words or pages.
14. Average amount of royalty, if provided. (If royalty is a percentage of wholesale or net, it is based on price paid by bookstores or distributors. If it is on retail price, it is based on the cover price of the book.)
15. Average amount paid for advances. (Whether a publisher pays an advance or not is noted in the listing.)

16. Whether they make outright purchases and amount paid.

17. Average first printing (number of books usually printed for a first-time author).

18. Average length of time between acceptance of a manuscript and publication of the work.

19. Whether they consider simultaneous submissions.

20. Length of time it should take them to respond to a query, a proposal, or a complete manuscript.

21. Availability and cost for writers' guidelines and book catalogs.

22. Nonfiction Section—Preference for query letter, book proposal, or complete manuscript, and whether they accept phone or fax queries.

23. Fiction Section—same as above.

24. Special Needs—if they have specific topics they need that are not included in the subject listing.

25. Ethnic Books—usually specifies which ethnic groups they target or any particular needs.

26. Tips—specific tips provided by the editor or the publisher.

Without a doubt, this market guide is the indispensable reference tool for writers who specialize in the religious market.

Inside Religious Publishing: The coeditors of this book are the coauthors of the book you are now holding in your hands. *IRP* is published by Zondervan Publishing House in Grand Rapids, Michigan. The publishing industry is usually a mystery to people who want to write and be in print. And religious publishing seems stranger yet. *Inside Religious Publishing* offers a "behind the scenes" look at what it takes to get started and to become a published author in the religious field. Even for already-established authors, this book helps expand horizons, stimulate new ideas, and enlarge opportunities. It is an excellent help for anyone writing and wanting to be successfully published.

IRP marshals the wisdom and experience of many of the best-known people in religious publishing, each writing in his or her areas of expertise. The contributors are editors, authors, agents, booksellers, and marketing specialists. For example, Sherwood E. Wirt writes on pursuing excellence, Philip Yancey writes on art and propaganda, and Wayne E. Oates writes on communicating the presence of God through writing. Other contributors include David R. Collins, D. Bruce Lockerbie, Andrew T. Le Peau, Dean Merrill, Judith E. Markham, Ed van der Maas, Jim Carlson, Robert Walker, Stephen Board, Bob Hudson, William H. Gentz, Michael Pearce Pfeifer, and Ted Andrew. Over thirty experts teach on fiction, nonfiction, movie scripts, curriculum, books, articles, and much more.

The book is divided into four sections. The first one focuses on general issues such as motivation, philosophy, spiritual concerns, writing pitfalls, and ethics for writers. The second part relates to books in particular, with chapters on editing, writing, working with agents, getting happily published, and other topics. The third section goes into other types of writing, such as magazine writing, curriculum, and audio-visual scripts. It also includes material on using the new electronic technology. The closing chapters look beyond the horizon into the future of the religious publishing scene.

Writers, whether beginners or polished professionals, can all profit from having this excellent collection of resource articles taking readers *Inside Religious Publishing*.

If you are serious about writing and publishing books and other religious material, these four resources will pay for themselves many times over. Together they represent an absolute treasure chest of quality information. Serious writers understand the need to build up their professional library with the better reference sources. (And don't forget to use Chapters 9 and 10 of *this* book!) Besides, as a good word carpenter, don't you want the finest tools?

Magazines

Three magazines to which you might want to subscribe are *The Writer, Writer's Digest*, and *The Christian Communicator*.

The Writer was founded in Boston in 1887. Each issue has articles on the art and craft of writing, a market listing for specialized markets, and departments such as "Prize Offers," "The Writer's Library," "Letters to the Editor," and a section which updates the ever-changing market situation. For examples, they would list which editor is moving to which publisher, what magazine is suspending publication, and so on. You can subscribe to *The Writer* at The Writer, Inc., 120 Boylston Street, Boston, Ma. 02116-4615.

Writer's Digest is more of a "popular" magazine in that it is more trendy. Each issue has articles by well-known writers on special topics of concern to contemporary writers. Departments cover current trends and topics, the writer's bookshelf, New York, Chicago, and Los Angeles market updates, and a look at the writer's life. Columns in each issue are on nonfiction, fiction, poetry, and photography. The magazine is published by Writer's Digest, 9933 Alliance Road, Cincinnati, Ohio 45242. This magazine was founded in 1920.

The Christian Communicator is the magazine for Christian writers and speakers. This monthly periodical is a member magazine of the Evangelical Press Association and is published by American Christian Writers, P.O. Box 110390, Nashville, TN 37222. Each issue has articles of interest to writers (examples: on successful self-editing, the kinship of fiction and nonfiction writing, and writing devotionals), pen tips (editorial changes at the publishing houses, new markets, etc.), recommendations on the best book and magazine markets, and interviews with writers and editors (people like Madeleine L'Engle, Wightman Weese, and Len Goss). Note: The magazine also has a manuscript critique service where they will critique your written work, offer ideas for improvement, and suggest markets when possible. For the critique service, teaching rather than publication is the goal, as they want to help Christian writers gain the requisite tools to polish and improve their writing skills. The fees for this service are quite reasonable. American Christian Writers also operates the Christian Writers Learning Center, which provides dozens of cassette tapes on many subjects taken from presentations at writers conferences all over the country.

Other magazines and newsletters you will want to consider are these:

Christian Author Newsletter. The Christian Writers Institute produces this bimonthly. It is full of information primarily for new writers. They are at 177 East Crystal Lake Avenue, Lake Mary, Florida 32746.

Christian Book Review. This bimonthly is the reader's guide to new Christian books, serving to promote the value of Christian books by doing essay-style reviews of many of the new ones appearing from the press. They also include the religious bestsellers lists. Their address is P.O. Box 1949, Wake Forest, North Carolina 27588.

Christianity and the Arts. This quarterly magazine emphasizes Christian expression in writing, the arts, dance, and music. The magazine also helps sponsor "Karitos," a Christian Arts Festival in Chicago—with musical performances, writing workshops, poetry reading, panel discussions, drama, an art show, and children's activities. Correspondence can be sent to P.O. Box 118088, Chicago, Illinois 60611.

Cross & Quill. This bimonthly newsletter is a publication of the Christian Writers Fellowship International. It is aimed at Christian writers, agents, editors, and writing conference directors. Information on it can be had by writing to Rt. 3 Box 1635, Jefferson Davis Road, Clinton, South Carolina 29325.

Exchange. This is a quarterly forum for Christian writers to share information and ideas. One can reach them at #104-15 Torrance Road, Scarborough, Ontario M1J 3K2, Canada.

Gotta Write Network LitMag. This is a general, or secular, semiannual publication emphasizing writers networks and writing techniques (especially fiction). Their address is 612 Cobblestone Circle, Glenview, Illinois 60025.

Inklings. This is a quarterly tabloid aimed at thinking Christians and spiritual seekers interested in literature and the arts. They provide reviews on culture, literature, books, theater, film, and the arts. They publish out of Denver, Colorado (P.O. Box 12181, zip: 80212-0181).

Tickled By Thunder. Articles on writing for writers, and information on writer's news. They also publish fiction and poetry inclusions. This quarterly is located at 7385-129 Street, Surrey, British Columbia V3W 7B8, Canada.

The Write Touch. This magazine is for new writers attempting to get in print. They publish a variety of different articles. Their address is P.O. Box 695, Selah, Washington 98942.

Writers Connection. A monthly newsletter on "the nuts and bolts" information on writing and publishing. Write to them at P.O. Box 24770, San Jose, California 95154-4770.

Writers Information Network. This is a bimonthly newsletter produced by the Professional Association of Christian Writers. Full of religious publishing industry news, market news, and information on conferences, computers, resources for writers, and more. Contains newsbreaks, cartoons, ideas, and facts. The address is Box 11337, Bainbridge Island, Washington 98110.

Writer's Resource Network. This newsletter is published bimonthly and contains news and resources for both writers and editors. Write to them at Box 940335, Maitland, Florida 32794.

Correspond with these publications and request information on subscriptions (or submissions). You might be pleasantly surprised to discover the many excellent resources available to help you in your ministry of writing.

Literary Market Place

Another essential and extremely valuable tool that you will want to acquaint yourself with is the *Literary Market Place*. This one is the single best and most authoritative reference guide to the entire North American book publishing industry that is available today. It is a good resource to consult in the library, for it is a large (almost 2,000 pages), professional reference volume and quite expensive. It is updated annually and published by R. R. Bowker, a Reed Reference Publishing Company, 121 Chanlon Road, New Providence, New Jersey 07974.

This *LMP* is called "the bible of American and Canadian publishing," because it is an exhaustive directory of the entire book publishing field. It includes all the houses, editors, agents, editorial services firms, etc., and it is one of the most valuable references anyone interested in publishing could ever consult. Why is it so valuable? Because of the absolute wealth of information it contains. For example, a recent edition is divided into 14 sections: (1) Book Publishing; (2) Associations; (3) Book Trade Events; (4) Courses, Conferences, and Contests; (5) Agents and Agencies; (6) Services and Suppliers; (7) Direct Mail Promotion; (8) Review, Selection, and Reference; (9) Radio, TV, and Motion Pictures; (10) Wholesale, Export, and Import; (11) Book Manufacturing; (12) Book Manufacturing (classified by services offered); (13) Magazine and Newspaper Publishers; and, (14) Names and Numbers.

Almost anything you might want to know about markets, publishers, agents, services and suppliers, associations and events, courses and conferences related to writing and publishing, and so on, are to be found in this extraordinary and exhaustive publishing reference volume. In short, this is the best effort at researching, collecting, indexing, and preparing information on the book publishing industry that one can find.

Christian Writing Conferences

An excellent resource for any writer, especially a beginning one, is a writers' conference and workshop. Writing guilds, seminars, and conferences are becoming increasingly more important and helpful in the religious publishing arena. Many acquisitions editors attend these conferences, and even offer teaching workshops at them, in an effort to scout potential authors and manuscripts. You may wish to attend one or more of the growing number of Christian writing conferences. Rubbing elbows with other authors and professional book editors can give you insights and inspiration you would otherwise miss, and go a long way towards honing your writing skills and enhancing your publishing possibilities.

Both of the authors have spoken at many of these conferences, and we strongly recommend them. We list below only some of the many fine conference opportunities. Attendance figures will vary, from a small conference (30 to 50 conferees attending) to a larger one (200 to 300 conferees attending). A more detailed listing of Christian conferences can be found in *The Christian Writers' Market Guide*, while writers conferences or book trade workshops of a more general or secular nature can be found in *Literary Market Place*.

JANUARY

American Christian Writers. Houston, Texas. Write: Reg Forder, Box 110390, Nashville, Tennessee 37222, or call 1-800-21-WRITE.

American Christian Writers Conference Directors Conference. Houston, Texas. Write: Reg Forder, Box 110390, Nashville, Tennessee 37222, or call 1-800-21-WRITE.

Florida Christian Writers Conference. Park Avenue Retreat Center, Titusville, Florida. Write: Billie Wilson, 2600 Park Avenue, Titusville, Florida 32780, or call 407-269-6702, ext. 202.

FEBRUARY

Christian Writers' Institute International Conference. Orlando, Florida. Write: Dottie McBroom, 177 East Crystal Lake Avenue, Lake Mary, Florida 32746-4244, or call 407-324-5465, or Fax 407-324-0209.

Glen Eyrie Writers' Workshops. Glen Eyrie Conference Center, Colorado Springs, Colorado. Write: Grace Saint, Box 6000, Colorado Springs, Colorado 80934, or call 719-594-2535. (Also in April, June, and October.)

Timber-Lee Christian Writer's Conference. Timber-Lee Christian Center, East Troy, Wisconsin. Write: Gene Schroeppel, N8705 Scout Road, East Troy, Wisconsin 53120, or call 414-642-7345.

Ventura County Writers Seminar. Ventura, California. Write: Julie Carobine, 10142 Fallen Leaf Court, Ventura, California 93004, or call 805-647-4566.

Washington Christian Writers Fellowship Seminar. Seattle, Washington. Write: Elaine Colvin, P.O. Box 11337, Bainbridge Island, Washington 98110, or call 206-842-9103.

Writers' Conference at Santa Fe. Santa Fe, New Mexico. Write: Ruth Crowley, Program Coordinator, Santa Fe Community College, Box 4187, Santa Fe, New Mexico 87502-4187, or call 505-438-1251.

Writers Weekend at the Beach. Ocean Park, Washington. Write: Pat Rushford, 3600 Edgewood Drive, Vancouver, Washington 98661, or call 206-695-2263.

MARCH

American Christian Writers. San Diego, California. Write: Reg Forder, Box 110390, Nashville, Tennessee 37222, or call 1-800-21-WRITE.

American Christian Writers. Seattle, Washington. Write: Reg Forder, Box 110390, Nashville, Tennessee 37222, or call 1-800-21-WRITE.

Central Arizona Christian Writers Workshop. Cottonwood, Arizona. Write: Mona Gransberg Hodgson, Box 999, Cottonwood, Arizona 86326-0999, or call 602-634-0384.

Colorado Christian Writers Conference. Boulder, Colorado. Write: Debbie Barker, 67 Seminole Court, Lyons, Colorado 80540, or call 303-823-5718.

Delmarva Christian Writers' Seminar. Dover, Delaware. Write: Sina McLaughlin, P.O. Box 1111, Dover, Delaware 19903-1111, or call 302-735-4774.

Professionalism in Writing School. Tulsa, Oklahoma. Write: Norma Jean Lutz, 4308 South Peoria, Suite 701, Tulsa, Oklahoma 74105, or call 918-749-5588.

The Salvation Army Christian Writers' Conference. Des Plaines, Illinois. Write: Marlene Chase, 10 West Algonquin Road, Des Plaines, Illinois 60016-6006, or call 708-294-2050.

Write to Be Read Workshops. Atlanta, Georgia. Write: Norman B. Rohrer, 260 Fern Lane, Hume Lake, California 93628, or call 209-335-2333.

Writers Workshop: From Pen to Publisher. Walla Walla Community College, Walla Walla, Washington. Write: Marcia Mitchell, 835 Valencia, Walla Walla, Washington 99362, or call 509-529-4672.

APRIL

Christian Writers Fellowship of Orange County Writer's Days. Garden Grove, California. Write: Louis Merryman, P.O. Box 538, Lake Forest, California 92630, or call 310-379-5646.

Greater Philadelphia Christian Writers' Conference. Downington, Pennsylvania. Write: Marlene Bagnull, 316 Blanchard Road, Drexel Hill, Pennsylvania 19026-3507, or call 610-626-6833.

Inspirational Writers Alive! Seminar. Amarillo, Texas. Write: Helen Luecke, 2921 South Dallas, Amarillo, Texas 79103-6713, or call 806-376-9671.

Minnesota Christian Writers Guild Spring Seminar. Minneapolis/St. Paul, Minnesota. Write: Sue Campbell, 3551 Virginia Avenue North, Minneapolis, Minnesota 55427, or call 612-545-1573.

Mount Hermon Christian Writers Conference. Mount Hermon, California. Write: David R. Talbott, Box 413, Mount Hermon, California 95041-0413, or call 408-355-4466.

Narramore Christian Writers Conference. Narramore Christian Foundation, Rosemead, California. Write: Clyde Narramore, 1409 North Walnut Grove Avenue, Rosemead, California 91770, or call 818-288-7000.

Pittsburg Christian Writers' Seminar. Pittsburg, Kansas. Write: LeAnn Campbell, 267 SW 1st Lane, Lamar, Missouri 64759, or call 417-682-2713.

Virginia Christian Writers Conference. Roanoke, Virginia. Write: Betty B. Robertson, P.O. Box 12624, Roanoke, Virginia 24027-2624, or call 703-342-7511.

Writers Helping Writers Workshop. Spokane, Washington. Write: Pat Pfeiffer, P.O. Box 104, Otis Orchards, Washington 97027-0140, or call 509-927-7670.

Writing for Publication. Pittsburgh Theological Seminary, Pittsburgh, Pennsylvania. Write: Mary Lee Talbot, 616 North Highland Avenue, Pittsburgh, Pennsylvania 15206, or call 412-326-5610.

MAY

African-American Christian Writers' Conference. Chicago, Illinois. Write: Stanley B. Long, c/o American Tract Society, P.O. Box 462008, Garland, Texas 75046.

American Christian Writers. Dallas/Fort Worth, Texas. Write: Reg Forder, Box 110390, Nashville, Tennessee 37222, or call 1-800-21-WRITE.

God Uses Ink Writers. Briercrest Bible College, Caronport, Saskatchewan. Write: Donna Lynn Erickson, 510 College Drive, Caronport, Saskatchewan S0H 0S0, Canada, or call 306-756-3214.

Greater Syracuse Christian Writer's Conference. Liverpool, New York. Write: Pat Spencer, 108 Woodpath Road, Liverpool, New York 13090, or call 315-652-3178.

Writer's World Conference. Akron, Ohio. Write: Tom Raber, Box 966, Cuyahoga Falls, Ohio 44223.

JUNE

American Christian Writers. Detroit, Michigan. Write: Reg Forder, Box 110390, Nashville, Tennessee 37222, or call 1-800-21-WRITE.

American Christian Writers. St. Louis, Missouri. Write: Reg Forder, Box 110390, Nashville, Tennessee 37222, or call 1-800-21-WRITE.

Andrews University Christian Writers and Communicator's Conference. Berrien Springs, Michigan. Write: Kermit Netteburg, Communications Department, Andrews University, Berrien Springs, Michigan 49104, or call 616-471-3618.

Bethel College Christian Writers' Conference. Mishawaka, Indiana. Write: Wayne Gerber, Adult Education, Bethel College, 1001 West McKinley, Mishawaka, Indiana 46545, or via telefax at 219-257-3357.

Boondocks Retreat. Dodge City, Kansas. Write: Linda Fergerson, 2216 Thompson, Dodge City, Kansas 67801, or call 316-225-1126.

Christian Writers Institute Conference and Workshop. Wheaton, Illinois. Write: Dottie McBroom, 177 East Crystal Lake Avenue, Lake Mary, Florida 32746, or call 407-324-5465.

God Uses Ink Writers Conference. Ancaster, Ontario. Write: Audrey Dorsch, Box 8800, Station B, Willowdale, Ontario M2K 2R6, Canada, or call 905-479-5588.

Mark Twain Writers Conference. Hannibal-LaGrange College, Hannibal, Missouri. Write: James C. Hefley, 921 Center Street, Hannibal, Missouri 63401, or call 800-947-0738.

Mississippi Valley Writers' Conference. Augustana College, Rock Island, Illinois. Write: David R. Collins, 3403 45th Street, Moline, Illinois 61265, or call 309-762-8985.

SDA Camp Meeting Writing Class. Auburn, Washington. Write: Marion Forschler, 18115-116th Avenue SE, Reston, Washington 98058-6562, or call 206-235-1435.

Seattle Pacific Christian Writers Conference. Seattle Pacific University, Seattle, Washington. Write: Linda Wagner, Humanities Department, Seattle Pacific University, Seattle, Washington 98119, or call 206-281-2109.

Southeastern Writers Conference. St. Simons Island, Georgia. Write: Pay Laye, Route 1 Box 102, Cuthbert, Georgia 31740, or call 912-679-5445.

Southern Christian Writers Conference. Samford University, Birmingham, Alabama. Write: Joanne Sloan, 3230 Mystic Lake Way, Northport, Alabama 35476, or call 205-333-8603.

St. David's Christian Writer's Conference. St. David's, Pennsylvania. Write: Carol Wedeven, 1 Old Covered Bridge Road, Newtown Square, Pennsylvania 19073, or call 610-356-8208.

Wesleyan Writers Conference. Wesleyan University, Middletown, Connecticut. Write: Anne Greene, c/o Wesleyan University, Middletown, Connecticut 06459, or call 203-347-9411.

Write-to-Publish Conference. Chicago, Illinois. Write: Lin Johnson, 9731 Fox Glen Drive #6F, Niles, Illinois 60714-5829, or call 708-296-3964. (Spring, fall, and summer seminars offered; write for other dates.)

JULY

Antioch Writers Workshop. Antioch College, Yellow Springs, Ohio. Write: Judy DuPolito, P.O. Box 494, Yellow Springs, Ohio 45387, or call 513-866-9060.

Christian Artists Seminar in the Rockies. Estes Park, Colorado. Write: Cam Floria, 425 West 115th Street, Denver, Colorado 80234, or call 303-452-1313.

Christian Communicators Conference at The Master's College. Santa Clarita, California. Write: Lowell (Doc) Saunders or Susan Titus Osborn, 3133 Puente Street, Fullerton, California 92635, or call 714-990-1532, or 1-800-WRITE 17.

Green Lake Christian Writer's Conference. Green Lake, Wisconsin. Write: Jan DeWitt, Program Department, American Baptist Assembly, Green Lake, Wisconsin 54941, or call 800-558-8898 or 414-294-3323.

Louisiana Christian Writers Guild Workshop. Shreveport, Louisiana. Write: Mark Sutton, 8900 Kingston Road, Shreveport, Louisiana 71118, or call 318-686-2898.

Michigan Northwoods Writers Conference. Glen Arbor, Michigan. Write: Robert Karner, 1 Old Homestead Road, Glen Arbor, Michigan 49636, or call 616-334-3072.

Midwest Writers Workshop. Ball State Univeristy, Muncie, Indiana. Write: Earl Conn, Department of Journalism, Ball State University, Muncie, Indiana 47306-0485, or call 317-285-8200.

Montrose Bible Conference Christian Writers Conference. Montrose, Pennsylvania. Write; Jill Renich Meyers, 204 Asbury Drive, Mechanicsburg, Pennsylvania 17055-4303, or call 712-766-1100.

Oregon Christian Writers' Coaching Conference. Salem, Oregon. Write: Kristen Ingram, 955 South 59th Street, Springfield, Oregon 97478-5452, or call 503-726-8320.

The Presbyterian Writers Guild Seminar. Cincinnati, Ohio. Write: Ann Barr Weems, 6900 Kingsbury Blvd., St. Louis, Missouri 63130, or call 314-725-6290.

Review and Herald Writer's Week. Hagerstown, Maryland. Write: Penny E. Wheeler, 55 West Oak Ridge Drive, Hagerstown, Maryland 21740, or call 301-790-9731.

Southeast Arizona Christian Writers Fellowship. Picture Rock Retreat Center, Tucson, Arizona. Call Bea Carlton 520-384-9232 or Neta Warawa 520-586-3246.

Southern Baptist Writers Workshop. Nashville, Tennessee. Write: Director, SBWW, 127 Ninth Avenue North, Nashville, Tennessee 37234, or call 615-251-2939.

Write to Be Read Workshops. Hume Lake, California. Write: Norman B. Rohrer, 260 Fern Lane, Hume Lake, California 93628, or call 209-335-2333.

YWAM Writers Seminar. Kona, Hawaii. Write: Beverly Caruso, 1621 Baldwin Avenue, Orange, California 92665, or call 714-637-1733.

AUGUST

American Christian Writers. Minneapolis, Minnesota. Write: Reg Forder, Box 110390, Nashville, Tennessee 37222, or call 1-800-21-WRITE.

Cape Cod Writers Conference. Cape Cod Conservatory, West Barnstable, Massachusetts. Write: Marion Vuilleumier, Cape Cod Writers Center, c/o Conservatory, Route 132, West Barnstable, Massachusetts 02668, or call 508-375-0516 or 508-775-4811.

Frontiers in Writing Seminar. Amarillo College, Amarillo, Texas. Write: Doris Meredith, P.O. Box 19303, Amarillo, Texas 79114, or call 806-352-3889.

The Glen Workshop, A Milton Center Writing Conference. Glen Eyrie Conference Center, Colorado Springs, Colorado. Write: The Glen Workshop, The Navigators, P.O. Box 6000, Colorado Springs, Colorado 80934, or call 1-800-944-GLEN.

Maranatha Christian Writers' Seminar. Muskegon, Michigan. Write: Leona Hertel, c/o Maranatha Bible and Missionary Conference, 4759 Lake Harbor Road, Muskegon, Michigan 49441-5299, or call 616-798-2161.

Southwest Writers Conference. Hilton Hotel, Albuquerque, New Mexico. Write: JoAnn Hamlin, 1338 Wyoming Blvd., NE, Suite B, Albuquerque, New Mexico 87122, or call 505-293-0303.

Texas Christian Writers Forum Conference. Houston, Texas. Write: Maxine E. Holder, 3606 Longwood Drive, Pasadena, Texas 77503-2221, or call 713-477-3716.

The Writing Academy Seminar. Nashville, Tennessee. Write: Ann Poppen, 6512 Colby, Des Moines, Iowa 50311-1713, or call 515-274-5026.

Writing for Christian Publishers. Regent University, Virginia Beach, Virginia. Write: Doug Tarpley, School of Journalism, Regent University, Virginia Beach, Virginia 23464, or call 804-532-7091.

SEPTEMBER

Cincinnati Bible College Christian Writers Workshop. Cincinnati, Ohio. Write: Dana Eynon, 2700 Glenway Avenue, Cincinnati, Ohio 45204, or call 513-244-8181.

Island Empire Christian Writers Seminars. Moreno Valley, California. Write: Bill Page, Unit 112, 23571 Sunnymead Ranch Parkway, Suite 103, Moreno Valley, California 92557-2867, or call 909-924-0610.

Northwest Christian Writers Conference. Post Falls, Idaho. Write: Sheri Stone, Box 1754, Post Falls, Idaho 83854-1754, or call 208-667-9730.

Northwest Ohio Christian Writers Seminar. Bowling Green, Ohio. Write: Nancy Kintner, 4235 Lyman Avenue, Toledo, Ohio 43612-1584, or call 419-478-1055.

Prescott Christian Writers Seminar. Prescott, Arizona. Write: Barbara Spangler, Box 26449, Prescott Valley, Arizona 86312, or call 602-772-6263.

San Diego Christian Writers Guild. San Diego, California. Write: Sherwood E. Wirt, 14140 Mazatlan Court, Poway, California 92064, or call 619-748-0565.

Southwest Christian Writers Seminar. Farmington, New Mexico. Write: Kathy Cordell, 91-Road 3450, Flora Vista, New Mexico 87415, or call 505-334-0617

Washington Christian Writers' Fellowship. Seattle, Washington. Write: Elaine Wright Convin, P.O. Box 11337, Bainbridge Island, Washington 98110, or call 206-842-9103.

Wenatchee Christian Writers Mini-Seminar. Wenatchee, Washington. Write: Shirley Pease, 1818 Skyline Drive #31, Wenatchee, Washington 98801-2302, or call 509-662-8392.

Word & Pen Christian Writers Club. Oshkosh, Wisconsin. Write: Beth Ziarnik, 1865 Indian Point Road, Oshkosh, Wisconsin 54901-1315, or call Don Derozier at 414-235-7905.

OCTOBER

American Christian Writers. Atlanta, Georgia. Write: Reg Forder, Box 110390, Nashville, Tennessee 37222, or call 1-800-21-WRITE.

American Christian Writers. Miami, Florida. Write: Reg Forder, Box 110390, Nashville, Tennessee 37222, or call 1-800-21-WRITE.

Black Mountains Christian Writers Retreat. Belmont, North Carolina. Write: Robert Waldrup, 3476 Boat Club Road, Belmont, North Carolina, 28012-9642, or call 704-825-7918.

Christian Writers Workshop. Northeastern Christian Junior College, Villanova, Pennsylvania. Write: Eva Walker Myer, 1860 Montgomery Avenue, Villanova, Pennsylvania 19085, or call 215-525-6780.

Columbus Christian Writers Fall Conference. Salt Fork Lodge, Cambridge, Ohio. Write: Brenda Custodio, 3069 Bocastle Court, Reynoldsburg, Ohio 43068, or call 614-861-1011.

Northeast Georgia Writers Conference. Gainesville, Georgia. Write: Elouise Whitten, 660 Crestview Terrace, Gainesville, Georgia 30501-3110, or call 404-532-3007.

Northern Virginia Christian Writers Fellowship. Dunn Loring, Virginia. Write: Jennifer Ferranti, P.O. Box 629, Dunn Loring, Virginia, 22027, or call 703-698-7707.

Oregon Association of Christian Writers Seminar. Aloha, Oregon. Write: Ed Demaree, Oregon Association of Christian Writers, 17768 SW Pointe Forest Court, Aloha, Oregon 97006, or call 503-297-2987.

Piedmont Writers Conference. Mt. Holly, North Carolina. Write: Doug Baltgegar, P.O. Box 902, Mr. Holly, North Carolina, or call 704-827-7242.

Right Writing Christian Writers' Workshop. Columbia, Missouri. Write: Teresa Parker, 237 East Clearview Drive, Columbia, Missouri 65202, or call 314-875-1141.

Sandy Cove Christian Writers Conference. Sandy Cove/ North East, Maryland. Write: Gayle Roper, RD 6 Box 112, Coatesville, Pennsylvania 19320, or call 610-384-8125.

Southwest Christian Writers Guild Conference. Dallas, Texas. Write: Debra Frazier, 1809 Waterford Lane, Richardson, Texas 75082, or call 214-783-6319.

Swan Valley Writers Guild Conference. Swan River, Manitoba. Write: Marlene Hohne, Box 2115, Swan River, Manitoba R0L 1Z0, Canada, or call 204-525-4652.

NOVEMBER

American Christian Writers. On-board Caribbean Cruise Conference, leaving from Fort Lauderdale. Write: Reg Forder, Box 110390, Nashville, Tennessee 37222, or call 1-800-21-WRITE.

American Christian Writers. Phoenix, Arizona. Write: Reg Forder, Box 110390, Nashville, Tennessee 37222, or call 1-800-21-WRITE.

Valley Christian Writers Conference. Fresno, California. Write: Ruth Duke, 6315 North 8th Street, Fresno, California, 93710, or call 209-431-6474.

Wordpower. Winnipeg, Manitoba. Write: Manitoba Herald, 3-169 Riverton Avenue, Winnipeg, Manitoba R2L 2E5, Canada, or call 204-669-6575.

Writers In The Redwoods Retreat. Occidental, California. Write: Elaine Wright Colvin, 6250 Bohemian Highway, Occidental, California 95465, or call 707-874-3507.

Libraries

Once you have reflected on the art of writing, and have in mind a tentative idea about a publisher, you will be ready to begin serious research on your chosen topic. The obvious place to begin such research is your local library. [You might also write to the Congregational Library of 14 Beacon Street, Boston, Massachusetts 02108, to receive their quarterly bulletin of religious books that can be borrowed by mail anywhere in the United States.]

Go to the Card Catalog and use the Subject Guide first. If, for example, you are writing a book on the positive effects of religious practices in the home, look at the cards under "Family." Depending on the holdings of that library, you might find many books specifically on religion and the family, or you might find few or none. Let your mind wander and freely associate. What else might your topic be listed under? Try "Religion" to see if there might be books on religion and the home. Use whatever key words you might have on your subject. In this case, "Home," "Family," and "Religious Practices" are but three such.

Peruse the books you find listed in the card catalog. Some will pertain directly to your topic, some will be of marginal value, and others will be of no use to you at all. Another way to find books is to browse through the shelves. To do this you need to know the general classification of your topic in the Dewey Decimal Classification. The example listed above, on religion in the home, is listed in the 249s in the Dewey Decimal System of Classification. Find that area in the library and see what is available. Some libraries have closed shelves which means that only an employee can get the books. This unfortunate system makes shelf browsing almost impossible.

If you are going to do any serious research in a library, you must have a working understanding of the *Dewey Decimal System of Classification* of books. Included below is a general summary of this system, and also the more detailed sub-classification for religion.

DEWEY DECIMAL CLASSIFICATION
GENERAL SUMMARY

000 GENERAL WORKS
010 Bibliography
020 Library Science
030 General Encyclopedias
040 General Collected Essays
050 General Periodicals
060 General Societies
070 Newspapers Journalism
080 Collected Works
090 Manuscripts & Rare Books

100 PHILOSOPHY
110 Metaphysics
120 Metaphysical Theories
130 Branches of Psychology
140 Philosophical Topics
150 General Psychology
160 Logic
170 Ethics
180 Ancient & Medieval Philosophy
190 Modern Philosophy

200 RELIGION
210 Natural Theology
220 Bible
230 Doctrinal Theology
240 Devotional & Practical
250 Pastoral Theology
260 Christian Church
270 Christian Church History
280 Christian Churches & Sects
290 Other Religions

300 SOCIAL SCIENCES
310 Statistics
320 Political Science
330 Economics
340 Law
350 Public Administration
360 Social Welfare
370 Education

500 PURE SCIENCE
510 Mathematics
520 Astronomy
530 Physics
540 Chemistry
550 Earth Sciences
560 Paleontology
570 Anthropology & Biology
580 Botanical Sciences
590 Zoological Sciences

600 TECHNOLOGY
610 Medical Sciences
620 Engineering
630 Agriculture
640 Home Economics
650 Business
660 Chemical Technology
670 Manufactures
680 Other Manufactures
690 Building Construction

700 THE ARTS
710 Landscape & Civic Art
720 Architecture
730 Sculpture
740 Drawing & Decorative Arts
750 Painting
760 Engraving
770 Photography
780 Music
790 Recreation

800 LITERATURE
810 American
820 English
830 German
840 French
850 Italian
860 Spanish
870 Latin

380 Public Services & Utilities
390 Customs & Folklore

880 Greek
890 Other Literature

400 LANGUAGE
410 Comparative
420 English
430 German
440 French
450 Italian
460 Spanish
470 Latin
480 Greek
490 Other Languages

900 HISTORY
910 Geography, Travel & Description
920 Biography
930 Ancient History
940 Europe
950 Asia
960 Africa
970 North America
980 South America
990 Pacific Islands

DEWEY DECIMAL CLASSIFICATION
RELIGION

200 RELIGION
201 Philosophy & Theories
202 Handbooks & Outlines
203 Dictionaries & Encyclopedias
204 Essays & Lectures
205 Periodicals
206 Organizations & Societies
207 Study & Teaching
208 Collections
209 History

210 NATURAL THEOLOGY
211 Knowledge of God
212 Pantheism
213 Creation of Universe
214 Theodicy
215 Religion & Science
216 Good & Evil
217 Worship
218 Immortality

219 Analogy

220 BIBLE

221 Old Testament
222 Historical Books
223 Poetic Books

250 PASTORAL THEOLOGY
251 Preaching (Homiletics)
252 Sermons
253 Pastor
254 Church & Parish Administration
255 Brotherhoods & Sisterhoods
256 Societies for Parish Work
257 Parish Education Work
258 Parish Welfare Work
259 Other Parish Work

260 CHRISTIAN CHURCH
261 Christian Social Theology
262 Government & Organization
263 Sabbath, Lord's Day & Sunday
264 Public Worship, Ritual & Liturgy
265 Sacraments & Ordinances
266 Missions
267 Religious Associations
268 Religious Education &
Sunday Schools
269 Revivals & Spiritual Renewal

**270 CHRISTIAN CHURCH
HISTORY**
271 Religious Orders
272 Persecutions
273 Heresies

224 Prophetic Books
225 New Testament
226 Gospels & Acts
227 Epistles
228 Revelation
229 Apocrypha

230 DOCTRINAL THEOLOGY

231 God
232 Christology
233 Man
234 Salvation
235 Angels, Devils, Satan

236 Eschatology
237 Future State

238 Christian Creeds
239 Apologetics

240 DEVOTIONAL & PRACTICAL

241 Moral Theology
242 Meditations
243 Evangelistic Writings
244 Miscellany
245 Hymnology
246 Christian Symbolism
247 Sacred Furniture & Vestments
248 Personal Religion
249 Family Worship

274 In Europe
275 In Asia
276 In Africa
277 In North America
278 In South America
279 In Other Parts of the World

280 CHRISTIAN CHURCHES & SECTS

281 Primitive & Oriental Churches
282 Roman Catholic Church
283 Anglican Churches
284 Protestantism
285 Presbyterian & Congregational Churches

286 Baptist & Immersionist Churches
287 Methodist Churches
288 Unitarian Church
289 Other Christian Sects

290 OTHER RELIGIONS

291 Comparative Religion
292 Greek & Roman
293 Teutonic & Norse Religions
294 Brahmanism & Buddhism
295 Zorastrianism & Related
296 Judaism
297 Islam & Bahaism
298
299 Other Non-Christian Religions

Some libraries use the **Library of Congress** system because it is capable of being divided into minute categories, and is easily expandable. The general outline of this system is as follows:

A   General Work—Polygraphy
B   Philosophy—Religion
C   History—Auxiliary Sciences
D   History and Topography (except America)

E-F	America
G	Geography—Anthropology
H	Social Sciences
I	Political Science
K	Law
L	Education
M	Music
N	Fine Arts
P	Language and Literature
Q	Science
R	Medicine
S	Agriculture—Plant and Animal Husbandry
T	Technology
U	Military Science
V	Naval Science
Z	Bibliography and Library Science

While you will want to consult books on your subject, you will also need to read articles in magazines and journals. It is possible that a book can be somewhat dated before it is even released from the press, but periodical articles are usually more timely and fresh. We are fortunate today that so many different indexes are available to help us find exactly what we are looking for in journal and magazine sources. Listed below are some of the better indexes you will want to consider using in your research.

Access—indexes about 160 general magazines and has a good listing of city and regional magazines
Art Index
Applied Science and Technology Index
Biography Index
Book Review Digest
Book Review Index
Business Periodicals Index

Catholic Periodical and Literature Index
Christian Periodical Index
Consumer Index to Product Evaluations and Information Sources
Cumulative Index to Periodical Literature Dissertation Abstracts
Education Index
Film Literature Index
Guide to Social Science and Religion in Periodical Literature
Guide to the Performing Arts
Historical Abstracts Humanities Index
An Index to Book Reviews in the Humanities
Index to Free Periodicals
Index to How-to-Do-it Information
Index to Jewish Periodicals
Index to New England Periodicals
Index to Periodical Articles By and About Blacks
Magazine Index—lists about 370 magazines, but is available only on microfilm
New Periodicals Index
The New Review of Books and Religion
New Testament Abstracts
New York Times Index
Old Testament Abstracts
Pastoral Care and Counseling Abstracts
The Philosopher's Index
Physical Education Index
Physical Education/Sports Index
Popular Periodicals Index
Psychological Abstracts
Reader's Guide to Periodical Literature
Religion Index One: Periodicals—prior to 1979 this index was known as *Index to Religious Periodical Literature*
Religious and Theological Abstracts

The Review of Books and Religion
Science of Religion Abstracts and Index of Recent Articles
Sociological Abstracts
Southern Baptist Periodical Index
Subject Index to Children's Magazines
The United Methodist Periodical Index

Many other indexes exist, but these will certainly be instrumental in assisting your quest for vital information in your research and writing work.

An unidentified news correspondent once wrote,

> Some men die of shrapnel
> Some go down in flames.
> But most men perish inch by inch
> Who play at little games.

Writing can also perish inch by inch, and so can the writer! Do not write if you intend to "play at little games." Remember the analogy of religious literature being like popcorn (or in many cases, just plain corn). Do your homework. Research your topic. Ask what others can teach you about it. Remember God's words to Aaron in Numbers 18:29: "Give it from the best that you receive."

9

WHERE TO SELL YOUR BOOKS

If you are anything like most writers we have known, you realize that you need to understand book markets in order to find a place for your work.

One of the things you need to be conscientious about is to scout out any publisher that might possibly have an interest in the kind of book on which you are working. Read periodicals like *Christianity Today, Moody Magazine, Charisma & Christian Life, Christianity & The Arts*, and the *Christian Review, Books & Culture*, to see which publishers advertise there. What kinds of titles do they advertise? Are they publishing on current topics? Do some of the publishing houses seem to specialize in particular books, such as books on the deeper Christian life, or books for an academic or professional audience? Do they publish issues books that address the critical questions facing Christians today in their personal lives, families, communities, and the wider culture? Or does the publisher appear to specialize in celebrity books or other books for the very popular reader? Who are some of the top-selling authors that each house represents? In other words, look at the books the publisher promotes in the different magazines, not to copy their style, but to get an idea of what is being published by the house in question and how they communicate.

Write to the various publishing companies that you consider appropriate—the houses that you would like to submit your material to—and request copies of their catalogs and authors' guidelines. Most have free catalogs they will be happy to send. Ask them to send you their author information and submission guidelines also. (Do this in writing or by FAX or phone.) Each publishing house that has any kind of an active publishing program will provide guidelines for submission. And these will be provided free of cost. These guidelines will tell you what the requirements for submission are and what you should send along with your book proposal. Some editors want to see samples of your writing, or samples from the actual manuscript you will be submitting. The guidelines will tell you what to send. Study them carefully, for they will give you specific instructions as to submission requirements and any special slant that a publisher wants. Get to know the editors of these houses; they are your entrance into the world of print.

In compiling this list of the better book markets, we corresponded with nearly all of the religious houses. If we did not receive personal replies from them, we often talked with them over the phone, or personally at book meetings. In some cases, we included information taken from their own guidelines, or from other market research sources. One thing to keep in mind is this: You can send a query letter or a proposal to more than one publisher at a time. There is nothing wrong with that. In fact, it is to your advantage to do so. Simultaneous submissions of actual manuscripts is another thing. A publisher does not want to invest money, time, and attention in the decision-making process only to find that other houses are looking at the same material and maybe have even made publishing offers. You don't want to sell your book to two or three publishers at the same time. Unforgivable!

ABINGDON PRESS
201 Eighth Avenue, South
Nashville, Tennessee 37203-3957
615-749-6290
FAX 615-749-6512

Mary Catherine Dean, Senior Editor of General Interest Books

Abingdon Press, **Cokesbury, Dimensions for Living,** and **Kingswood Books** are the publishing arms of The United Methodist Church. (See also **The United Methodist Publishing House.**) Abingdon publishes around 120 books per year and handles ecumenic religious books such as Bible studies, minister's aids, professional titles, academic texts, lay inspirational, as well as children's materials. Their publishing mission is to help others know God and serve their neighbor, and their books are meant to inform, inspire, and educate members of the Christian community at large, as well as the general public. They also publish ethnic books for African-Americans, Native-Americans, and Asian-Americans, and books on United Methodist history, doctrine, and polity. Abingdon has about 825 titles currently in print. For nonfiction proposals, submit a prospectus detailing how your book is different from others on the market, along with two sample chapters.

ABBOTT-MARTYN PRESS (See STAR SONG PUBLISHING GROUP)

ACCENT PUBLICATIONS
4050 Lee Vance View
Colorado Springs, Colorado 80918
719-535-2905

Mary B. Nelson, Managing Editor

Accent is a division of **Cook Communications Ministries.** They do evangelical Christian church resource products, publishing a significant amount of curriculum material for adult, youth, children's and preschool Sunday school classes, and vacation Bible schools. Accent Publications is committed to communicating biblical truths in an easily understood manner with contemporary relevance. Their writers must be baptistic. No phone calls. Query first if interested in writing curriculum, as curriculum writing assignments are by assignment only after completing various tests and passing. State your qualifications and background for writing curriculum and age level expertise. For nonfiction writing projects, of which Accent publishes five to eight per year, these include books for the general reader in family relationships, self-help, personal growth and fulfillment, and so on. They have about 130 titles in print. Send for their guidelines and catalog (include SASE) before sending manuscript material.

ACTA PUBLICATIONS
4848 North Clark Street
Chicago, Illinois 60640
312-271-1030
FAX 312-271-7399

Gregory Pierce, Publisher
Gregory F. Augustine, Co-Publisher

ACTA stands for "Assisting Christians to Act." This Catholic house publishes ten general books per year that will be useful for the faith of average Christian readers. They want innovative, accessible, provocative books for thoughtful Catholics and other Christians. They also do audio and video tapes for the Christian market. ACTA Publications has about 75 book titles in print, and their imprints include **Buckley Publications** and **National Center for the Laity**. Guidelines and a catalog are available. Query first.

ALBA HOUSE
2187 Victory Boulevard
Staten Island, New York 10314
718-761-0047
FAX 718-761-0057

Aloysius W. Milella, Editor in Chief
Victor L. Viberti, Acquisitions Editor

Alba House is a Catholic publishing firm that publishes devotional material, Bible study helps, books on prayer, pastoral care, spirituality, sociology, education, and biographies. They publish from 45 to 50 books per year, and they have 230 titles in print. Send a query letter with SASE.

THE ALBAN INSTITUTE
4550 Montgomery Avenue, Suite 433-N
Bethesda, Maryland 20814-3341
301-718-4407
FAX 301-718-1958

Celia Allison Hahn, Editor in Chief

The Institute is nondenominational and publishes practical guidance for church life and leadership. Their books are ecumenical and parochial, and their market primarily is clergy and lay leadership. They want the books they publish to encourage and equip congregations to be vigorous and faithful and to minister within their faith communities and in the world. The Institute publishes eight to ten books per year, and they

163

have over 100 titles in print. No unsolicited manuscripts. Send a query and ask for the "Alban Institute Book Publishing Program Guidelines for Authors."

ALBURY PRESS
2448 E. 81 Street, Suite 5600
Tulsa, Oklahoma 74137-4256
918-582-2126
FAX 918-494-3665

John Mason, President

Albury Press is a new publishing house interested in publishing frontlist titles from prominent charismatic leaders. The press is privately owned, but operates out of the Harrison House building. They plan to release about fifteen titles per year.

ALPINE PUBLICATIONS
P.O. Box 7027
Loveland, Colorado 80537
303-667-2017

Betty Jo McKinney, Publisher

This publisher deals with books for working women along with dog and horse nonfiction titles. Alpine publishes five or so books per year, and they have about 40 titles in print. Send a query with SASE.

AMERICAN CATHOLIC PRESS
16160 South Seton Drive
South Holland, Illinois 60473-1863
708-331-5485

Joan Termini, Manager
Michael Gilligan, Editorial Director

American Catholic Press does ten or so books each year in the area of Catholic worship resources. Outside of materials for the Roman Catholic liturgy, the only other publishing interest for them is new music resources for church services. They do not want poetry or fiction. This press has 12 titles now in print. Query with a proposal and some sample chapters.

AMG PUBLISHERS
6815 Shallowford Road
Chattanooga, Tennessee 37421
615-894-6060
FAX 615-894-6863

Dale Anderson, Vice President and Editorial Director

AMG publishes Bible study and Bible reference materials to edify the church and to encourage further individual study. Their focus is on pastoral helps, and they do not publish fiction, allegories, or children's works. AMG is a division of Evangelical/AMG International, and does from seven to ten books per year. Currently they have about 100 titles in print. On first contact, they want the writer to send a well-presented query letter along with a book proposal with a good book description.

AMHERST PRESS
3380 Sheridan Drive
Suite 365
Amherst, New York 14226
(No phone calls or faxes accepted)

Ed Gahona, Owner/Editor
Susan Mason, Non-fiction Editor

This new general publisher works with all categories and genres, except poetry and children's books. Their first 2 books were published in 1996. The mission of Amherst Press is to expand voices of new writers. Their guidelines and catalog are available. Submit a full manuscript and cover letter with SASE. They report in 2 to 3 weeks.

ANCHOR (See DOUBLEDAY)

ANCHOR BIBLE REFERENCE LIBRARY (See DOUBLEDAY)

AUGSBURG BOOKS (See AUGSBURG FORTRESS PUBLISHERS)

AUGSBURG FORTRESS PUBLISHERS
Box 1209, 426 South Fifth Street
Minneapolis, Minnesota 55440
612-330-3300
FAX 612-330-3455

Marshall Johnson, Editorial Director of Fortress Press
Ronald Klug, Editorial Director of Augsburg Books

Augsburg Fortress is the publishing house of the Evangelical Lutheran Church in America. They publish 110 to 120 books per year. On the **Augsburg Books** side of the Augsburg Fortress equation, they publish in the areas of reference books, contextual theology, Bible studies, books on various social concerns, books for the family, spirituality, and inspirational/devotional works for children (especially children's books with a Christmas theme and historical fiction for 10-14 year olds) and adults. On the **Fortress Press** side, they have a heavy emphasis on books for the academic market in theology, biblical texts, church history studies, studies in preaching and worship, and books for counselors and professors. They also publish ethnic books for African-Americans, Hispanics, and Native-Americans. 1,200 Augsburg Fortress titles are currently in print. They ask for a query letter only, after which they may ask for an abstract and sample chapters.

AUGUST HOUSE PUBLISHERS
P. O. Box 3223
Little Rock, Arkansas 72203
501-372-5450
FAX 501-372-5579

Liz Smith Parkhurst, Vice President and Editor in Chief

This publisher has Methodist connections and publishes mostly American folklore and books on storytelling. In the religious arena, they are looking for books that contain only stories for retelling in churches, Sunday schools, and for use in devotions. On occasion, they also publish a select number of ethnic books for African-Americans, Mexican Americans, and other multicultural titles. They do ten to twenty books per year and have around 100 titles in print. Query only.

AVE MARIA PRESS, INC.
P. O. Box 428
Notre Dame, Indiana 46556
219-287-2831
FAX 219-239-2904

Frank J. Cunningham, Director of Publications

Ave Marie is a not-for-profit Catholic publishing company owned by the Indiana Province of the Congregation of Holy Cross and located on the campus of Notre Dame University. They usually publish twenty books per year, with slightly under 200 titles currently in print. Their specialty publishing categories are spirituality, ministry, prayer books, and religious education. They want to serve the ever-changing spiritual, formative, and informational needs of individual Christians and church-related institutions. They do not want to see any fiction or personal testimony projects. They do accept unsolicited manuscripts, but it is better to ask for their guidelines and catalog and then to send a query letter and book proposal.

BAKER BOOKS/BAKER BOOK HOUSE
P. O. Box 6287
Grand Rapids, Michigan 49516-6287
616-676-9185
FAX 616-676-9573

Allan Fisher, Director of Publications
Daniel Van't Kerkhoff, Acquisitions Editor, Baker Books
Jim Weaver, Editor of Academic Books, Baker Books
Jane Campbell, Editor, Chosen Books
William J. Petersen, Editorial Director, Fleming H. Revell

Baker's combined imprints publish around 235 books per year, with a 1,700-title backlist. Their imprints include **Baker Books, Chosen Books, Fleming H. Revell, Raven's Ridge,** and **Wynwood Press.** Baker is a major evangelical house that produces works for both lay and academic/professional reading audiences, and the Baker publishing program reflects the diversity of the evangelical movement. Their mission is to publish writings that promote historic Christianity and irenically express the concerns of evangelicalism. The books they produce are for the personal enrichment and spiritual growth of all readers. Their interests are broad and varied, and includes ministers' worship aids, theology, history, fiction, and devotions. They are interested in mysteries and contemporary women's fiction from a Christian worldview without being preachy. They do not want to see any romances, historical fiction, fantasy, exposes, personal stories, biographies, or poetry, but they do want to publish more material by and for Blacks. They intend their books to strengthen the Church. Guidelines and catalogs are available and manuscripts may be sent with SASE. For nonfiction projects, send for their brochure entitled "Preparing a Proposal for Baker, Revell, and Chosen Books" before submitting any material. For fiction, send a proposal and three chapters only.

BALLANTINE BOOKS
A Division of **RANDOM HOUSE, INC.**
201 East 50th Street
New York, New York 10022
212-751-2600
FAX 212-572-4912

Linda Grey, President and Publisher

The Ballantine Publishing Group publishes general fiction and nonfiction, but occasionally they do publish religion titles. With their various imprints, including **Ballantine Books, Del Ray, Fawcett,** and **Ivy Books,** they publish nearly 500 books per year. Almost 5,000 Ballantine, Del Rey, Fawcett, and Ivy Books titles are currently in print. They do not provide guidelines or tip sheets. They would prefer at first to see only an outline and two sample chapters, accompanied by a self-addressed stamped envelope. Do not send the entire manuscript.

BANTAM BOOKS
1540 Broadway
New York, New York 10036
216-354-6500

Toni Burbank, Vice President and Executive Editor
Leslie Meredith, Executive Editor
Tom Dupree, Ann Harris, Robert Weisbach, Senior Editors

Bantam, a division of Bantam Doubleday Dell Publishing Group, Inc., publishes religious fiction and nonfiction that appeals to a large, general audience and that crosses over into the secular trade market. This includes a large number of books in the new age category, under the **New Age Books** imprint. They want fresh ideas in many kinds of religious and inspirational categories from authors of experience and authority for readers young and old. They want no humor books, nor books dealing with conquest over adversity—unless the author is well-known. Unless an author is already a celebrity or well-known in some other way, Bantam accepts manuscripts only from professional agents. Other Bantam imprints are **Golden Apple, Peacock Press,** and **Sweet Dreams.** Query only. After an invitation, send a proposal and two or three chapters, along with an author biography.

BARBOUR AND COMPANY, INC.
P. O. Box 719
Uhrichsville, Ohio 44683
614-922-6045
FAX 614-922-5948

Tim Martins, President
Stephen Reginald, Vice President, Editorial
Susan Johnson, Managing Editor, Barbour Books
Rebecca Germany, Editor, Heartsong Presents

Barbour, along with their other imprints **Heartsong Presents** (their line of romance fiction), **The Christian Library,** and **Inspirational Library,** publishes high quality "bargain" books for the Christian bookselling market, including trade books, Bibles, devotionals, and reference. These are mostly reprints, or inspirational books for the promotional market. (Their mail-order division, Christian Book Bargains, is now owned by Christian Book Distributors, a catalog mail-order Christian business.) Barbour does not do Bible study materials, theology, or any academic titles. They publish twenty to thirty books per year, and have 300 titles currently in print. Send for their author guidelines and catalog and include SASE. They prefer a query with a proposal and a couple of sample chapters.

BARCLAY PRESS
110 South Elliott Road
Newberg, Oregon 97132
503-538-7345
FAX 503-538-7033

Dan McCracken, General Manager

Barclay Press is associated with the Friends Church (Quaker). They publish three to five books per year in the areas of spirituality and social issues, and they have 30 titles in print. They will not provide guidelines but they will send a free catalog. Writers may contact them via a query letter.

BEACON HILL PRESS (See NAZARENE PUB-LISHING HOUSE)

BEACON PRESS
25 Beacon Street
Boston, Massachusetts 02108
617-742-2110
FAX 617-723-3097

Kathleen Montgomery, Executive Vice President, UUA
Susan Worst, Religion Editor

As Beacon Press is affiliated with the Unitarian Universalist Association of Congregations, their publishing mission is to do books promoting the values of the Association within and beyond the denomination. Beacon publishes nonfiction titles in fields consonant with the social values and intellectual interests of liberal religion. Controversial and liberal books addressed at exploring the human condition would be of special interest. They publish in the following categories/ genres: General nonfiction, religion and theology, spirituality, current affairs, anthropology, women's studies, history, philosophy, environmental studies, Jewish studies,

African-American studies, Asian-American studies, and Native American studies. Beacon is not interested in seeing fiction, poetry, inspirational literature, books for children, or self-help books. Fifty to sixty books are published each year by this house, and they have nearly 300 titles on their backlist. They want to see a cover letter, a curriculum vitae, the work's table of contents, and two or three sample chapters.

BEECH TREE BOOKS (See WILLIAM MORROW AND COMPANY, INC.)

BETHANY HOUSE PUBLISHERS
Division of Bethany Fellowship, Inc.
11300 Hampshire Avenue South
Minneapolis, Minnesota 55438
612-829-2500
FAX 612-829-2768

Carol Johnson, Editorial Director
Steven R. Laube, Acquisitions Editor
Kevin Johnson, Editor for Nonfiction
Sharon Madison, Manuscript Review Editor

Bethany House publishes a broad range of books for a broad range of Christian readers, from children through adults. They use human interest stories of God at work among people, Bible study tools, personal growth, devotionals, contemporary issues, marriage and family, and some inspiration. They are especially interested in books on the deeper Christian life, spirituality, and both women's and men's issues. Their fiction program is quite active and successful, especially in historical fiction. They do not want to see books on music, cookbooks, diet books, prophecy, poetry, exercise books, textbooks, or personal experience books. Bethany does from seventy-five to eighty-five books each year, and they have nearly 600 titles currently in print. For both fiction and nonfiction, send a query letter, chapter by chapter synopsis, and a couple of finished chapters as samples.

BETHEL PUBLISHING
1819 South Main
Elkhart, Indiana 46516
219-293-8585
FAX 219-522-5670

Richard Oltz, Senior Editor

Bethel is the publishing arm of the Missionary Church. For many years Bethel functioned in a limited capacity, serving the denomination's curriculum and printing needs alone. Now the house has entered the wholesale field of Christian family products sold through various bookstores, including fiction (adult, teen, historical, topical, present day), and children's materials (primarily 10-13 year old readers, but other ages are acceptable). They do not acquire theological studies, poetry, or pre-school and elementary age stories. Material should be evangelical in approach and tenor. They publish around ten books per year with 30 titles currently in print. Guidelines and catalog are available. Best to send a query first, then the full manuscript.

BIBLE DISCOVERY
20 Lincoln Avenue
Elgin, Illinois 60120
708-741-0800
FAX 708-741-0499

Bible Discovery was the imprint of Cook Communications Ministries that focused on Bibles and Bible story reference books for children that effectively bridge Scripture to a child's life. This publishing program is now under the Chariot label (see Chariot Books). They are looking for new ways to use Scripture for 8-14 year olds, as well as Bible portions for 0-3s and 3-8 year olds. The ideas have to be clear, concise, and age-appropriate. Writers should contact **The Writer's Edge** editorial service, a service that links writers and publishers, located at P. O. Box 1266, Wheaton, Illinois, 60189.

BLUE DOLPHIN PUBLISHING, INC.
P. O. Box 1920
Nevada City, California 95959-1920
916-265-6925
FAX 916-265-0787

Paul M. Clemens, President
Linda Maxwell, Wendy Kelly, Editors

Blue Dolphin publishes twelve to fifteen books per year in most categories of religion. Their specialty is in comparative spiritual traditions, lay and transpersonal psychology, self-help, health, healing, relationships, and "whatever helps people grow in their conscious evolution." They also have some interest in books on early Christianity, personal mysticism, ecology titles, anthropology, education, and books on men's and women's issues. **Pelican Pond Publishing** is another of their imprints. They have about 50 titles now in print. They will accept poetry only from previously published poets. Send the complete manuscript.

BOB JONES UNIVERSITY PRESS
1700 Wade Hampton Blvd.
Greenville, South Carolina 29614
803-242-5100
FAX 803-242-5100

George Collins, Editor in Chief
Gloria Repp, Acquisitions Editor

Bob Jones Press publishes around thirty El-hi textbooks a year for Christian schools on earth sciences, history, language arts, literature, and mathematics. They also do five to ten books per year for children under the **Light Line** and **Pennant Books** imprints. They have a special need for realistic and historical fiction for readers from the upper elementary grades through the teens. They are also looking for biographies with a high moral tone, humor, and works on problem realism. BJU Press has over 300 titles in print. Some of their books go out under the **Unusual Publications** imprint. For both fiction and nonfiction, send a proposal with five sample chapters. Send the whole manuscript if it is complete.

BRANDEN PUBLISHING COMPANY, INC.
Division of Branden Books
Box 843, 17 Station Street
Brookline Village, Massachusetts 02147
617-734-2045
FAX 617-734-2046

Adolph Caso, Editor

Branden publishes mostly in general or secular categories (fifteen books or so each year), but they do several religion books each year, especially Eastern and African religions as they relate to Christianity. They have slightly less than 300 titles currently in print. Query letter only for nonfiction works.

BRENTWOOD CHRISTIAN PRESS
4000 Beallwood Avenue
Columbus, Georgia 31904
404-576-5787

Jerry L. Luquire, Executive Editor

Brentwood publishes collections of sermons on family topics for the mainline groups, poetry, and books on how the

Bible relates to today. In fiction, they do stories of faith overcoming daily problems. **Pastor's Choice Press** is a subsidiary of Brentwood which publishes sermon notes, outlines, illustrations, and other things pastors might find interesting—but they do only *subsidy* publishing under the PCP imprint. Guidelines are available, but no catalog. Send the complete manuscript.

BRIDGE-LOGOS PUBLISHERS, INC.
North Brunswick Corporate Center
1300 Airport Road, Suite E
North Brunswick, NJ 08902
908-435-8700
FAX 908-435-8701

Guy J. Morrell, President
Catherine J. Barrier, Editor in Chief

The former **Logos International**, the corporate predecessor of Bridge Publishing, Inc. (which was a division of Valley Books Trust in the UK) and the first true charismatic publishing house, is now publishing under the auspices of Bridge-Logos Publishers. The company is looking for quality Christian books written from a solid biblical perspective on various topics, including evangelism, discipleship and spiritual growth, spiritual warfare, revival, the Spirit-filled life, matrimonial relationships, education, the family, church growth, daily devotionals, Christian testimony, and Bible study. They also have an interest in books on topical issues, such as politics, sports, abortion, human sexuality, freedom from substance abuse and other bondages, etc., when discussed from a thoroughly biblical viewpoint. Although primarily interested in nonfiction, Bridge-Logos is willing to review proposals for good Christian fiction and good Christian juvenile material. As for poetry, they generally do not accept it, but they will consider publishing the work of previously established authors or those with exceptional merit. Bridge-Logos also publishes works that have become the fabric of the charismatic literary heritage under the imprint known as **The Logos Library.** Other Bridge-Logos imprints include **Logos, Haven Books, Bridge,** and **Open Scroll.** They do around twenty-five books per year and would prefer queries with letter or detailed manuscript proposals, but they will accept unsolicited manuscripts. **Selah House Publishing,** an affiliate of Bridge-Logos Publishers, produces materials that don't fit the Bridge-Logos editorial focus, but in this imprint the authors provide most of the funding for publishing. In submitting to Bridge-Logos, with the proposal, send a brief synopsis of the work, a detailed chapter by chapter outline, and author biographical information.

BRIDGEPOINT (See VICTOR BOOKS)

BRISTOL BOOKS
P. O. Box 4020
Anderson, Indiana 46013-0020
317-644-0856
FAX 317-622-1045

James S. Robb, Editor

Bristol Books is the imprint of Bristol House, Ltd., which publishes books from a Wesleyan Christian perspective. However, as almost all of the manuscripts they end up publishing come from their established list of authors or other persons they know personally, very few books from authors they are not connected with will be considered. They do about ten books per year, and they have no guidelines to offer prospective authors. For nonfiction submissions, send a proposal and two sample chapters.

BROADMAN & HOLMAN PUBLISHERS
127 Ninth Avenue, North
Nashville, Tennessee 37234
615-251-2000
FAX 615-251-3870

Kenneth H. Stephens, Publisher
Bucky Rosenbaum, Manager, Books Section
Vicki Crumpton, Acquisitions and Development Editor

This house is a division of the Sunday School Board of the Southern Baptist Convention, but one does not need to be a Southern Baptist to publish with them. Their books are intended to contribute to the effectiveness of churches and to the personal growth of individual Christians. They publish sixty to seventy titles per year that bring a commitment to traditional Christian values in the areas of religion (mostly Southern Baptist), Christian living, Bible study helps, professional development for ministers (practical theology), books for church leadership and church-staff workers, marriage and family, juvenile, children's fiction (but they only publish children's fiction in a series and they have decided not to publish juvenile fiction), general nonfiction, inspirational, and biography. They are no longer interested in seeing poetry, children's picture books, adult fiction, exposes of prominent persons or organizations, and art/gift books. **Church Street Press** (Connie Powell, Editor) is the imprint of the Baptist Sunday School Board specializing in books on church music. These books can be aimed at children, youth, adults, both general and academic. They release 3 to 4 books each year. Query them and expect a reply in 1 to 2 weeks. Broadman & Holman has some 700 titles currently in print. They do provide submission guidelines, and they prefer a query/proposal in the format of those guidelines.

BROWN PUBLISHING
P. O. Box 539
Dubuque, Iowa 52004
319-588-1451
FAX 319-589-4705

Ernest T. Nedder, Publisher
Mary Jo Graham, Senior Editor

This Catholic press, which publishes fifty plus titles each year, is primarily seeking school and parish texts, along with easy-to-use self-help books. No author guidelines are available. They prefer seeing the complete manuscript.

BUCKLEY PUBLICATONS (See ACTA PUBLI-CATIONS)

CAMERON PRESS, INC.
155 Thornwood Drive
Marlton, New Jersey 08053
609-983-5937
FAX 609-983-5331

Lynn Guise, Editor

Cameron is an evangelical house that published ten titles per year in the area of Christian living books. They are also interested in adult fiction suitable for series. They do not want to see children's books. Writer's guidelines are available. Send a query and a proposal.

CAMPION BOOKS (See LOYOLA PRESS)

WILLIAM CAREY LIBRARY
1705 North Sierra Bonita Avenue
Pasadena, California 91104
818-798-4067
FAX 818-794-0477

David Shaver, General Manager

William Carey is very specialized in its publishing program, including only books and studies of church growth and world missions. They do ten to fifteen titles per year and have 90 in print at this time. Query only.

CATHEDRAL MUSIC PRESS (See MEL BAY PUBLICATIONS, INC.)

THE CATHOLIC UNIVERSITY OF AMERICA PRESS
303 Administration Building
620 Michigan Avenue, N.E.
Washington, D.C. 20064
202-319-5052
FAX 202-319-5802

David J. McGonagle, Director

This university press publishes scholarly books for the academic community and academic libraries. They also publish textbooks for classroom use. Most of the things they produce are specifically for Roman Catholics. The press is not interested in doing books for the popular religious reading audience. They do around twenty titles per year, and have about 250 titles currently in print. Send a query letter and a two-page summary abstract.

CHALICE PRESS
P. O. Box 179
1316 Convention Plaza
St Louis, Missouri 63166-0179
314-231-8500
FAX 314-231-8524

Stephen Cranford, Chairman
David P. Polk, Editor

Chalice Press is a division of the Christian Board of Publications of the Christian Church (Disciples of Christ). This publisher does twelve to fifteen nonfiction titles per year in the area of Protestant religion, and they have 100 books now in print. They look for informed treatments of current social issues, books on preaching, and books on stewardship. They also publish hymnals and are now looking for a greater number of female and ethnic minority writers. Guidelines are available. Send a full proposal and two sample chapters.

CHARIS BOOKS (See SERVANT PUBLICATIONS)

CHOSEN BOOKS
2956 Valera Court
Vienna, Virginia 22181
703-242-2080
FAX 703-242-2080

Jane Campbell, Editor

Chosen is owned by **Baker Book House.** They are looking for well-crafted volumes of charismatic emphasis that recognize the gifts and ministry of the Holy Spirit and help the reader live a more empowered and effective Christian life. Their narratives must have a strong theme and reader benefits. They are not looking for straight autobiographies, however, nor do they publish fiction, poetry, children's books, academic works, or Bible studies. They publish fifty to sixty titles per year and have more than 100 now in print. Guidelines are available. They want to see a proposal with sample chapters.

CHRISM BOOKS (SEE GOSPEL PUBLISHING HOUSE)

CHRISTIAN CLASSICS
Box 30
Westminster, Maryland 21158
410-848-3065
FAX 410-857-2805

John J. McHale, President and Director of the Press

This Catholic house is owned by **Thomas More Press,** a division of mainline Catholic **Tabor Publishing** (which is itself a division of RCL Enterprises). They produce mostly Catholic books of theology, spirituality, reference, biography, and history. Their subjects also include psychology and general nonfiction religious material. Christian Classics produces ten to fifteen books per year; they have 75 titles now in print. They appreciate the query approach.

CHRISTIAN EDUCATION PUBLISHERS
Box 261129
San Diego, California 92196-1129
619-578-4700

Arthur L. Miley, Publisher
Carol Rogers, Managing Editor

Christian Education Publishers is an evangelical Bible club house that produces materials for ages two through high school. They do novels, picture books, and story books. Their fiction features children in a current setting learning a significant Bible truth. The Bible studies and curriculum are for ages 2-3 through high school. The Christian education materials (reproducible) are for teachers to use in teaching the Bible to children—primarily activity books of games, puzzles, and crafts that encourage children in Bible learning. Fiction for take-home papers is also considered, but no full-length fiction is wanted. They publish twenty-five or so books each year. **Rainbow Books** is another imprint of CEP. All writing is by assignment. Query first. Request guidelines and an application, then review their stated club objectives and indicate which age you prefer writing for.

THE CHRISTIAN LIBRARY (See BARBOUR AND COMPANY, INC.)

CHRISTIAN LIFE BOOKS (See CREATION HOUSE)

CHRISTIAN LIGHT PUBLICATIONS
1066 Chicago Avenue
Harrisonburg, Virginia 22801
703-434-0768

Merna B. Shank, Acquisitions

CLP publishes tracts, Sunday school, vacation Bible school, and Christian day school curriculum, along with general Christian books. They do a small number of books each year, and have 70 titles in print. Query only.

CHRISTIAN LITERATURE CRUSADE, INC.
701 Pennsylvania Avenue, Box 1449
Fort Washington, Pennsylvania 19034-8849
215-542-1240
FAX 215-542-7580

Ken Brown, Publishing Manager
Willard Stone, Submissions Editor

CLC publishes some ten to twenty conservative evangelical books per year. They have 250 titles in print. Since they operate as part of a worldwide literature mission, their output is limited to books that will fit their missionary outlook.

Currently they are looking for evangelism, discipleship and deeper life, and missionary biographies (especially for young people). They are also looking for a small number of fictionalized biographies of well-known people. Do not send poetry. With appropriate SASE they will send guidelines and a catalog. Send a query letter with a proposal and three chapters.

CHRISTIAN MEDIA
Box 448
Jacksonville, Oregon 97530
503-899-8888

James Lloyd, Editor and Publisher

This press is interested in media-oriented materials that focus on Christian music, video, film, broadcasting, and drama. They also do prophetic books that interpret the end times (but not books that take the rapture position), eschatology, and books on politics. No guidelines. Query only.

CHRISTIAN PUBLICATIONS, INC.
3825 Hartzdale Drive
Camp Hill, Pennsylvania 17011
717-761-7044
FAX 717-761-7273

Jonathan Graf, Editorial Director
David E. Fesenden, Associate Editor

Christian Publications and **Horizon Books** are wholly owned by and are the official publishing houses of The Christian and Missionary Alliance. They publish twenty-five books per year, and they have 320 titles currently in print. All their books have to adhere to the doctrinal statement of the Alliance, but they are also open to writers outside of their denomination. Their purpose is to propagate the faith to the Alliance constituency in particular, to the broader evangelical constituency worldwide, and to non-Christians. Therefore, the primary theme of most of their books is the deeper Christian life (especially on sanctification) and evangelism. They also publish in the area of missions (usually denominational). Fiction is published for adults, teens, and children. Their National Ministries Division has a line of reprint books that challenge the believer by classic authors such as A. W. Tozer and A. B. Simpson. These publications are offered to ministries for use as promotional items, love gifts, or premiums. They do not want to see poetry and sci-fi. Writers should ask for their author's guide. They want to see a query along with some writing samples.

CHRISTIAN SCHOOLS INTERNATIONAL
Box 8709, 3350 East Paris Avenue, S.E.
Grand Rapids, Michigan 49518-8709
616-957-1070
FAX 616-957-5022

Sheri D. Haan, Director
Judy Bandstra, Editor

Christian Schools International, or **CSI Publications**, publishes elementary and secondary school textbooks, teacher resources, and aids and curriculum guides. They do fifteen titles each year and have 135 now in print. Query.

CHRISTIAN UNIVERSITIES PRESS
781 Woodmont, #345
Bethesda, Maryland 20814
301-654-7114
FAX 301-654-7336

Robert West, Editor in Chief

185

CUP is an imprint of International Scholar's Publications. They do mainstream scholarship with a Christian theme, and publish twenty-five to thirty titles per year, including some dissertations and scholarly monographs. They are looking for theology, reference materials, and books on the missionary and renewal movements. Guidelines are available. Send a proposal and two sample chapters.

THE CHRISTOPHER PUBLISHING HOUSE
24 Rockland Street
Hanover, Massachusetts 02339
617-826-7474
FAX 617-826-5556

Harold Walsh, President
Nancy A. Lucas, Managing Editor

This house publishes ten to twelve adult nonfiction and fiction religious tradebook titles each year in hardcover and paperback. About 120 of their books are now in print. Their guidelines are available. Send the complete manuscript.

CHURCH GROWTH INSTITUTE
P. O. Box 4404
Lynchburg, Virginia 24502
804-525-0022
FAX 804-525-0608

Larry A. Gilbert, Director
Cindy G. Spear, Editor

Church Growth Institute materials are meant to benefit the local church, including topics dealing with leadership and administrative duties, ministering in the local church, evangelism, stewardship, and Christian growth. The books they publish must be practical and easy for the average Christian to understand. In the future CGI may begin to produce a broader range of curriculum-type material that applies biblical principles to Christian living and Christian growth suitable for small group Bible studies or Sunday school curriculum. Currently they are looking for books on church growth, books on how to start special ministries, and leadership training materials. They are not interested in reference books. Most published works are through assignments, and they publish ten to twenty books per year, with 35 currently in print. Query or submit outline and brief explanation of writing project.

CISTERCIAN PUBLICATIONS, INC.
Wallwood Hall, WMU Station
Kalamazoo, Michigan 49008
616-387-8920
FAX 616-387-8921

Ernest Breisach, President
E. Rozanne Elder, Vice President and Editorial Director

Cistercian is operated by the Order of Cistercians of the Strict Observance (Roman Catholic). They produce up to ten books per year in the nonfiction categories of Christian living, theology, and historical theology, but they want Christian monastic studies only. They have 150 books in print. Guidelines and catalog are available. Send a proposal and two sample chapters.

CLARENDON PRESS (See OXFORD UNIVERSITY PRESS)

CLIFFSIDE PUBLISHING HOUSE
11535 Old Highway 16
Grassy Creek, North Carolina 28631
910-982-9285

Brodrick Shepherd, President

This house specializes in publishing two or three books per year on the return of Christ and the end of the world. They are looking for apocalyptic studies, prophecy, and commentaries on end-time theories. Guidelines are available. Query with a proposal and two or three sample chapters.

COKESBURY (See ABINGDON PRESS)

COLLEGE PRESS PUBLISHING COMPANY, INC.
P. O. Box 1132
Joplin, Missouri 64802
417-623-6280
FAX 417-623-8250

John M. Hunter, Editor

College Press and its imprint, **Forerunner Books,** are associated with The Christian Churches/Churches of Christ. They wish to publish inductive studies of the Bible that challenge the objective and rational approach to learning. They want their books to equip the church to fulfill the primary responsibility of carrying out the Great Commission, and to help Christians today to cope with the world around them. They are especially interested in Bible studies (biblical exposition), apologetics, exegetical studies, and nonfiction topical and inspirational books. There is no interest in poetry, books on prophecy, and non-biblical works. They will not publish anything contrary to the Bible, so writers must be sure to use scriptural documentation in their work. Full manuscripts are permissible, but not preferred. Better to query with a proposal and samples.

COMPANION PRESS
167 Walnut Bottom Road
Shippensburg, Pennsylvania 17257
717-532-3040
FAX 717-532-9291

Keith Carroll, Publisher

This non-denominational publisher also operates under the **Destiny Image** imprint. They do twenty to thirty books each year (a high percentage of them as subsidy projects) for the general Christian reader. Guidelines and catalog are available. They will take a query or a complete manuscript.

CONCORDIA PUBLISHING HOUSE
3558 South Jefferson Avenue
St. Louis, Missouri 63118-3968
314-268-1000
FAX 314-268-1329

John W. Gerber, President
David V. Koch, Chief Editor, Books
Mervin A. Marquardt, Managing Editor
Bruce Cameron, Academic and Theological Editor
Ruth Geisler, Family and Children's Resources Editor

Concordia is the publishing arm of the Lutheran Church—Missouri Synod. They publish sixty to seventy books per year that are consistent with the teachings of the Lutheran Church—Missouri Synod and that consciously and actively promote the Christian faith and life. Many of their books are published for

Hispanic, Chinese, African-American, Hmong, and Vietnamese readers. Their interests are in well-researched books on religion, resources for congregational ministries and leaders, books on classic and contemporary theology, Christian living books, and aids for family living. They are not publishing poetry or fantasy novels (they publish very little adult fiction). The St. Louis-based house recently announced plans to enter the Christian mysteries market for kids eight to twelve. They will be looking for books that are suspenseful and have a sense of the unknown, but that stress values-building. Concordia has over 1,000 titles currently in print. Guidelines are available in their booklet, "What Authors Should Know." They want to see a summary statement of the writing project and a brief autobiography.

CONTEMPORARY DRAMA SERVICE (See MERI-WETHER PUBLISHING LTD.)

THE CONTINUUM PUBLISHING GROUP
370 Lexington Avenue, Suite 1700
New York, New York 10017-6503
212-953-5858
FAX 212-953-5944

Justus George Lawler, Senior Editor

Continuum publishes religious studies, history, sociology, psychology and social thought, women's studies, literature and criticism, and works in the performing arts. They offer more than one hundred new publications a year, along with a 700-title backlist. Send a query letter first.

COOK COMMUNICATIONS MINISTRIES
4050 Lee Vance View
Colorado Springs, Colorado 80918
719-536-0100
FAX 719-536-3279

David Mehlis, President
Dan Brokke, Senior Vice President

The imprints of Cook Communications Ministries (formerly David C. Cook Publishing Company) include **Chariot Books** (children's books), **Chariot Family Publishing** (application of Christian beliefs to life), **Lion Books** (Christian books targeted to the general market for both children and adults), **SSP** (Scripture Press Publications are meant to serve the church and provide the best resources for a wide variety of publications), and **Victor Books** (contemporary and traditional Christian books that challenge, inspire, inform and entertain). Their program now includes Christian books, cards, worship music, toys, and magazines. The mission of the book imprints is to meet the needs of Christian education, and to promote and contribute to the teaching and putting into practice of loving God and loving each other—by creating and disseminating Christian communications materials and services to people throughout the world. These imprints publish about sixty books per year, with over 500 titles in print. Most of their books are both fun and educational and aimed at the Christian family, modeling Christian living and Christian character traits. They go primarily to the home, rather than to the church. Each book is designed to help readers better understand themselves, their relationship to God, and the message of the Bible. Cook Communications prefers that writers work with **The Writer's Edge** editorial service, a service that links writers and publishers, located at P.O. Box 1266, Wheaton, Illinois, 60189.

CORNELL UNIVERSITY PRESS
Box 250, Sage House
512 East State Street
Ithaca, New York 14850
607-277-2338
FAX 607-277-2374

191

Bernhard Kendler, Executive Editor
Roger Haydon, Editor and Acquisitions Coordinator

Cornell publishes general nonfiction scholarly books and monographs. They do about 160 per year at the press, including ten or a dozen specifically in the area of religion, particularly philosophy of religion and church history or historical theology (medieval and early modern). They have 2,200 titles in print. Guidelines are available. Query first.

CORNERSTONE PRESS CHICAGO
939 West Wilson, Suite 202-C
Chicago, Illinois 60640
312-561-2450
FAX 312-989-2076

Jane Hertenstein, Associate Editor

Cornerstone is a division of Jesus People USA, which is now a part of the Evangelical Covenant Church of America. They publish ten or a dozen books a year on general religious subject matters, spiritual works, investigative journalism, children's picture books, books on music, humor, the arts, art history, and poetry. Recently Cornerstone debuted a fiction line. They sometimes publish under their **Mere Bones** imprint. Send a proposal and some sample chapters.

CRAIG PRESS (See PRESBYTERIAN AND RE-FORMED PUBLISHING COMPANY)

CREAGER PUBLISHING (See PELICAN PUB-LISHING COMPANY, INC.)

CREATION HOUSE
190 North Westmore Drive
Altamonte Springs, Florida 32714
407-862-7565
FAX 407-869-6051

Steve Strang, Publisher
Deborah Poulalion, Editorial Manager

Creation House and **Christian Life Books** are both part of Strang Communications, the publishers of the non-denominational *Charisma & Christian Life* and *Ministries Today* magazines. They publish fifteen to twenty-five books per year that serve the evangelical Christian market, and they have special access to the charismatic and Pentecostal parts of evangelicalism. There are some 150 books now in print. They are currently looking for books of Spirit-filled interest, devotional life, practical Christian living, Bible study, and some fiction (though they publish little fiction). These books must show how they will appeal to their target market of charismatics and Pentecostals. They do not want to see poetry or children's books. Write for their guidelines for submissions. They want to see a cover letter, a one-to-two-page summary of the manuscript, a brief table of contents, and some excerpts from the work.

CREATION LIFE PUBLISHERS, INC. (See MASTER BOOKS)

CREATIVE KEYBOARD PUBLICATIONS (See MEL BAY PUBLICATIONS, INC.)

CROSS CULTURAL PUBLICATIONS, INC.
P. O. Box 506
Notre Dame, Indiana 46556
219-272-0889
FAX 219-273-5973

Elizabeth Pullapilly, President
Cyriac K. Pullapilly, General Editor

Under the imprint **Cross Roads Books**, this publisher does about twenty titles per year, mostly in intercultural scholarly topics. They have fifteen such titles in print. They are open to well-researched and well-written books on intercultural and interfaith matters, especially if they lend themselves to classroom use as textbooks. Their published titles include books in history, biography, philosophy, religion, ethics, comparative religion and literature, historical novels, science, mythology, literary criticism, and fiction. Send a query and a proposal, along with one chapter.

THE CROSSROAD PUBLISHING COMPANY, INC.
370 Lexington Avenue
New York, New York 10017
212-532-3650
FAX 212-532-4922

Michael Leach, Executive Vice President and Publisher

Crossroad is part of the German-based Herder and Herder Verlag family of international publishing companies committed to publishing quality books intended to inform, build community, inspire, enlighten, and heal. The company publishes a wide range of titles including scholarly books for seminarians, teachers, and clergy, as well as for laypeople. Topics include religion and philosophy, religious education, theology, history, spirituality, counseling and self-help, and world religions. Bible study materials are also included in their list. A new imprint for this house is called **Herder**, intended to expand Crossroad's publishing program into greater theological discourse at the lay and professional levels. **Meyerstone** is also a Crossroad imprint. They publish nearly 100 books per year and have about 800 now in print. Writers should send a query letter and an initial outline.

CROSS ROADS BOOKS (See CROSS CULTURAL PUBLICATIONS, INC.)

CROSSWAY BOOKS
1300 Crescent Street
Wheaton, Illinois 60187
708-682-4300
FAX 708-682-4785

Lane T. Dennis, President
Leonard G. Goss, Vice President of Editorial and Editor in Chief
Frederick J. Rudy, Vice President of Operations
Ted Griffin, Managing Editor
Lila Bishop, Associate Editor
Steve Hawkins, Assistant Editor
Jill Carter, Editorial Associate

Crossway Books, the book publishing division of **Good News Publishers**, is a major publisher of serious Christian books and a highly creative house that publishes many of the leading Christian authors of the day. Crossway is committed to publishing books that help bring readers to a knowledge of Christianity and help them understand and live in a world becoming increasingly hostile to faith. Each book they publish has to be consistent with what the Bible teaches, and it must stand within the stream of historic Christian truth as affirmed by genuine Christians through the ages and reaffirmed in classic Reformation orthodoxy and its heritage. In general, they seek to publish books that provide a fresh understanding and a distinctively Christian examination of questions confronting Christians and non-Christians in their personal lives, families, churches, communities, and the wider culture. The main types of nonfiction they publish fall into these categories: Issues books, books on the deeper Christian life, and Christian academic and professional books. In nonfiction, they do not want to see celebrity books, popular trend books (diet exercise, self-help, recovery, etc.), popular experience books, or cultural synthesis books. The main types of fiction they publish are supernatural, fantasy, science fiction, Christian realism, historical, mystery, Western, and children's. They are not interested in seeing romance novels, horror novels, biblical novels, issues novels, or end-times/prophecy novels. Crossway publishes fifty to sixty books per year, with a backlist of over 300 titles. They provide catalogs and submissions guidelines and ask to see a full book proposal with two sample chapters.

CSI PUBLICATIONS (See CHRISTIAN SCHOOLS INTERNATIONAL)

C. S. S. PUBLISHING COMPANY
628 South Main Street
Lima, Ohio 45804
419-227-1818
FAX 419-228-8184

Fred Steiner, Editorial Director

CSS is an unaffiliated religious publisher that serves the needs of pastors, worship leaders, and parish program planners in the broad Christian mainline of the American church. This house likes to put out books on topics relating to the Christian faith, including lectionary-based worship resources, sermons, worship aids, Bible studies, devotions, materials for Sunday schools, retreats, and evangelism. They also publish dramas. While most of their materials are for the clergy, they are also interested in the lay market. They publish about forty books per year, 20% through their subsidy operation, **Fairway Press**. (Fairway publishes books on a cooperative basis, meaning that the author puts up some of the money for publishing costs.) They have about 400 books currently in print. They do provide manuscript submission guidelines as well as updated manuscript needs list. For both fiction and nonfiction submissions, they prefer that writers send the entire manuscript.

**CUSTOM COMMUNICATIONS SERVICES, INC./
SHEPHERD PRESS**
77 Main Street
Tappan, New Jersey 10983
914-365-0414

Norman Shaifer, President

This house publishes histories of individual congregations, denominations, or districts. They do around fifty
of these on a yearly basis, and they especially want stories
of larger congregations that have played a role in the growth
and development of their communities. Send a query, a
proposal, and two sample chapters.

DESTINY IMAGE (See COMPANION PRESS)

DIMENSION BOOKS
P. O. Box 811
Denville, New Jersey 07834
201-627-4334

Thomas P. Coffey, President

This house does twenty to twenty-five nonfiction books
per year, and has around 200 titles now in print. They
publish in the areas of religion (Catholic), Christian
spirituality, music, biography, psychology, and psychiatry.
They do provide guidelines, and prefer to see a query and
some sample chapters.

DIMENSIONS FOR LIVING (See ABINGDON PRESS)

DISCIPLESHIP RESOURCES
Box 840
1908 Grand Avenue
Nashville, Tennessee 37202
615-340-7068
FAX 615-340-7006

David Hazelwood, Executive Editor
Craig Gallaway, Editorial Director

Discipleship Resources is a division of the Board of Discipleship of the United Methodist Church. They do twenty to twenty-five titles per year on leadership in ministry, the ministry of the laity, spiritual gifts, and ethnic titles related to African-Americans, Hispanics, and Asian Americans. They are looking for books that keep in touch with the real needs of the church and that examine specific areas of ministry in the church. There are over 300 Discipleship Resources titles now in print. They want to see a book proposal and two sample chapters.

DISCOVERY HOUSE PUBLISHERS
Box 3566
Grand Rapids, Michigan 49501-3566
616-942-9218
FAX 616-957-5741

Robert K. DeVries, Publisher
Carol Holquist, Associate Publisher
Tim Beals, Editor

Discovery House does ten to fifteen books a year aimed at the general CBA trade market. They are affiliated with the Radio Bible Class and now have 65 titles in print. They want books "that feed the soul with the Word of God." Guidelines are available. Query only.

DON BOSCO MULTIMEDIA
Box T, 475 North Avenue
New Rochelle, New York 10802
914-576-0122
FAX 914-654-0443

James Hurley, Publisher
James T. Morgan, Editor

This company is a subsidiary of Salesian Society Inc. Six to twelve titles on religious, trade, and youth and family ministries are published by Don Bosco Multimedia per year. There are about 100 titles currently in print under this imprint as well as **Patron Books** and **Salesiana Publishers.** They want book projects that are directed towards young people to help them develop life skills as Christians. Guidelines and catalogs are available. Query only.

DOUBLEDAY
Division of Bantam Doubleday Dell Publishing
1540 Broadway
New York, New York 10036
212-354-6500
FAX 212-302-7985

William Barry, Vice President and Deputy Publisher
Eric Patrick Major, Vice President, Religious Publishing

Among many other lines, Doubleday publishes books on religion and spirituality for the general trade and special interests markets, including Bibles, religion, biography, history, material for scholarly biblical commentaries as well as inspirational books relating to Jewish, Catholic, and evangelical groups. Their fiction program covers mysteries, romance, westerns, and science fiction. Over 1,200 Doubleday titles are now in print. Besides the Doubleday imprint, they publish under **Anchor, Anchor Bible Reference Library,** and **Main Street.** They wish to see a query, chapter index, topic summary, and sample chapters.

EDEN PUBLISHING
8635 West Sahara Avenue, Suite 459
Las Vegas, Nevada 89117
702-796-6959
FAX 702-796-0282

Barbara Griffin Dan, Publisher

This is a Christian publisher of educational and inspirational books meant to touch the heart and minister to the human spirit. Eden does about ten books per year. Query letter first.

EDICIONES CERTERA (See INTERVARSITY PRESS)

EDUCATIONAL MINISTRIES, INC.
165 Plaza Drive
Prescott, Arizona 86303-5549
602-771-8601
FAX 602-771-8621

Robert Davidson, President
Suzanne Rood Cox, Projects Editor
Linda Davidson, Editor

This company has 120 titles currently in print, and publishes ten books each year on Christian educational resource materials for the mainline Protestant religious market. They are looking for material to be compiled into books on various activities used in the church during the Lenten season. Send the complete manuscript.

EDITORIAL PROTAVOZ (See KREGEL PUBLICATIONS)

WILLIAM B. EERDMANS PUBLISHING COMPANY
255 Jefferson Avenue, S.E.
Grand Rapids, Michigan 49503
616-459-4591
FAX 616-459-6540

Jon Pott, Vice President and Editor in Chief
Amy Eerdmans, Children's Book Editor

This house specializes in Protestant scholarly and academic books in theology, biblical studies, Christian history, ethics, philosophy of religion, spirituality, and Christian life. Their backlist includes many reference volumes in the theological and biblical studies field. Eerdmans also does children's inspirational and regional (Michigan) books. They want their books to bridge the gap between the evangelical and mainline worlds. They do a limited amount of fiction for adults, but are active in children's fiction. Eerdmans publishes eighty to one hundred books each year and has 1,000 backlist titles now in print. They will send a catalog and writer guidelines. On first contact, they prefer seeing a query letter and some sample chapters.

ELEMENT BOOKS
42 Broadway
Rockport, Massachusetts 01966
508-546-1044
FAX 508-546-9882

Delbert Riddle, Managing Director
Paul Cash, Acquiring Editor

Element is affiliated with Element Books, Ltd., and produces books for the very broad religious market, including titles on alternative health, psychology, new age religion, world religion, and philosophy. They do not want scholarly books or books on limited-interest subjects. They publish up to fifty books a year, and have 325 titles now in print. Guidelines are available. Query only.

EMERALD BOOKS
P. O. Box 635
Lynnwood, Washington 98046
206-771-1153
FAX 206-775-2383

Warren Walsh, Editor

This press publishes five books each year in the areas of Christian living and youth. They are also looking for Christian fiction. Guidelines will be sent upon request. Send a proposal and two chapters (for fiction, send four chapters).

ENCOUNTER BOOKS (See ST. PAUL BOOKS AND MEDIA)

EVANGELICAL PRESS (See PRESBYTERIAN AND REFORMED PUBLISHING COMPANY)

FAIRWAY PRESS (See C. S. S. PUBLISHING COMPANY)

FAITHWARE (See LIGUORI PUBLICATIONS)

FAME PUBLISHING, INC.
820 South MacArthur Blvd.
Suite 105-220
Coppell, Texas 75019
214-393-1467
FAX 214-462-9350

Margaret J. Kinney, President

Fame is a nondenominational house publishing three to five titles per year. They have 13 titles now in print of books covering a wide variety of topics, including political themes, Christian living, and health-related. They do not want books that are contrary to Scripture, and they are now considering beginning a line of Christian fiction. Send a proposal and some sample chapters.

FELL PUBLISHERS, INC. (See LIFETIME BOOKS)

FOCUS ON THE FAMILY PUBLISHING
8605 Explorer Drive
Colorado Springs, Colorado 80920-1051
719-531-3400
FAX 719-531-3481

Dean Merrill, Vice President, Resource Group
Al Janssen, Director of Book Publishing
Gwen Weising, Managing Editor
Ken Wall, Editor

Focus on the Family directs its activities primarily toward "the preservation of the home." The book publishing division of this communications complex is looking mostly for writers who have a public speaking or teaching ministry who do books with a unique slant that are practical and applicable to the lives of their constituents. They do from fifteen to twenty adult titles each year. Almost all of their books emphasize marriage and family relationships, as well as the importance of Christian values in people's lives. They do not want to see poetry, adult fiction, or devotionals. Focus has nearly 100 titles now in print. They do provide author's guidelines and a catalog. When submitting a proposal, include a one-page synopsis, and outline of the chapters, with a two- or three-sentence description of each chapter, and the first two chapters of the proposed manuscript.

FORERUNNER BOOKS (See COLLEGE PRESS PUBLISHING COMPANY, INC.)

FORTRESS PRESS (See AUGSBURG FORTRESS PUBLISHERS)

FORUM BOOKS (See FRANCISCAN PRESS)

FRANCISCAN PRESS
1800 College Avenue
Quincy, Illinois 62301-2699
217-228-5670
FAX 217-228-5672

Terrence J. Riddell, Director

This press is associated with Quincy University (Catholic) and also publishes under the imprints of **Herald Books** and

Forum Books. They are looking for books in moral theology, Franciscan history, and the life and writings of St. Francis, St. Clare, and St. Bonaventure. Franciscan has nearly 350 books in print, and they publish five to ten new titles each year. No guidelines are available, but they will send a free catalog. Send a query letter.

> **FRANCISCAN UNIVERSITY PRESS**
> Franciscan Way
> Steubenville, Ohio 43952
> 614-283-6358
> FAX 614-283-6442
>
> Sterling Spears, Director
> Celeste Gregory, Editor

FUP is a division of the Franciscan University of Steubenville. They have about 40 titles in print, and they do five to ten titles a year in Catholic apologetics, devotionals, and biblical studies. Most of their books are authored by university professors and associates. Send a proposal and a single chapter.

> **THE FRIENDS OF ISRAEL GOSPEL MINISTRY, INC.**
> P. O. Box 908
> Bellmawr, New Jersey 08099
> 609-853-5590
> FAX 609-853-9565
>
> Amy Julian, Director of Publications

The Friends of Israel publish a small number of books and booklets each year from a strictly nontechnical and dispensational perspective on the prophecies associated with Israel. They also publish the magazine *Israel My Glory*. While their publications are almost always done by their own in-house staff, one may send a query letter.

FRIENDS UNITED PRESS
101 Quaker Hill Drive
Richmond, Indiana 47374
317-962-7573
FAX 317-966-1293

Ardith Talbot, Editorial Manager

This Friends United Meeting (Quaker) publishing house does six to ten books per year in history, spirituality, and Quaker studies. As their purpose is to energize and equip Friends, they are restricted to Quaker authors (their authors must be a part of the Society of Friends—Friends United Meeting). The authors are restricted to Quaker history and Quaker theology and spirituality. Meeting these criteria would allow them to consider the publication of a manuscript. They have some 50 titles in print. Send a proposal or a complete manuscript.

FRIENDSHIP PRESS
475 Riverside Drive, Room 860
New York, New York 10115
212-870-2586
FAX 212-870-2550

Audrey A. Miller, Executive Director
Margaret Larom, Editor

Friendship is a subsidiary of the National Council of Churches of Christ, USA. They publish general religious books, ecumenical titles, books on the multicultural society, and books in the social sciences. They also publish material on the global perspective, mission education, liberal political issues, peace and justice education, spiritual reflection, and some fiction. They publish for all age groups, with church people as the primary reading audience, and do anywhere from ten to twenty books each year. They have 225 or so titles in print. Guidelines and catalog are available. Send the complete manuscript.

GARBORG'S HEART 'N HOME
2060 West 98th Street
Bloomington, Minnesota 55431
612-888-5727
FAX 612-888-4775

Joan Garborg, Editor

Garborg's produces devotionals and inspirational daily thoughts called "DayBrighteners" for different markets. They do about twenty of these a year. Guidelines are available. Send a sample of thirty day thoughts or quotes.

GATEWAY EDITIONS (See REGNERY PUBLISHING INC.)

C. R. GIBSON COMPANY
32 Knight Street
Norwalk, Connecticut 06856
203-847-4543
FAX 203-847-7613

Frank Rosenberry, President
Marilyn M. Jensen, Vice President and Publisher

Gibson publishes gift books, special occasion gift books, recordbooks, children's books, and greeting cards. They have also done some fiction and some poetry. They do about fifteen book-length titles per year, and have over 120 in print. Guidelines are available. For nonfiction, send a proposal and one sample chapter. For adult and children's fiction, send a proposal and one sample chapter. For poetry, send the complete manuscript.

MICHAEL GLAZIER BOOKS (See THE LITUR-
GICAL PRESS)

GOLD 'N' HONEY (See QUESTAR PUBLISHERS)

GOLDEN APPLE (See BANTAM BOOKS)

GOOD NEWS PUBLISHERS (See CROSSWAY
BOOKS)

GOSPEL LIGHT PUBLICATIONS (See REGAL
BOOKS)

GOSPEL PUBLISHING HOUSE
Division of Publication
1445 Boonvile Avenue
Springfield, Missouri 65802-1894
417-831-8000
FAX 417-862-8558

Joseph Kilpatrick, Director of Publications
David A. Womack, Manager, Ministry Resources
Development

Gospel Publishing House is a denominational publisher
and a division of the General Council of the Assemblies of
God. All of their books must take the doctrinal viewpoint that
is compatible with their denominational positions. The kinds
of books published by GPH include Bible study, biography,
Christian education, Christian living, deaf education,
devotional, doctrinal, evangelism, healing, history of the
Assemblies of God, books on the Holy Spirit, missionary
studies, books for pastors, prophecy, and youth books. Imprints
of GPH include **Chrism Books, Logion Press,** and **Radiant
Books.** They publish around twenty-five titles per year and

have about 75 now in print. They provide a copy of their mission statement, and the guidelines entitled "Writing for Assemblies of God Publications." Query before submitting any work. Include a brief description of your plans for the manuscript.

GREAT QUOTATIONS
1967 Quincy Court
Glendale Heights, Illinois 60139-2045
708-582-2800, ext. 116
FAX 708-582-2813

Patrick Caton, Senior Editor

This publisher releases 50 books each year in the areas of gifts, women's interests, and humor. Their books are light reading, impulse buy merchandise that appeals to women as gifts. They want to see a cover letter and 5 sample pages, with SASE.

GREENLEAF PRESS
1570 Old La Guardo Road
Lebanon, Tennessee 37087
615-449-1617
FAX 615-449-4018

Rob Sherer, Editor

Greenleaf Press is a general publisher that specializes in biography, historical fiction, and historical non-fiction. About 6 books are released each year. Send a query with sample chapters. They emphasize that writers should treat their audience with respect. Write real stories for real people.

GREENWILLOW BOOKS (See WILLIAM MORROW AND COMPANY, INC.)

GROUP PUBLISHING, INC.
P. O. Box 481
Loveland, Colorado 80539
303-669-3836
FAX 303-669-3269

Thom Schultz, President
Paul Woods, Senior Editor
Susan Lingo, Book and Curriculum Acquisitions Editor
Kirk R. Gilmore, Magazines Director

The emphasis for this house is on youth ministry, for which they publish fifty to sixty books each year. Their books are geared to those who work with junior through senior high, mostly in a church setting. They want how-to books, devotionals, Bible studies, and some reference. They are also the publishers of **Group's Hands-On Bible Curriculum**, as well as three Group magazines, *Children's Ministry, Group*, and *Jr. High Ministry*. MinistryNet is Group's online, interactive ministry resource. They have about 250 book titles in print. Query letters first, then proposal and two sample chapters.

GROUP'S HANDS-ON BIBLE CURRICULUM (See GROUP PUBLISHING, INC.)

HANNIBAL BOOKS
921 Center Street
Hannibal, Missouri 63401
314-221-2462

James C. Hefley, President
Marti Hefley, Editor

Hannibal is the book publishing division of Hefley Communications, Inc., which produces the Mark Twain

Writers Conference. They have 25 titles in print, and each year they do about five new ones that impact readers for Christ. They especially want crossover books. They publish "Country Classics," stories about growing up in families with traditional values, and Christian issue documentaries of intense personal interest. Rarely do they publish fiction, and almost never do they publish books by first-time authors. Query letter only.

HAPPY DAY BOOKS (See STANDARD PUBLISHING COMPANY)

HARPERCOLLINS PUBLISHERS (See HARPER SAN FRANCISCO GROUP)

HARPER SAN FRANCISCO GROUP
1160 Battery Street
San Francisco, California 94111-1213
415-477-4400
FAX 415-477-4444

Thomas Grady, Vice President and Publisher
Barbara Moulton, Senior Editor
John Shopp, Senior Editor
Patricia Klein, Editor

Harper San Francisco is the religious publishing division of the large general trade house, **HarperCollins Publishers.** They publish seekers-market or personal-need books for the general reader and are interested in books on spirituality, recovery, theology and biblical studies, translations, religion and philosophy of religion, liturgy and preaching, and sociological and psychological studies. Their books for the believer's market range from evangelical to Catholic in content. The division publishes approximately 150 titles per year. They also publish more popular materials for the general lay audience, especially in the area of New Age, and many other books on non-Christian spirituality. They want to see an annotated outline, one or two sample chapters, and a curriculum vitae.

HARRISON HOUSE PUBLISHERS
2448 E. 81 Street, Suite 5600
Tulsa, Oklahoma 74137-4256
918-582-2126
FAX 918-494-3665

Keith Provance, President

This press emphasizes charismatic books that proclaim the truth and power of the Gospel with excellence, challenging Christians to live victoriously, grow spiritually, and know God intimately. Most of the books they publish are by and for full-time ministers who have a specific message for the church. Their publishing areas include biography, religion, and self-help. They do thirty-five or so books per year and have about 400 in print. They are not looking for testimony books at this time, and they no longer publish fiction. They want writers to use the query approach.

HARVEST HOUSE PUBLISHERS, INC.
1075 Arrowsmith Street
Eugene, Oregon 97402
503-343-0123
FAX 503-342-6410

Robert C. Hawkins, Jr., President
Eileen Mason, Vice President, Editorial
Carolyn McCready, Editorial Director

Harvest House is a progressive evangelical publishing house that publishes books to "help the hurts of people" and nurture spiritual growth. They do several adult and youth

211

"how-to" books, as well as other more popular treatments of Christianity. All topics must be original, relevant, and examined from a biblical standpoint with an emphasis on contemporary application. They focus on "how to" books, but they publish in many different areas, including adult and juvenile fiction, biblical study, Bible study methods and aids, Christian education, Christian living, contemporary issues, counseling, cults, devotionals, discipling, ethics, evangelism, family life, leadership, marriage and family, prayer, stewardship, theology, witnessing, and women. **Marcon Publishers** is a Harvest House imprint of books meant for distribution into the ABA or general market. Gift books and cookbooks will be added to their diverse publishing program. They wish to see an outline, project synopsis, and the first three chapters. This house docs roughly eighty books per year and has more than 350 titles on their backlist. They provide writer's guidelines that should be read carefully before submitting any material.

HAVEN BOOKS (See BRIDGE-LOGOS PUBLISH-ERS, INC.)

HAWORTH PASTORAL PRESS (See THE HAWORTH PRESS, INC.)

THE HAWORTH PRESS, INC.
10 Alice Street
Binghamton, New York 13904-1580
607-722-5857
FAX 607-722-1424

Bill Cohen, Publisher
William Clements, Senior Editor

The Haworth Press publishes some 200 books per year in the general social and behavioral sciences, but under their

Haworth Pastoral Press imprint they do five to ten books on pastoral care and psychology and social work with a pastoral perspective. Their backlist amounts to 1,000 titles. Send a proposal and two sample chapters.

HEARTSONG PRESENTS (See BARBOUR AND COMPANY, INC.)

HENDRICKSON PUBLISHERS, INC.
Box 3473
Peabody, Massachusetts 01961-3473
508-532-6546
FAX 508-531-8146

David L. Townsley, Editorial Director
Philip H. Anderson, Acquisitions Editor
Partick Alexander, Senior Academic Editor

Hendrickson publishes books of a more academic perspective in the areas of biblical studies, theology, philosophy, homiletics, and studies of the original biblical languages. They do about fifteen books per year and have about 150 titles currently in print. They have also developed a more pentecostal line of material. Writer guidelines are provided. Send two or three sample chapters from manuscripts, with a proposal.

VIRGIL W. HENSLEY, INC.
6116 East 32nd Street
Tulsa, Oklahoma 74135
918-664-8520
FAX 918-664-8562

Terri Kalfas, Editor

This press is looking for books that cut across denominational lines, but should always stay within the bounds of the Christian faith. For fiction, only book-length manuscripts will be considered. Christianity must be essential to the plot of the story. For nonfiction, the basis for the work must also be Christianity. No personal prophecy, testimonials, sermon collections, poetry, or short stories will be considered. They produce five to ten titles annually, with 15 titles now in print. Send a book proposal and the first three chapters from the work.

HERALD BOOKS (See FRANCISCAN PRESS)

HERALD PRESS
616 Walnut Avenue
Scottdale, Pennsylvania 15683
412-887-8500
FAX 412-887-3111

David Garber, Book Editor
Michael A. King, Book Editor

Herald Press is part of the Congregational Literature Division of **Mennonite Publishing House** (owned by the Mennonite Church). Each year they release a variety of new books for adults, young people, and children (primarily for ages 9 and up). They want books that promote justice and peace and that are consistent with Scripture as interpreted in the Anabaptist/Mennonite tradition. They do thirty books annually (almost always with writers belonging to their denomination), and have about 450 books currently in print. Book proposals should be in these areas: missions and evangelism, family life, current issues, peace and justice, personal experience, adult and juvenile fiction, Bible study, inspiration, devotional, church history, Christian ethics, and theology. They also do ethnic titles for Native Americans (with a California focus), the Amish, and the Mennonites. Guidelines and catalogs are available. Send a one-page summary of the book, a one- or two-sentence summary of each chapter, the first chapter and one other chapter.

HERDER (See THE CROSSROAD PUBLISHING COMPANY, INC.)

HERE'S LIFE PUBLISHERS (See THOMAS NELSON PUBLISHER'S, INC.)

HONOR BOOKS
P. O. Box 55338
Tulsa, Oklahoma 74155
918-585-5033
FAX 918-584-5536

Cris Bolley, Editor in Chief

The niche for Honor Books is evangelical and motivational gift books that illustrate the character of God. Topics of interest to them include business ethics, family and personal character-building, self-improvement books, and seasonable gift books that celebrate special events in an individual's life. They will not accept any material that "comes against" an individual or group of individuals, and they are also not open to seeing poetry or autobiographies. They do about twenty-five books annually, with 50 titles currently in print. Query first with an outline, chapter synopsis, or table of contents. Include a sample chapter or a sample of your writing style.

HOPE PUBLISHING (See PELICAN PUBLISHING COMPANY, INC.)

HOPE PUBLISHING HOUSE
P. O. Box 60008
Pasadena, California 91116
818-792-6123
FAX 818-792-2121

Faith Annette Sand, Publisher

Hope, a program unit of the Southern California Ecumenical Council, publishes religious books of interest to the faith community. Their past titles include books on marriage, trusting God, books on women's faith, philosophy, psychology, personal memoirs, and books on social change (rape, abortion, etc.). They produce in the neighborhood of ten titles per year and also publish under the **New Paradigm Books** imprint. Thirty-five titles comprise their backlist. Query letter only.

HORIZON BOOKS (See CHRISTIAN PUBLICATIONS, INC.)

HOWARD PUBLISHING COMPANY, INC.
3117 North 7th Street
West Monroe, Louisiana 71291
800-858-4109 or 318-396-3122
FAX 800-342-2067 or 318-397-1882

Gary Myers, Vice President, Editorial
Philis Boultinghouse, Editor

This non-denominational press looks for books that speak to the heart, deepen the faith, and inspire holiness in Christians' lives. Each year they publish five to ten nonfiction titles that attempt to meet serious and relevant needs for the evangelical readership. There are some 40 titles in print at Howard. They will accept either a proposal or a finished manuscript.

HUNTINGTON HOUSE PUBLISHERS
104 Row 2, Suites A1 and A2
Lafayette, Louisiana 70508
318-237-7049
FAX 318-237-7060

Mark Anthony, Editor in Chief

The company's goal is to educate and keep readers abreast of critical current events. They publish adult nonfiction books on current affairs and political topics, controversial religious topics, how-to books, books on globalism and the "New Age" movement, biographies, children's books, and novels. They provide writer's guidelines and suggestions for formatting manuscripts. Huntington publishes twenty-five to thirty books per year and they have 75 titles in print. Recently they absorbed **Prescott Press Publishers**. Send a query plus a two- to four-page synopsis.

ICAN PRESS BOOK PUBLISHERS, INC.
ICAN Press Building
616 Third Avenue
Chula Vista, California 91910
619-425-8945
FAX 619-425-2829

Dahk Knox, Editor in Chief
Josette Rice, Senior Editor

Topics included in the publishing program at ICAN Press have been career development, professional growth, psychology, management, leadership, communications, health, business, self-esteem, self-confidence, and selected fiction. But they are now looking for inspirational books, personal success stories, books on prophecy, novels with end-times themes, books identifying cults, and Christian children's stories. The fiction they publish needs morals, must keep a quick pace, have a simple style, and be a quick read. They have thirty books in print. Send a query with a proposal. If the manuscript is available, send that as well.

ICS PUBLICATIONS
2131 Lincoln Road, N.E.
Washington, D.C. 20002
202-832-8489
FAX 202-832-8967

Stephen Payne, Editorial Director

This Catholic house is operated by the Institute of Carmelite Studies and publishes about ten titles on a yearly basis. They mostly want translations of Carmelite classics and introductions to the Carmelite traditions (the Carmelites are a contemplative religious order also engaged in various other kinds of ministry). ICS also does popular commentaries on Carmelite authors, such as Teresa of Avila, John of the Cross, and so on. Send a query, an outline, and a sample chapter.

IGNATIUS PRESS
2515 McAllister Street
San Francisco, California 94118
415-387-2324
FAX 415-387-0896

Joseph Fessio, Editor

Ignatius publishes some forty books each year almost exclusively for the general Catholic market. Their backlist consists of 350 titles. Query only.

INSPIRATIONAL LIBRARY (See BARBOUR AND COMPANY, INC.)

INTEGRATION BOOKS (See PAULIST PRESS)

INTERNATIONAL SCHOLAR'S PUBLICATIONS (See CHRISTIAN UNIVERSITIES PRESS)

INTERVARSITY PRESS
Box 1400
Downers Grove, Illinois 60515
708-887-2500
FAX 708-964-1251

Kenneth DeRuiter, Executive Director
Andrew T. LePeau, Editorial Director
James Hoover, Managing Editor
Rodney Clapp, Academic and General Books Editor
Daniel G. Reid, Reference and Academic Books Editor

InterVarsity Press is the publishing arm of InterVarsity Christian Fellowship of the USA and operates within the framework of IVCF's Purposes and Statement of Faith. They provide a full line of books from an evangelical Christian perspective to an open-minded audience—Bible study guides, popularly written story-oriented books, academic and theological books, and issue-oriented books of interest to pastors, teachers, and educated Christians. The manuscripts they consider must be biblically based and reflect mature understanding. They must reflect the Lordship of Christ in all of life, be audience-oriented, develop readers in Christlikeness, exhibit high standards of quality, have integrity, be responsibly biblical, and be consistent with IVCF. They must also be broadly evangelical, prophetic, and financially viable. InterVarsity will consider material in virtually every area in which Jesus' teachings are thoughtfully applied. Some of the areas where they publish are reference, academic/text, Bible study guides, humor, fiction, self-help, and contemporary issues. Besides InterVarsity Press, their other imprints are **LifeGuide Bible Studies, Saltshaker Books,** and **Ediciones Certera.** They do provide guidelines and a statement of editorial philosophy. InterVarsity, which publishes about seventy-five books per year and has a backlist of about 650 titles, does not accept unsolicited manuscripts, and they ask

219

writers to work through The Writer's Edge editorial service in order to get their materials in the hands of IVP editors. This service is located at P. O. Box 1266, Wheaton, Illinois, 60189.

JESUIT WAY (See LOYOLA PRESS)

JEWS FOR JESUS BOOKS
60 Haight Street
San Francisco, California 94102
415-864-2600
FAX 415-552-8325

Steven Lawson, Director of Publications

Jews for Jesus publishes three to five books each year exclusively on Jewish evangelism and messianic topics. Most of these books are done by people on their staff, but outside of this they want especially to have books from other Jewish believers. They also publish under the **Purple Pomegranate** imprint. There are no guidelines. Query only.

JOSSEY-BASS INC., PUBLISHERS
350 Sansome Street
San Francisco, California 94104
415-433-1740
FAX 415-433-0499

Debra Hunter, Vice President and Editorial Director
Sara Polster, Editor, Religion in Practice
Rachel Anderson, Managing Editor

Jossey-Bass is the professional publishing division of Simon & Schuster, Inc. They publish professional titles (about 100 per year) in business, business management, training, general education, the social and behavioral sciences and the health-related fields (health and health education). They have over 1,000 titles now in print. In late 1996 or early 1997 Jossey-Bass will launch a new line of books for professionals in religion, Religion in Practice. They will address for the religion professional the same themes addressed for professionals in the secular marketplace: leadership and empowerment. The new line will be interdenominational and interfaith in its offerings. Send a query letter.

JOY PUBLISHING
P. O. Box 827
San Juan Capistrano, California 92675
714-493-4552
FAX 714-493-6552

Woody Young, President

Joy publishes a small number of books, mostly titles having to do with Christian writing and resource materials for Christian writers. Query letter first.

JUDSON PRESS
Box 851
Valley Forge, Pennsylvania 19482-0851
215-768-2118
FAX 215-768-2056

Harold Rast, Publisher
Kristy Arnesen Pullen, Associate Publisher
Mary Nicol, Managing Editor

Judson Press is the denominational publisher for the American Baptist Churches in the USA. Their purpose is to create and widely distribute quality educational resources that encourage sound biblical principles, that encourage, support, and challenge not only American Baptists but also the wider Christian community. Their books must be based on sound biblical principles. Among other things, they publish practical how-to books for local church leaders, worship aids, Bible studies, books for women, and books for the African-American population. Judson does fifteen to twenty book projects per year and they have about 200 titles currently in print. They provide a brochure on publishing your book with the press, and ask for a full proposal with a sample chapter.

KINDRED PRESS
4169 Riverton Avenue
Winnipeg, Manitoba R2L 2E5
Canada
204-669-6575
FAX 204-654-1865

Marilyn Hudson, Director

This Mennonite Brethren press publishes Bible studies, juvenile devotionals, and other resources for the churches within their denomination. All submissions have to be in keeping with the tenets of that denomination. They publish a limited amount of fiction for all ages. Guidelines are available. For nonfiction and fiction, send a proposal and three sample chapters.

KINGSWOOD BOOKS (See ABINGDON PRESS)

JOHN KNOX PRESS (See THE WESTMINSTER PRESS)

KREGEL PUBLICATIONS
P.O. Box 2607
Grand Rapids, Michigan 49501
616-451-4775
FAX 616-451-9330

James R. Kregel, President
Dennis Hillman, Senior Editor
Harold Kregel, Vice President for Spanish Publishing Division

Kregel publishes ministry and preaching related materials from an evangelical Protestant perspective, and their goal is to provide solidly evangelical, biblical books for the vocational Christian worker and Christian reader. They are open to any biblically based or expositional study for pastors or students, or church- or ministry-related books. They are not interested in seeing any fiction, poetry, cookbooks, curriculum, or sports-related items. Kregel publishes about fifty to sixty titles per year, and they have over 400 books in print. Their Spanish imprint is **Editorial Protavoz** (where they have over 200 Spanish titles in print). They do provide a catalog and guidelines, and they request a query letter only.

LANGMARC PUBLISHING
P. O. Box 33817
San Antonio, Texas 78265-3817
210-822-4273
FAX 210-822-5014

R. J. Roberts, Editor
Renee Hermanson, Editor

LangMarc is a Lutheran house publishing five to ten general religious trade books a year that focus on spiritual growth, inspiration, congregational helps, and materials for teens. They have 15 books in print. Query with a proposal and two to three sample chapters.

LARSON PUBLICATIONS
4936 Rte. 414
Burdett, New York 14818
607-546-9342
FAX 607-546-9344

Paul Cash, Director

This house is affiliated with the Paul Brunton Philosophic Foundation, the purpose of which is to make philosophic ideas available to as many individuals as possible who wish to pursue spirituality in an independent manner. The primary theme of most of their books is spiritual philosophy, including metaphysical, spiritual, and mythological topics. They actively develop new works with leading visionaries and scholars in the spiritual philosophy field who are making significant contributions as well as restore to print some of the works by great minds no longer available to the general public. They publish five books per year and have about 50 in print. They want to see a query with sample chapters and SASE.

LEE & SHEPARD BOOKS (See WILLIAM MORROW AND COMPANY, INC.)

LIFEGUIDE BIBLE STUDIES (See INTERVARSITY PRESS)

LIFETIME BOOKS
2131 Hollywood Blvd., Suite 204
Hollywood, Florida 33020
305-925-5242
FAX 305-925-5244

Donald L. Lessne, President
Brian Feinblum, Senior Editor

Lifetime Books is an imprint of **Fell Publishers, Inc.,** a general house that publishes three to five religious titles per year, usually in the area of spirituality. They have a backlist of about 160 titles. They do not want books about the coming end times or books on particular interpretations of the Bible. Guidelines and catalog are available. Query first.

LIGHT LINE (See BOB JONES UNIVERSITY PRESS)

LIGUORI PUBLICATIONS
One Liguori Drive
Liguori, Missouri 63057-9999
314-464-2500
FAX 314-464-8449

Robert Pagliari, Editor in Chief
Audrey Vest, Managing Editor

This publisher is operated by a Catholic religious order, the Redemptorists (Catholic religious congregation of men), but their publishing is a collaborative effort of Redemptorists and lay people. Their mission is to spread the Good News of Christ through the print and electronic media. They publish general interest trade titles featuring books on religion, problem-oriented books, self-help, and devotional books, along with practical pastoral material targeted to parishes. Curriculum and study guides are also produced. They do not want to see fiction or any children's material at this time. All publications must be from a Catholic-Christian perspective. Liguori publishes sixty to seventy books each year; they have about 300 titles currently in print. **Triumph Books** and **Faithware** are also Liguori imprints. They appreciate the query approach, with a clear indication of what else in on the market in the field and an explanation of what make one's manuscript special.

LILLENAS PUBLISHING COMPANY
Box 419527
Kansas City, Missouri 64141
816-931-1900
FAX 816-753-4071

John Mathias, Director
Paul M. Miller, Editor

Lillenas publishes play scripts and full-length sketches, which they consider a major form of proclamation in the church. They provide material for worship and entertainment and education, and are affiliated with the **Nazarene Publishing House** (they are the drama and music division for the house). The two categories of plays they handle are those with some spiritual direction and wholesome plays for schools and dinner theaters that are not necessarily specifically religious. Their purpose is to provide creative and practical resources for church and school programs. The program material can include readings and recitations, short dialogs, puppet scripts, and exercises (mostly for children). For all submissions, they want writers to find a new point of view. Read some Lillenas scripts. Allow an actor or director to read your work. Become acquainted with theater/stage terminology. Write the script with regard for the visual approach, for theater is seeing as well as hearing. Unless poetry is seasonal, they have no outlet for it. They provide contributor's guidelines. Use the query approach, but submit six to ten scripts.

LION BOOKS
4050 Lee Vance View
Colorado Springs, Colorado 80918
719-536-0100
FAX 719-536-3279

David W. Toht, Publisher

Lion Books, an imprint of **Cook Communication Ministries,** unfold the Christian faith in a straightforward and attractive manner written for a wide, general readership. They publish fifty titles per year, and have 300 titles in print. Lion appeals to both the churchgoer and those exploring new spiritual vistas with books from a positive Christian viewpoint. While their books are written from a Christian perspective, their goal is to publish books that meet the needs of readers who may not consider themselves Christians. They publish young adults and family books with evangelical Protestant themes, adult fiction and nonfiction, as well as gift and reference books. They do not want end times books, romance novels, missionary or conversion stories, or books endorsing New Age or occult beliefs. Send for their guidelines and catalog. Query only.

LITTLE DEER BOOKS (See STANDARD PUB-LISHING COMPANY)

THE LITURGICAL PRESS
P. O. Box 7500
St. John's Abbey
Collegeville, Minnesota 56321
612-363-2213
FAX 612-363-3299

Michael Naughton, Director
Mark Twomey, Managing Editor

This Benedictine press is a division of The Order of St. Benedict, Inc. They produce about sixty books a year, mostly liturgical, scriptural, and pastoral books for the scholarly, academic, and professional audiences. They also publish under **Michael Glazier Books** and **Pueblo Books**. About 900 titles are currently in print with this house. Guidelines and catalog are available. Send a query letter and a formal book proposal.

LIVING BOOKS (See TYNDALE HOUSE PUB-LISHERS, INC.)

LIVING FLAME PRESS
325 Rabro Drive
Hauppauge, New York 11788
516-348-5251

Nancy Benvenga and Emily Teutshman, Editors

This ecumenical Catholic publisher produces ten titles a year in theology, liturgy, and pastoral issues. They are looking for well-researched and well-written books on pastoral issues of a timely nature. They do some fiction, but they do not want biblical novels based on outdated (or literal) understandings of the Bible. Guidelines are available. Send a proposal and some sample chapters.

LOIZEAUX BROTHERS
P. O. Box 277
3301C Route 66
Neptune, New Jersey 07753
908-922-6665
FAX 908-922-9487

Peter I. Bartlett, President
Marjorie Carlson, Managing Editor

Loizeaux publishes about twenty titles per year in biblical commentaries and other books of serious Christian thought from a conservative, evangelical worldview. They have some 125 titles in print. Send query.

LOGION PRESS (See GOSPEL PUBLISHING HOUSE)

LOGOS INTERNATIONAL (See BRIDGE-LOGOS PUBLISHERS, INC.)

THE LOGOS LIBRARY (See BRIDGE-LOGOS PUBLISHERS, INC.)

LOYOLA PRESS
3441 North Ashland Avenue
Chicago, Illinois 60657
312-281-1818
FAX 312-281-0555

Joseph F. Downey, S.J., Editorial Director
George A. Lane, Director
Jeremy Langford, Editor
June Skinner Sawyers, Editor

Founded in 1912 by Jesuit priests as a textbook publisher, Loyola University Press is now officially Loyola Press (the word "University" was dropped because they do little if any scholarly publishing). The house publishes twelve to fifteen titles per year in college, high school and elementary school textbooks, literature, theology, Jesuit studies, and Christian (predominately Catholic) philosophy and history, along with specific titles on Chicago. Their backlist consists of 450 active titles. They are looking for books written more or less out of the Catholic tradition. **Campion Books** is their imprint for trade books. Their **Wild Onion** and **Jesuit Way** imprints are dedicated to Chicago-interest and Jesuit studies titles, respectively. They are looking for authors and ideas that will fit into their various imprints. Send a query, a proposal, and some sample chapters.

LURA MEDIA, INC.
7060 Miramar Road, Suite 104
San Diego, California 92121-2347
619-578-1948
FAX 619-578-7560

Marcia Broucek, Owner
Lura Jane Geiger, Publisher and Editor in Chief

This is an ecumenical press doing five to ten personal growth titles per year. Aside from personal experience books, they also specialize in books emphasizing spiritual and feminine themes. There are about 35 titles on their backlist. They prefer seeing a book proposal accompanied by a sample chapter.

MAGPIE BOOKS (See WINSTON-DEREK PUB-LISHERS)

MAIN STREET (See DOUBLEDAY)

MARCON PUBLISHERS (See HARVEST HOUSE PUBLISHERS, INC.)

MARKOWSKI INTERNATIONAL PUBLISHERS
One Oakglade Circle
Himmelstown, Pennsylvania 17036
717-566-0468
FAX 717-566-6423

Michael A. Markowski, Owner
Marjorie L. Markowski, Editor

This publisher releases 6 to 10 books each year that deal with personal development, motivation, inspiration, and self-help. **Success Publishers** is their imprint name. They prefer to see complete manuscripts, but they do not publish children's books.

MARMAC (See PELICAN PUBLISHING COM-PANY, INC.)

MASTER BOOKS
P. O. Box 26060
Colorado Springs, Colorado 80936-6060
719-591-0800
FAX 719-591-1446

Ron Hillestad, General Manager

Master is a division of **Creation Life Publishers, Inc.** They publish material dealing with creation science, biblical science, scientific material for children's books (biblical creationism), and books on the creation/evolution debate. They do five to ten publishing projects per year, and have about 50 titles now in print. Occasionally they also publish pamphlets and booklets, and computer games. Query with sample chapters.

MEL BAY PUBLICATIONS, INC.
P. O. Box 66, Four Industrial Drive
Pacific, Missouri 63069
314-257-3970
FAX 314-257-5062

William A. Bay, Vice President
L. Dean Bye, General Manager

This press specializes in inspirational religious books, children's picture books, juvenile plays, and music books. (Their music publications are under two imprints: **Cathedral Music Press** and **Creative Keyboard Publications.** Their real specialty is in method books for virtually all instruments, and they publish a complete line of songbooks containing songs from around the world.) They do about twenty-five inspirational titles a year (130 per year considering all their publications) and prefer seeing a full manuscript upon submission. In the case of musical submissions, they also want to receive a cassette recording.

MENNONITE PUBLISHING HOUSE (See HERALD PRESS)

MERCER UNIVERSITY PRESS
1400 Coleman Avenue
Macon, Georgia 31207
912-752-2880
FAX 912-752-2264

Edd Rowell, Director

Mercer University Press is especially interested in scholarly books in the field of history, philosophy, theology, and religion, including history of religion, philosophy of religion, Bible studies, and ethics. They have 325 titles in print in these areas. Submit outline and synopsis, along with some sample chapters.

MERE BONES (See CORNERSTONE PRESS CHICAGO)

MERIWETHER PUBLISHING LTD.
885 Elkton Drive
Colorado Springs, Colorado 80907
719-594-4422
FAX 719-594-9916

Arthur L. Zapel, Editor

With over 60 titles now in print, Meriwether publishes around fifty nonfiction books on Christian education, theater/drama, performing arts, and creative worship (clowning, mime, storytelling, banner-making, etc.) per year. They serve both schools and churches. Their backlist titles include theater anthologies, scenebooks, acting/directing texts, comedy improvisation, stagecraft, and costuming books. They also publish some children's picture books. Their **Contemporary Drama Service** publishes about thirty-five religious plays per year, primarily fresh approaches to the familiar biblical Christmas and Easter stories, as well as sketches and playlets for children on Bible adventures and other things. As an interdenominational house, they are looking for a non-denominational slant. They are not interested in seeing devotionals, self-help materials, adult fiction, and biographies. They ask possible contributors to study their catalog and to submit material that seems to fit with the books and plays they have already published. For plays, think simple. They want their dramas to witness in a powerful way, so they want legitimate drama with honest conflict and resolution. Thirty minutes maximum length; no complicated scenery or lighting. Include a synopsis and brief statement of objectives. For plays, send the complete manuscript. Ask for a copy of their complete catalog for an indication of the types of things they do.

MEYERSTONE (See THE CROSSROAD PUBLISHING COMPANY, INC.)

MISTY HILL PRESS
5024 Turner Road
Sebastopol, California 95472
707-823-7437

Sally C. Karste, Editor

This small press does a handful of titles on a yearly basis, some religious, but most are in the area of historical fiction for children. Send for their guidelines. Query letter only.

MOODY PRESS
820 North La Salle Blvd.
Chicago, Illinois 60610
312-329-2101
FAX 312-329-2144

Greg Thornton, Vice President and Executive Editor
James S. Bell, Jr., Editorial Director

Moody Press is the book publishing arm of the non-denominational Moody Bible Institute, publishing sixty to eight-five books per year. Their mission is to produce books that educate, edify, and evangelize. Moody publishes many kinds of books, both fiction and nonfiction, that meet the needs of Christians of all ages and all walks of life, so long as they are based on the teaching of the Bible without being "preachy." This includes financial and current issue books, fiction, family/marriage, men's issues, evangelism, Christian education, and some texts. The approach should be fresh, appealing, and relevant. They do not publish short stories, game or cartoon books, sermons, theses, poetry, picturebooks, or cookbooks. Nor are they interested right now in personal experience stories. **Northfield Publishing** is an imprint of Moody specially designed for the secular trade bookstore. Northfield is more general in nature, aimed at readers who are not necessarily Christians but who are interested in more information about how to integrate principles from the Bible with their lives. There are some 700 Moody backlist titles that are currently in print. Send a proposal with sample chapters.

THOMAS MORE PRESS
205 West Monroe, 6th Floor
Chicago, Illinois 60606
312-609-8880
FAX 312-609-8891

John Sprague, President
Joel Wells, Editor

This Catholic house is associated with the Thomas More Association of Chicago. They produce five to ten books on religion and spirituality a year, and they are looking for serious but not necessarily scholarly manuscripts on theology, commentary, reflection, and reference. Guidelines are available. Send a complete manuscript or a full proposal with sample chapters.

MOREHOUSE PUBLISHING
871 Ethan Allen Highway
Ridgefield, Connecticut 06877
203-431-3927
FAX 203-431-3964

Deborah Grahame-Smith, Senior Editor

This firm specializes in Anglican religious publishing, including titles representative of theology, spirituality, ethics, religious education, liturgics, marriage, parenting, singles, youth, seniors, current social issues, and primary and secondary texts. They publish fifteen to twenty titles per year, and have about 350 titles now in print. Morehouse serves the church by developing curriculum and publishing books of specific interest in the religious market—academic, devotional, reference, juvenile. They want nothing apocalyptic, no autobiographies or personal witness or healing stories, and no adult fiction. While they have published a very select few children's books over the years, their children's books publishing program is under review, and they are not currently accepting juvenile fiction. Submit query letter with three sample chapters.

MORNING STAR PRESS
Box 1095
Grand Central Station
New York, New York 10163
212-661-4304

Kathleen Shedaker, Publisher

Two or three religious or inspirational books are published each year by this press, which is associated with the Morning Star Chapel. Their purpose in publishing is to encourage all Christians to live a more serious Christian life. They do not provide catalogs or guidelines. Query first.

JOSHUA MORRIS PUBLISHING, INC.
221 Danbury Road
Wilton, Connecticut 06897
203-834-9878
FAX 203-834-0811

Sally Lloyd Jones, Editorial Director
Doreen Beauregard, Editor

Joshua Morris, a subsidiary of the Reader's Digest Association, is an evangelical Anglican children's book packager and publisher of both fiction and nonfiction products (seventy-five to one hundred titles per year). They look for educational books on biblical or general themes with a Christian approach that will bring the Gospel to life for children. They want their books to have the interactive task of involving, entertaining, challenging, and inspiring young readers. Over 1100 titles are in print at this house. Send proposal and at least one sample chapter.

WILLIAM MORROW AND COMPANY, INC.
1350 Avenue of the Americas
New York, New York 10019
212-261-6500
FAX 212-261-6595

Debbie Mercer-Sullivan, Managing Editor

Morrow is a subsidiary of The Hearst Corporation and a general trade publisher that does five or so religious titles each year (out of around 600 total titles per year). They publish religious fiction, poetry, arts, history, juvenile, and how-to books. **Beech Tree Books, Greenwillow Books,** and **Lee & Shepard Books** are some of Morrow's imprints. Manuscripts and proposals in both fiction and nonfiction should be submitted only through a literary agent.

MOTT MEDIA, INC., PUBLISHERS
1000 East Huron Street
Milford, Michigan 48042
313-685-8773
FAX 313-685-8776

Joyce Bohn, General Manager

Mott Media no longer publishes books for the Christian trade market, since their trade line was purchased by Baker Book House. But they do continue to publish for the Christian school and home school movements (six to ten projects per year). The company also owns and operates the Evangelical Book Club. Classroom and supplementary materials should be orthodox in Christian doctrine and geared to the conservative evangelical spectrum. Mott has around 100 titles currently in print. Send a brief description of the writing project, an assessment of the reading market, and an explanation of why the project differs from others already available on the market.

MOUNT OLIVE COLLEGE PRESS
643 Henderson Street
Mount Olive, North Carolina 28365
919-658-2502

Pepper Worthington, Editor

Associated with Mount Olive College, this small press publishes five titles per year in religious nonfiction, fiction, and poetry. Some of the other types of books they have published include drama, devotionals, books on travel, essays, cookbooks, photography titles, literary criticism, and children's books. About 20 titles form their backlist. They provide a catalog and guidelines. For nonfiction, send a proposal and a sample chapter. For fiction, send a synopsis and a sample chapter. For poetry, send six sample poems.

MULTNOMAH PRESS (See QUESTAR PUBLISHERS)

MUSTARD SEED BOOKS (See STAR SONG PUBLISHING GROUP)

MYSTERY INK (See THOMAS NELSON PUBLISHER'S, INC.)

NATIONAL BAPTIST PUBLISHING BOARD
6717 Centennial Blvd.
Nashville, Tennessee 37209
615-350-8000
FAX 615-350-9018

Kenneth H. Dupree, Director of Publications

The National Missionary Baptist Convention of America operates the publishing board for this African-American publisher. Their mission is to provide quality Christian resources for African-American churches. They are now looking for biblically based children's fiction. They prefer seeing the complete manuscript. Phone queries are not discouraged.

THE NATIONAL CATHOLIC REPORTER PUBLISHING COMPANY (See SHEED & WARD)

NATIONAL CENTER FOR THE LAITY (See ACTA PUBLICATIONS)

NAVPRESS PUBLISHIING GROUP
7899 Lexington Drive
Colorado Springs, Colorado 80920
719-548-9222

Kathryn Yanni, Editorial Director
Debby Weaver, Submissions Editor
Erik Thrasher, Associate Publisher, Pinon Press

NavPress is a division of The Navigators, and they develop evangelical Protestant materials on discipleship, spiritual growth, and Bible study that are practical, relevant, and life-related. Their books must be biblically rooted and culturally relevant, and their publishing topics include parenting, finances, self-help, creation/evolution, marriage, theology, and Christian living. While they continue to publish some fifty projects per year and have about 250 titles now in print, neither NavPress nor their **Pinon Press** imprint (their general trade imprint comprised of books that speak to pressing societal issues in an engaging, accessible fashion) are any longer accepting any unsolicited submissions, proposals, or queries.

NAZARENE PUBLISHING HOUSE
Box 419527
6401 The Paseo
Kansas City, Missouri 02108
816-931-1900
FAX 816-753-4071

Michael R. Estep, Director, Communications Division
Hardy Weathers, Director of the Press
Shona Fisher, Editorial Coordinator

Beacon Hill Press is the publishing logo of the Nazarene Publishing House, the publishing arm of the Church of the Nazarene, producing around 50 to sixty-five titles per year. There are almost 400 titles in print. The drama publishing division is **Lillenas Publishing Company.** Beacon Hill is an evangelical house that publishes a wide range of material from juvenile to college texts. They want to see practical, lay-oriented books on personal growth and applied Christianity. They will also consider inspirational, devotional, and Bible study book projects. The scope also includes social action themes and fiction for the adult reading audience that has a Christian heartbeat. For both fiction and nonfiction, they want writers to use the query approach, but also to send a proposal and at least two chapters.

NEIBAUER PRESS
20 Industrial Drive
Warminster, Pennsylvania 18974
215-322-6200
FAX 215-322-2495

Nathan Neibauer, President and Editor

Neibauer Press is a division of the Louis Neibauer Company, Inc., and has about 25 titles now in print. They do five to ten new books each year for evangelical Protestant church leaders. They are looking for books on stewardship and church growth, and they also publish tracts, bulletin fillers, and pamphlets. No guidelines are available, but a catalog can be sent. Send a query letter.

THOMAS NELSON PUBLISHERS, INC.
Nelson Place at Elm Hill Pike
Nashville, Tennessee 37214
615-889-9000
FAX 615-391-5225

Joseph Moore, Executive Vice President
Byron Williamson, President, NelsonWord Publishing Group
Frank Couch, Vice President, Bible Division
Lila Empson, Senior Editor, Oliver-Nelson Books
Janet Thoma, Vice President, Janet Thoma Books
Rolf Zettersten, Executive Vice President and Publisher, Royal Media

Nelson has formed the **NelsonWord Publishing Group,** which encompasses three divisions: **Word Publishing, Thomas Nelson Publishers,** and **Thomas Nelson Bibles.** Thomas Nelson is one of the oldest publishing firms in the country. They publish 250 books per year for Christian readers of all ages, including Bibles, inspirational and motivational books for the religious marketplace, books on the validity of the historic Christian belief and Christian experience, books on biblical reference, fiction with Christian themes for adults and teens, counseling, seniors and aging, singles, career planning, theology, etc. All children's books must be a complete package since they don't supply illustrations. **Here's Life Publishers,** formerly affiliated with Campus Crusade for Christ, is now an imprint of Thomas Nelson, as are **Oliver-Nelson Books,** and **Janet Thoma Books.** (The fiction imprint, **Jan Dennis Books,** has been cut, while the **Two Rivers** imprint of books designed for the general market has been "put on the shelf.") A new imprint, **Mystery Ink,** is geared to doing books for the mystery genre. In addition to publishing Bibles, books, and music, Nelson has another organizational unit specializing in media and magazines, **Royal Media.** (See also **Word Publishing, Inc.**) Nelson has about 400 book titles currently in print. Send a full proposal and three sample chapters.

NEW AGE BOOKS (See BANTAM BOOKS)

NEW HOPE
Box 12065
Birmingham, Alabama 35202-2065
205-991-8102
FAX 205-991-4990

Cindy McClain, Editor and Group Manager

New Hope is run by the **Woman's Missionary Union,** an auxiliary to the Southern Baptist Convention. They publish around ten books per year that have a missions or ministry emphasis. They want their books to lead to spiritual growth toward a missions lifestyle or toward active involvement either in missions or in the support of missions. In other words, they are looking for "how-to" books for missions. New Hope also publishes for the Hispanic market. Guidelines and a catalog are provided. Send a book proposal and three sample chapters.

NEW LEAF PRESS
P. O. Box 311
Green Forest, Arkansas 72638
501-438-5288
FAX 501-438-5120

Tim Dudley, President
Jim Fletcher, Acquisitions Editor

This New Leaf is not to be confused with the Atlanta-based distributor of metaphysical, spiritual, and alternative books and products of the same name. This house is a Christian publisher releasing thirty to forty new titles per year, with an emphasis on prophecy, self-help, and inspirational gift books. The goal of this Pentecostal/charismatic press is to publish books that will introduce readers to Christianity and to bring balance to the church. They are currently looking for books that meet the needs of the family, books written specifically for women, and books that would fit into their gift line. Most of the books they publish have been solicited. Their backlist amounts to nearly 200 titles. Include a cover letter, table of contents, and synopsis of the chapters.

NEW PARADIGM BOOKS (See HOPE PUBLISHING HOUSE)

NEW SOCIETY PUBLISHERS
4527 Springfield Avenue
Philadelphia, Pennsylvania 19143
215-382-6543
FAX 215-222-1993

Barbara Hirshkowitz, Editor
T. L. Hill Editor

New Society is a division of the New Society Educational Foundation, Inc., which publishes from twelve to fifteen titles per year emphasizing fundamental social change through nonviolent action. They have around 100 titles currently on their backlist in the nonviolent traditions in Christianity and Judaism, cooperative economics, cooperative management, women's and antinuclear issues, ecology, Third World, sustainable living, and environmental issues. They are looking for books emphasizing nonviolent action from the world religions. Query only.

NEWMAN PRESS (See PAULIST PRESS)

NORTHCOTE BOOKS (See HAROLD SHAW PUB-LISHSERS)

NORTHFIELD PUBLISHING (See MOODY PRESS)

NORTH WIND (See HAROLD SHAW PUBLISHERS)

NOVALIS
223 Main Street
Ottawa, Ontario K1S 1C4
Canada
612-236-1393
FAX 612-236-1393

Michael O'Hearn, Acquisitions Editor

This house, affiliated with the University of St. Paul, does fifteen or so titles per year on sacramental preparation. They also publish materials on Christian funeral rites. Novalis provides no guidelines. Send a query letter with a proposal and sample chapters.

OLIVER-NELSON BOOKS (See THOMAS NELSON PUBLISHERS, INC)

OMEGA PUBLICATIONS
P. O. Box 4130
Medford, Oregon 97510
503-826-1030

Jeani McKeever, Editor

Omega publishes two or three titles per year. They do fiction and nonfiction with a heavy emphasis on popular end-time themes, and also does some Bible study and family-related material. Query letter only.

OMF BOOKS (See HAROLD SHAW PUBLISHERS)

ONE HORN PRESS (See WINSTON-DEREK PUB-LISHERS)

OPEN COURT PUBLISHING COMPANY
332 South Michigan Avenue, Suite 2000
Chicago, Illinois 60604-9968
312-939-1500
FAX 312-939-8150

Andre W. Carus, President and General Manager
David Ramsay Steele, Editorial Director, General Books Division
Kerri Mommer, Assistant Editor, General Books Division

Open Court is a subsidiary of Carus Publishing Company, the publishers of *Cricket: The Magazine for Children.* They also have a fairly large textbook division (1,200 titles in print) that does elementary texts in reading, language, arts, and mathematics. The General Books Division does several titles each year in comparative religion and religious issues, along with philosophy, philosophy of religion, history, psychology, and economics. A special interest for this house is religions of other cultures, especially oriental. This division has some 225 titles in print. Send a query with two sample chapters.

OPEN SCROLL (See BRIDGE-LOGOS PUBLISH-ERS, INC.)

ORBIS BOOKS
Walsh Building
P. O. Box 308
Maryknoll, New York 10545-0308
914-941-7636
FAX 914-945-0670

Robert Ellsberg, Editor in Chief
William R. Burrows, Managing Editor

Orbis is owned and operated by the Catholic Foreign Missions Society of the Maryknoll Fathers and Brothers, and publishes fifty to sixty books per year. They publish religious studies and theology from and on Asia, Africa, and Latin America, and they are interested in religious developments in those areas. Their emphasis is on global justice and peace issues and the First World response to the Third World challenge relating to the themes of justice, and peace. They also publish in the area of ecology, social justice and social concerns, women's religious studies, liberation theology, interreligious matters, and mission theology. Orbis has a backlist of over 650 titles now in print. They provide guidelines and a catalog. Send a query letter, outline, and sample chapters.

OUR SUNDAY VISITOR PUBLISHING
200 Noll Plaza
Huntington, Indiana 46750
219-356-8400
FAX 219-356-8472

Greg Erlandson, Editor in Chief
Jacquelyn M. Murphy, Editor

This Catholic press does about thirty books each year to help Catholics become more aware of and secure in their faith—and to help them relate their faith to others. All of their books relate to the Catholic church. Their main interest is in solid devotional books that are not first person, well-researched church histories or lives of the saints, and catechetical books. OSV also wants Catholic viewpoints on current issues, reference and guidance, Bible study and devotional books, religion, educational, parenting, biography, and Catholic heritage books. They have about 250 book titles in print. Send a fully fleshed-out book proposal rather than the complete manuscript.

OXFORD UNIVERSITY PRESS
200 Madison Avenue
New York, New York 10016
212-679-7300
FAX 212-725-2972

Cynthia Read, Senior Editor
Nancy Lane and Robert Miller, Humanities Editors

Oxford Press emphasizes Bibles, scholarly textbooks, historical studies in American religion, biblical studies, theological works, professional and reference books in the humanities, etc. Oxford publishes more than sixty books each year and they have nearly 7,000 titles currently in print on their backlist. They also publish under the imprint **Clarendon Press.** They want a proposal, a cover letter, outline, and sample chapters.

PACIFIC PRESS PUBLISHING ASSOCIATION
Box 7000
Boise, Idaho 83707-7000
208-465-2500
FAX 208-465-2531

Robert Kyte, General Manager
Russell Holt, Vice President, Editorial Development

This Seventh-Day Adventist press publishes about thirty titles each year and has over 500 now in print on their backlist. In nonfiction, they want inspirational, devotional, family life, and Christian living books. In fiction, they want stories based on events that actually happened but are handled with good fiction techniques. They are also looking for books for the ethnic market. Guidelines and catalog are available. Send a query letter and a proposal, with one or two sample chapters for both fiction and nonfiction submissions.

PALISADES (See QUESTAR PUBLISHERS)

PANTHEON BOOKS (See SCHOCKEN BOOKS)

PARACLETE PRESS
P. O. Box 1568
Orleans, Massachusetts 02653
508-255-4685
FAX 508-255-5705

Lillian Miao, CEO
David Manuel, Editor

Paraclete is a division of Creative Joys, Inc. They do five to seven devotionals and personal testimonials each year, and have 40 titles currently in print. They are looking for manuscripts reflecting deeper spirituality of inter-denominational appeal, as well as books that encourage non-Christians to examine the claims of Christ. This press does not provide guidelines, but will send a catalog. Send a book proposal and two sample chapters.

PARAGON HOUSE
370 Lexington Avenue
New York, New York 10017
212-953-5950
FAX 212-953-9540

Michael Giampaoli, Director and Publisher

Paragon features books on philosophy, religion, culture, criticism, reference, academic/scholarly, history, new age enlightenment, and Jewish studies. They publish some twenty books a year, and have a backlist of 350 titles. A query letter is requested.

PASTORAL PRESS
225 Sheridan Street, NW
Washington, D.C. 20011-1492
202-723-1254
FAX 202-723-2262

Virgil C. Funk, Publisher
Lawrence J. Johnson, Director

Pastoral Press is a division of the National Association of Pastoral Musicians. The press publishes ten to fifteen professional and scholarly books on religion and theology per year. They have over 100 titles in print. Send a query letter.

PASTOR'S CHOICE PRESS (See BRENTWOOD CHRISTIAN PRESS)

PATRON BOOKS (See DON BOSCO MULTIMEDIA)

PAULIST PRESS
997 MacArthur Blvd.
Mahwah, New Jersey 07430
201-825-7300
FAX 201-825-8345

Donald Brophy, Managing Editor

Paulist publishes ecumenical theology, Roman Catholic studies, and books on scripture, liturgy, spirituality, church history, philosophy, and religion and public affairs. Their program is oriented toward adult-level practical and socially conscious nonfiction, with the exception of a few story books for children. Paulist publishes one hundred books each year and has about 700 in print. Their books must have a sense of the Western spiritual traditional. They are not seeking any poetry, fiction, or personal testimonies. Other Paulist imprints are **Integration Books, Newman Press,** and **Stimulus Books.** Writers should inquire before sending any manuscripts. For children's books, send just the text and not the illustrations.

PEACOCK PRESS (See BANTAM BOOKS)

PEAKE ROAD (See SMYTH & HELWYS PUBLISHING, INC.)

PELICAN POND PUBLISHING (See BLUE DOLPHIN PUBLISHING, INC.)

PELICAN PUBLISHING COMPANY, INC.
P. O. Box 3110
Gretna, Louisiana 70054-3110
504-368-1175
FAX 504-368-1195

Milburn Calhoun, Publisher
Nina Kooij, Editor

Pelican has a Baptist orientation but publishes forty to fifty books a year for a variety of lay readers as well as the clergy. They consider themselves a "niche" publisher, providing books with specific hooks that fill a void; they have about 500 titles currently in print. Bible studies, inspirational books, self-help titles (especially if the author is an established lecturer), Americana, educational stories for children, and motivational books are among their releases. They also publish fiction that reflects a particular faith or a particular time and place, also some ethnic fiction for blacks, Hispanics, Native Americans, Asian-Americans, etc. They are not seeking books on prayer, poetry, or personal stories. Other imprints in their publishing program are **Creager Publishing, Hope Publishing,** and **Marmac.** They do provide guidelines for authors. Pelican does not accept unsolicited manuscripts, so submit query with outline/synopsis and sample chapters.

PENNANT BOOKS (See BOB JONES UNIVERSITY PRESS)

PENTECOSTAL PUBLISHING HOUSE
8855 Dunn Road
Hazelwood, Missouri 63042
314-837-7300
FAX 314-837-4503

Marvin Curry, General Manager

This house is a subsidiary of the United Pentecostal Church International. They look for manuscripts covering Protestant pentecostalism, foreign languages, Bible study, and self-help. Also publishing under the name **World Aflame Press,** they produce ten to fifteen titles per year and have 135 titles now in print. Send query.

THE PILGRIM PRESS/UNITED CHURCH PRESS
700 Prospect Avenue E.
Cleveland, Ohio 44115-1100
216-736-3700
FAX 216-736-3703

Lynne M. Deming, Publisher
Kim Sadler, Denominational Resources Editor
Richard Brown, Editor

The Pilgrim Press is the publishing arm of the United Church of Christ and is a division of the United Church Board for Homeland Ministries. They publish religious books and curriculum, mostly for the denomination, but also books on social issues, church growth, education and women's issues, and occasionally African-American and Native American books. About twenty-five individual titles appear from this press each year; they have over 200 titles in print. They are looking for academic trade books on social issues and the moral life, gender studies, spirituality, and counseling/self-help. Guidelines are available. Send query letter, proposal, and a couple of sample chapters.

PILLAR BOOKS AND PUBLISHING COMPANY
5840 South Memorial Drive, Suite 111
Tulsa, Oklahoma 74145
918-665-3240
FAX 918-663-7690

Elizabeth Sherman, Editor

Pillar publishes books on Bible-based teaching on a variety of subjects and books on living the balanced yet powerful Christian life. They want Bible teaching materials of sound doctrine, commentaries, and scholarly studies on topical subjects. They do ten books a year and have 25 in print. They prefer that writers send entire manuscripts plus biographical information and market analysis.

PINON PRESS (See NAVPRESS PUBLISHING GROUP)

POCKET GUIDES (See TYNDALE HOUSE PUBLISHERS, INC.)

POWER BOOKS (See FLEMING H. REVELL COMPANY)

PRENTICE HALL, INC.
One Lake Street
Upper Saddle River, New Jersey 07428
201-236-7000

Charlyce Jones Owen, Humanities Editor

The Prentice Hall Humanities and Social Sciences Division is part of the Unit of Higher Education of the Simon & Schuster Educational Group. Primarily they publish religious books for clergy and academic and scholarly audiences, but they are also interested in inspirational guides for women, Bible study materials, and religious books generally applicable to living in today's world. Their texts for the academic setting include studies in history, biblical studies, world religions, theology, and some reference works. Query letter only.

PRESBYTERIAN AND REFORMED PUBLISHIING COMPANY
P. O. Box 817
Phillipsburg, New Jersey 08865
908-454-0505
FAX 908-859-2390

Bryce H. Craig, Director
Barbara Lerch, Acquisitions Coordinator
Thom E. Notaro, Editor

P&R is not owned by any denomination, but is affiliated by worldview with those groups that follow the Westminster Confession of Faith. Therefore, all their books are consistent with that Confession, in both the shorter and larger catechisms. They also publish under the logos of **Craig Press** and **Evangelical Press**. They do about ten books per year (they have 250 titles in print) with titles ranging from scholarly works advancing biblical and theological research to highly readable and practical books designed to help lay readers grow in Christian thought and service. Their publishing areas include theology, Christian living, Christian perspectives, apologetics, cults, comparative religions, eschatology, the biblical perspective on social issues, mission and ministry, church management, and pastoral textbooks. P&R wants new, engaging, and insightful applications of Reformed theology to modern life. They do not wish to see poetry, autobiographies, or theology inconsistent with the Westminster Standards. Send manuscript proposal, three sample chapters, and SASE.

PRESCOTT PRESS PUBLISHERS
P. O. Box 53777
Lafayette, Louisiana 70505
318-237-8578
FAX 318-237-7060

David England, Editor in Chief
Kay Walters, Associate Editor

This house was recently acquired by **Huntington House Publishers.** They publish ten to fifteen titles each year of varying themes in both fiction and nonfiction and want their books to make an impact on the entire market—both secular and Christian. Their publishing focus has been on family issues, self-help, political activism, spiritual inspiration, and other issues aimed at preserving ethical and family values. Their primary goal is to present a conservative Judeo-Christian perspective to the marketplace. They also want to assist, whenever possible, first-time authors to get their works published. Guidelines are available. Present an outline and chapter by chapter synopsis and a table of contents.

PROBE BOOKS
1900 Firman Drive, Suite 100
Richardson, Texas 75081-6796
214-480-0240
FAX 214-644-9664

Rick Road, Director of Publications
Louis D. Whitworth, Senior Editor

Probe is an independent, evangelical non-denominational house. As a subsidiary of Probe Ministries, Probe Books supports the ministry goal of equipping Christians to respond to the challenges of our culture. To do this they publish five to ten books per year that reclaim the primacy of Christian thought and values in the West. Their books are written to educated people at about the undergraduate level, though some are more appropriate for a more sophisticated reading audience. The special interest categories for Probe are apologetics and issues-oriented books, and they also want Christian approaches to all the academic disciplines, as well as books on national social, medical, political, educational, and family issues. They want well-educated authors of credible reputation and scholarship. They are not interested in seeing fiction, poetry, devotionals, Bible studies, prophecy books, children's literature, or personal stories. They have 20 books currently in print. Guidelines are available. Send a query with SASE.

PUEBLO BOOKS (See THE LITURGICAL PRESS)

PURPLE POMEGRANATE (See JEWS FOR JESUS BOOKS)

QUESTAR PUBLISHERS
Box 1720
Sisters, Oregon 97759
503-549-1144
FAX 503-549-2044

Dan Rich, President and Publisher
David Kopp, Vice President, Editorial
Thomas Womack, Editor
Rod Morris, Editor
Lisa Bergren, Managing Editor, Palisades

Multnomah Press was acquired by Questar in 1992, and now is the Questar imprint for both youth and adult books, while **Gold 'n' Honey** is their imprint for children's books (and the imprint for the popular Beginner's Bible). Questar publishes from thirty-five to forty titles per year, emphasizing children's books, with about 375 titles in print on their backlist. They want to publish literature that is contemporary while remaining faithful to the Scriptures. Some of the areas in which they have published are fiction (some published under the **Palisades** imprint—their new romance line), biblical studies, critical social concerns, Christian growth, family enrichment, devotionals, gift books, and religious texts. In fiction, they emphasize light fiction, and are looking not for "religious" stories but stories that are clean, moral, and uplifting. Most of their nonfiction is geared toward self-improvement or general inspiration. Send a proposal and two or three sample chapters. For fiction, send a two-page synopsis and three sample chapters.

QUINTESSENTIAL BOOKS
P. O. Box 2566
Shawnee Mission, Kansas 66201
913-384-8871
FAX 913-831-3663

Janette L. Jasperson, Vice President of Editorial

A nondenominational publisher of five to ten titles per year, Quintessential wants "hard-hitting" books that are solidly based on Scripture. However, they are not looking for books on the cults or on eschatology, nor do they want children's books. In fiction, they are looking for all the genres except romance. Most of their books are reprints of out-of-print titles. Send a cover letter with an explanation of the book project.

RADIANT BOOKS (See GOSPEL PUBLISHING HOUSE)

RAINBOW BOOKS (See CHRISTIAN EDUCATION PUBLISHERS)

RAINBOW BOOKS
P. O. Box 430
Highland City, Florida 33846-0430
813-648-4420
FAX 813-648-4420

Betsy A. Lampe, Editorial Director

Rainbow is a publisher of general nonfiction books concerning how-to, self-help, and some religious reference. They have around 100 titles in print and do about ten to fifteen per year. They are not looking for fiction or religious titles with a doomsday thrust. Query only.

RAVEN'S RIDGE (See BAKER BOOK HOUSE)

REALLY READING! BOOKS (See STANDARD PUBLISHING COMPANY)

REGAL BOOKS
2300 Knoll Drive
Ventura, California 93003
805-644-9721
FAX 805-644-4729

Kyle Duncan, Editorial and Acquisitions Director
Jean Daly, Curriculum Editor

Regal Books is the book publishing division of **Gospel Light Publications** (where the primary business is church and Sunday school curriculum). They publish fifteen to twenty book projects a year and aim their publications primarily at lay audiences with the goal being to help them grow in Christian faith and knowledge. They publish conservative, evangelical books dealing with Christian education, missions, Bible studies, self-help, Christian living, and church growth. There are about 200 Regal books currently in print. Query first, since they are accepting very few manuscripts at this time.

REGULAR BAPTIST PRESS
1300 North Meacham Road
Schaumburg, Illinois 60173-4888
708-843-1600
FAX 708-843-3757

Vernon D. Miller, Executive Editor

The book publishing program of the Regular Baptist Press, a division of the General Association of Regular Baptist Churches, is currently limited to their denominational constituency including pastors, professors in their schools, and

257

personnel in their missions agencies. And since their primary business is curriculum, they are producing very few book titles (seven per year). Query only.

REGENCY PRESS
P. O. Box 2306
Bandera, Texas 78003
210-796-7215

Gayle Buck, Editor

Regency is seeking romantic-based fiction, either contemporary or historical. The fiction must include Christian themes where the characters lives show spiritual growth, but the story should be without blatant teaching or preaching. Send a story synopsis with three sample chapters.

REGNERY PUBLISHING INC.
422 First Street, S.E., Suite 200
Washington, D.C. 20003-1803
202-546-5005
FAX 202-546-8759

Alfred S. Regnery, Publisher and President
Richard Vigilante, Executive Editor

Within a general, trade house Regnery does a small number of books yearly for both the Catholic and the evangelical Protestant reading audiences. These books, though religious, usually relate to politics, history, current affairs, biography, and public policy, and they are aimed at an alert market. Their total publishing operation does from twelve to fifteen books per year, and they have 160 titles now in print. They also publish under the **Gateway Editions** imprint. A catalog is provided. Send a proposal and two sample chapters.

RELIGION IN PRACTICE (See JOSSEY-BASS INC., PUBLISHERS)

RELIGIOUS EDUCATION PRESS
5316 Meadow Brook Road
Birmingham, Alabama 35242-3315
205-991-1000
FAX 205-991-9669

James Michael Lee, Publisher
Nancy J. Vickers, Managing Director

This press publishes serious books of more scholarly interest to pastors and professional religious educators. These include Catholic and Protestant books in the behavioral sciences, education, and theology and religion. The press does about five books a year while maintaining close to 75 titles on their backlist. Guidelines and a catalog are available. Send a query letter only.

RENLOW PUBLISHING
P. O. Box 951
Middletown, Ohio 45042

D. E. Margerum, Publisher/Editor

This general publisher also does a few inspirational and religious titles each year. Contact them with a query and sample chapters.

RESOURCE PUBLICATIONS, INC.
160 East Virginia Street, Suite 290
San Jose, California 95112-5876
408-286-8505
FAX 408-287-8748

William Burns, Publisher
Kenneth Guentert, Editor

Resource Publications wants imaginative resources for professionals, including church professionals in mainstream

Catholic and Protestant settings. As such, they are not an evangelical house or general interest publisher. They look for authors who see a book as an aid to their work, rather than writers who feel their work is done once they've sold it to a publisher. They do about twenty books per year in the liturgical, catechetical, and pastoral (or caregiving) field, most with an emphasis on peer counseling. What they do not want to see are inspirational books and "fundamentalist" novels. They have 100 books in print. Guidelines are available. Query on nonfiction. For fiction, they are only interested in short skits or read-aloud stories for storytellers. Query.

RESURRECTION PRESS, LTD.
P. O. Box 248
Williston Park, New York 11596
516-742-5686
FAX 516-746-6872

Emilie Cerar, Publisher

This Catholic press produces ten or so titles a year meant to inform and empower readers to creatively pursue Christian lifestyles. They work in the areas of spirituality, pastoral resources, healing, and spiritual formation and growth. They are also looking for books on problems in church and society, self-help projects, spirituality for the active Christian, and liturgical and pastoral materials for guiding and updating parish ministries. Resurrection publishes for the popular Catholic and general Christian markets. They are not now interested in poetry or fiction. They also publish under the **Spirit Life** imprint, and they have about 30 books in print. Guidelines and catalog are available. Query with a sample chapter.

FLEMING H. REVELL COMPANY
P. O. Box 6287
Grand Rapids, Michigan 49516-6287

616-676-9185
FAX 616-676-9573

William J. Petersen, Editorial Director
Linda Holland, Senior Editor

Revell is now owned and operated by **Baker Book House.** For the last 125 years Fleming H. Revell has sought to publish books that applied head knowledge of technical theology to the heart's spiritual growth. They do about fifty to sixty titles per year and have nearly 600 backlist books in print. Most of their publishing is aimed at adult laypersons who are growing and maturing in their Christian faith, and they appeal to the Protestant-evangelical tradition. They look for fiction and nonfiction book manuscripts that show how Christ has changed or strengthened lives. They want "niche" books by people with recognized ministries and platforms. Other Revell imprints are **Power Books** and **Spire.** Query and send for their brochure entitled "Preparing a Proposal for Baker, Revell, and Chosen Books" before submitting a proposal and two chapters for nonfiction and a synopsis and two chapters for adult fiction.

REVIEW AND HERALD PUBLISHING ASSOCIATION

55 West Oak Ridge Drive
Hagerstown, Maryland 21740-7390
301-791-7000
FAX 301-790-9734

Raymond H. Woolsey, Vice President, Editorial
Tim Crosby, Acquisition Editor

Review and Herald is a Seventh-Day Adventist house publishing forty books per year for the members of the SDA. These books include SDA religion, health, nutrition, and education. R & H is no longer accepting fiction. They have 800 active titles on their backlist. Guidelines and a catalog are available. Send a proposal with two or three sample chapters, or send the complete manuscript.

RICHARD OWEN ROBERTS, PUBLISHERS
123 North Washington, Box 23
Wheaton, Illinois 60189
708-752-4122

Richard Owen Roberts, Publisher

This press does a varied number of books each year, sometimes under the imprint **International Awakening Press,** mostly of scholarly theological and missiological material that has the capacity to shape the minds and hearts of people along biblical lines. They have about 65 books in print and do provide a book catalog. Send a summary letter of inquiry.

RIVERSIDE (See WORLD BIBLE PUBLISHERS INC.)

ROD & STAFF PUBLISHERS, INC.
Highway 172
Crockett, Kentucky 41413-0003
606-522-4348
FAX 606-522-4348

Duane E. Miller, Editor

This publisher specializes in religious story books, as well as church and Sunday school materials. They do about 25 titles each year and have 150 in print. Query letter.

ROPER PRESS (see TREASURE PUBLISHING)

ROYAL MEDIA (See THOMAS NELSON PUBLISHER'S, INC.)

SALESIANA PUBLISHERS (See DON BOSCO MULTIMEDIA)

SALTSHAKER BOOKS (See INTERVARSITY PRESS)

SCARECROW PRESS INC.
52 Liberty Street
Box 4167
Metuchen, New Jersey 08840-1279
908-548-8600
FAX 908-548-5767

Norman Horrocks, Vice President, Editorial
Danielle Salti, Associate Editor

Scarecrow is a part of the Grolier Company, and publishes five or so titles per year pertaining to research in religion, usually volumes of interest to libraries and scholarly readers. They do 125 titles per year in reference, bibliography, scholarly monographs, literature, religion, women's studies, library software, and so on. They have an active backlist of 1,500 titles. Best to query.

SCHOCKEN BOOKS, INC.
201 E. 50 Street
New York, New York 10022
212-572-2402
FAX 212-572-6030

Arthur Samuelson, Editorial Director
Bonny Fetterman, Editor

Schocken Books is the religious imprint of **Pantheon Books,** which is itself a division of Random House. Pantheon/ Schocken does about seventy-five books per year and has over

500 titles in print. Schocken publishes mostly for the Judaic market, both ancient and modern studies, but they have also done some books on the Gospels. Send a query letter only.

SCYTHE PUBLICATIONS (See WINSTON-DEREK PUBLISHERS)

SELAH HOUSE PUBLISHING (See BRIDGE-LOGOS PUBLISHERS, INC.)

SERVANT PUBLICATIONS
Box 8617
Ann Arbor, Michigan 48107
313-761-8505
FAX 313-761-1577

Bert Ghezzi, Vice President, Editorial
Heidi Hess, Managing Editor
Beth Feia, Editor

Servant is an ecumenical house and publishes from thirty-five to forty books per year under two imprints: **Vine Books** for evangelical Protestants and **Charis Books** for Catholics. The primary theme of both book lines is encouragement for the Christian life. Their books must be ecumenically sensitive, as they cannot attack another denomination nor can they proselytize. Both imprints do books on adult fiction, practical Christian living and teaching, theology, inspiration, the church today, Bible study, meditations, works on prayer, self-help, and the Charismatic movement. They will work with agents on some projects but only after they have pursued the author and developed a relationship with him or her. They will accept nonfiction proposals only from previously published authors. Academic writings are not sought. They have about 200 titles in print, and author guidelines are available. Send query letter, book proposal with outline, and two sample chapters. Also include a succinct and convincing explanation of why the book is unique and needed.

GENERAL CONFERENCE OF SEVENTH-DAY ADVENTISTS
12501 Old Columbia Pike
Silver Spring, Maryland 20904
301-680-5075
FAX 301-622-9627

Beverly Rumble, Editor

This Seventh-Day Adventist press specializes in books on education that present ideas for teaching in a Christian school, along with a variety of topics pertinent to SDA education. They do not publish Sunday school curriculum, nor do they want poetry, material for general exhortation, or cutesy stories. While it is preferred that their writers belong to the denomination, that is not absolutely necessary. Writers guidelines are available. They want writers to use the query approach.

HAROLD SHAW PUBLISHERS
388 Gundersen Drive
P. O. Box 567
Wheaton, Illinois 60189
708-665-6700
FAX 708-665-6793

Stephen Board, President and Publisher
Joan Guest, Managing Editor

Shaw is interested in books that expound the knowledge most worth having and that help people live the Christian faith in a work-a-day world. They want their books to include materials of value in the study of Scripture as well as those making a discerning observation about timeless elements of the human experience. Some devotional reading is produced, and Bible studies, along with more literary works. **Northcote Books** and **OMF Books** (Overseas Missionary Fellowship) are other imprints that Shaw publishes under or distributes for, along with the **Wheaton Literary Series** representing prose and poetry of high literary, academic, and artistic merit. Another new line is **North Wind**, a series of imaginative literature, biographies, and popular theology to encourage readers to follow God's call to purposeful and holy living. They do about thirty books each year and want things of practical or general interest to evangelical Christians. They are looking for books on personal or spiritual development, family issues, and also projects on mental health issues. They are not currently interested in personal stories, poetry, fiction, or devotional material. This house has around 250 titles in print. Send query, synopsis/proposal, and two to three sample chapters.

SHEED & WARD
Box 419492, 115 East Armour Blvd.
Kansas City, Missouri 64141-6492
816-531-0538
FAX 816-931-5082

Robert Heyer, Editor in Chief

This ecumenical Catholic house is a division of The National Catholic Reporter Publishing Company. They do thirty to thirty-five titles per year, mostly nonfiction in spirituality and ethics, and have about 200 books now in print. They are currently looking for books on euthanasia, health care, leadership, the sacraments, and books for small groups or priestless parishes. They are not looking for fiction or any books that look at Scripture from anything but a Catholic perspective. Send for guidelines. For first contact, they want writers to send a proposal and some sample chapters.

SHEPHERD PRESS (See CUSTOM COMMUNICATIONS SERVICES, INC.)

SHINING STAR
Box 299
Carthage, Illinois 62321
217-357-3981
FAX 217-357-3987

Mary Tucker, Editor
Becky Daniel, Editor

Shining Star, affiliated with Good Apple, Inc., publishes about twenty supplementary products (not curriculum) for the school market each year. They do Bible-based stories, games, activity books, puzzles, and crafts, all with strong spiritual emphases or that have to do with Christian values and truths. Their purpose is to have their books reflect the evangelical faith to the entire Christian community, as well as to edify the total person. The house seeks to provide teachers and parents with reproducible activities that will help them teach God's truths to children. They are not currently interested in long stories or poems, especially ones that sound more interesting to adults than to children. Send sample ideas or write for their themes and guidelines.

SKIPJACK PRESS, INC.
P.O. Box 2460-MBS
Ocean City, Maryland 21842
410-524-0319
FAX 410-524-0932

Fran Munday, Editor

This small press publishes two to five books a year mostly in the area of grief theology, but they are also interested in the topic of solidarity (especially on Central American issues). While grief is difficult to write about, there are many books already in print—so they are looking for something unique in the writing approach. They do not want things that are fundamentalistic or any inspirations quoting God. They would like a query letter with two sample chapters.

SMYTH & HELWYS PUBLISHING, INC.
6316 Peake Road
Macon, Georgia 31210-3960
912-752-2117
FAX 912-752-2264

Cecil P. Staton, President and Publisher
Scott Nash, Senior Vice President, Editorial Division

Smyth & Helwys, a publishing house of Christian resources, does approximately thirty titles per year meant to exhibit a sensible theology, avoiding the extremes of both the right and the left. Their books are intended to be well-informed but quite readable. Their publishing program is mostly nonfiction at this point, emphasizing biblical studies and spirituality. They also publish theology and doctrine on a selective basis. They are trying to develop a line of fiction and children's books, and they want to do more in the area of church-life related books (worship, preaching, education in the church, etc.). **Peake Road** is a new imprint with plans to publish twenty to thirty hardcover and trade titles a year that will be crossovers for the CBA and ABA markets. There are some 80 titles in print at this house. Best to query.

SONPOWER YOUTH RESOURCES (See VICTOR BOOKS)

268

SON-RISE PUBLICATIONS
143 Greenfield Road
New Wilmington, Pennsylvania 16142
800-358-0777
FAX 412-946-8700

Florence W. Biros, Acquisitions Editor

This press does five or six books each year, but about half of what they print is subsidy published. They want Christian teaching tools and books of testimony, and they are looking for a historical novel series. Query only.

SOWER'S PRESS
P. O. Box 666306
Marietta, Georgia 30066
770-565-8202
FAX 770-977-3784

Jamey Wood, Editor

Sower's Press publishes books to further establish ministries of speakers and teachers. They release 2 or 3 books each year. Submit a query with sample chapters. Expect a report in about a month. Their categories of special interest are marriage and family.

SPIRE (See FLEMING H. REVELL COMPANY)

SPIRIT LIFE (See RESURRECTION PRESS, LTD.)

SP PUBLICATIONS, INC. (See VICTOR BOOKS)

SQUEAKY SNEAKER BOOKS (See STAR SONG PUBLISHING GROUP)

SUMMIT PUBLISHING, LTD.
Denvigh House, Denvigh Road
Milton Keynes, MK1 1YP
England
011-44-190-836-8071
FAX 011-44-190-831-5408

Noel Halsey, President

Summit is committed to publishing high quality books by established as well as new charismatic evangelical Christian authors. In this country, Summit works very closely with **Creation House** in Altamonte Springs, Florida. Send a cover letter, a one-to-two-page summary of the manuscript, a brief table of contents, and some excerpts from the work.

STANDARD PUBLISHING COMPANY
8121 Hamilton Avenue
Cincinnati, Ohio 45231
513-931-4050
FAX 513-931-0904

Eugene H. Wigginton, Vice President and Publisher
Mark Taylor, Director, New Product Development
Theresa Hayes, Acquisitions Editor

Standard, a division of Standex International, is a publisher of curriculum and classroom resources, along with children's books (including children's picture books) and fiction, doing about seventy-five total titles per year. Their books include church growth, leadership in the church, and the deeper spiritual life. They are looking for training materials, bulletin board helps, tips for teachers, idea and craft books for teachers, devotional books for children and teens, object talk books, classroom activity books, and material for Christmas, Easter, Thanksgiving, Mother's Day, and Father's Day program books. They do not want to see poetry, juvenile fiction, fantasy, biographies, commentaries, books on prophecy, reference works, adult devotional material, or general books on Christian living. Their list of authors includes clergy and laity of mainline Protestant and Evangelical denominations, as well as Roman Catholic churches. They publish under **Happy Day Books, Little Deer Books, and Really Reading! Books.** Standard has a backlist of some 3,000 books in print. Writers guidelines are available for children's books, program books, and Christian education books. For fiction, send the entire manuscript. For Christian education books, send a query and two sample chapters. For picture books, send the full manuscript.

ST. ANTHONY MESSENGER PRESS
1615 Republic Street
Cincinnati, Ohio 45210
513-241-5615
FAX 513-241-0399

Norman Perry, Editor in Chief
Lisa A. Biedenbach, Managing Editor

St. Anthony publishes twelve to fifteen books per year that are practical and popular resources to nurture Catholic Christian life in our culture. This includes aids for liturgy and the sacraments, aids to prayer and spirituality, theology, books on Scripture and the church, parish ministry resources, and Franciscan resources. The style of their books is popular—easy to read, practical, concrete, and filled with examples. While some of their books cross over to other Christian denominations, all of them are geared to Roman Catholics. They seek the imprimatur (the license to publish from the Catholic episcopal authority) and therefore their books have nothing in them against Catholic faith and morals. Currently they are looking for Catholic identity books, pastoral ministry books, Scripture study resources, and books on Catholic history. Guidelines and catalog are available. There are about 100 St. Anthony titles now in print. They respond more quickly to a query than to a whole manuscript, so send a query, a brief description, and an outline.

ST. BEDE'S PUBLICATIONS
P. O. Box 545
Petersham, Massachusetts 01366-0545
508-724-3407
FAX 508-724-3574

Scholastica Crilly, Editor

St. Bede's is a Catholic press that publishes Christian spirituality, monastic spirituality, theology, and religious college textbooks. They do in the neighborhood of ten nonfiction titles a year, and they have around 70 titles in print. They do not publish fiction or poetry. Guidelines and catalog are available. Send a query letter only.

ST. PAUL BOOKS AND MEDIA
50 St. Paul's Avenue
Boston, Massachusetts 02130
617-522-8911
FAX 617-541-9805

Mary Wickenhiser, Editorial Director

St. Paul is a Catholic press, which is a division of Daughters of Saint Paul, that produces thirty to forty titles per year. They want "easy reading" books written for the average person, and they are also looking for juvenile fiction. Most of their backlist (of 900 titles) includes Roman Catholic catechisms, inspirational and liturgical books, books on papal teaching, some sociology, and some biography. They also publish under the imprint named **Encounter Books**. Send a query letter first.

STARBURST PUBLISHERS
P.O. Box 4123
Lancaster, Pennsylvania 17604
717-293-0939
FAX 717-293-1945

Ellen Hake, Editorial Director

Starburst publishes inspirational Bible-based books and fiction that address contemporary issues and the concerns of today to the Christian marketplace. They also operate as a general interest house, doing books in areas such as how-to, self-help, cooking, nutrition and health, personal finance, family and parenting, psychology, recreation, and nature and the environment. In adult fiction (they do not publish children's fiction), they want adventure, fantasy, historical, mainstream/contemporary, romance, and western. The fiction must be very unique or by an established author before it will be considered. They average ten to fifteen total titles per year. Author guides are available. Send query letter, outline, target audience, and three sample chapters. For nonfiction, include a brief analysis of the competition.

STAR SONG CONTEMPORARY CLASSICS (See STAR SONG PUBLISHING GROUP)

STAR SONG PUBLISHING GROUP
2325 Crestmoor
Nashville, Tennessee 37215
615-269-0196
FAX 615-385-2708

Matthew A. Price, Vice President, Editorial

Star Song was founded as a contemporary Christian music company. It now publishes twenty to twenty-five books per year as the book and educational division of Star Song under these imprints: **Abbott-Martyn Press, Star Song Contemporary Classics, Mustard Seed Books,** and **Squeaky**

Sneaker Books. The specialty of this publishing group is adult fiction, juvenile fiction, general interest categories, academic books, and worship. Some poetry is accepted (but query for poetry). They are looking for books by and for African-Americans. All products are to be biblically and spiritually sound, aesthetically superlative, accessible to the broadest number of people, and able to function as a tool for the furtherance of the Kingdom of God. They now have about 50 titles in print. They want a query letter, summary, brief marketing proposal, and two sample chapters.

STILLPOINT PUBLISHING INTERNATIONAL, INC.
P. O. Box 640, Meetinghouse Road
Walpole, New Hampshire 03608
603-756-9281
FAX 603-756-9282

Dorothy Seymour, Senior Editor

Stillpoint Publishing & Institute for Life Healing does books and tapes to awaken the human spirit. They publish five to ten nonfiction manuscripts per year, with a focus on human consciousness and spiritual ecology. They seek unique perspectives on personal growth and spiritual development, holistic health and healing, sacred ecology (eco-spirituality), and spirituality in business, community, and society. They do not want any direct or straight channeling books, nor do they publish fiction, poetry, or straight autobiography. Stillpoint has nearly 40 titles now in print. For first contact, send a cover or query letter, author biography, complete table of contents, and some sample material.

STILL WATERS REVIVAL BOOKS
4710-37A
Edmonton, Alberta T6L 3T5
Canada
403-450-3730

Reg Barrow, President

Fifteen titles per year are published by Still Waters, a press of the Reformed Church. They want Reformed and Reconstructionist books written for educated laypeople. Nothing non-Reformed or premillennial is considered. The books must agree with the doctrinal system found in the Westminster Confession of Faith, but must be applied to our modern world. No guidelines are provided. Send a proposal and two sample chapters.

STIMULUS BOOKS (See PAULIST PRESS)

SWEET DREAMS (See BANTAM BOOKS)

TABOR PUBLISHING (See CHRISTIAN CLASSICS)

JANET THOMA BOOKS (See THOMAS NELSON PUBLISHER'S, INC.)

TREASURE PUBLISHING
MCS 1000
829 South Shields
Ft. Collins, Colorado 80521
800-284-0158

Mark Steiner, President

Treasure Publishing is a new company that was recently formed after the sale of **Roper Press,** formerly of Dallas, Texas. This house does curricula for various grades of Sunday school, but primary consideration will also be given for book manuscripts on direct Bible studies, Bibles stories, or any medium that shows clearly the relevance of the Word to life. Material related to evangelism, personal discipleship, and Christian living are also on their publishing agenda. They also want fiction, but it is essential that it has an integration of the Christian message into the story or character. They have no interest in "tacked on" pithy afterthoughts. Roper does about five books a year and has approximately 100 titles in print. They do not publish biographies or autobiographies, or any reference works. Send a query letter with sample chapters and author background.

THE TRINITY FOUNDATION
P. O. Box 700
Jefferson, Maryland 21755
301-371-7155

John W. Robbins, President and Editor

Trinity publishes five or so books each year in philosophy and theology that advocate a systematic presentation of the whole doctrine of God. The patron saint and guiding light of this house is the late philosopher Gordon Clark, so get to know his work. A catalog is available. Use the query approach.

TRINITY PRESS INTERNATIONAL
P. O. Box 851
Valley Forge, Pennsylvania 19482-0851
610-768-2120
FAX 610-768-2056

Harold Rast, Director and Publisher
Laura Barrett, Managing Editor

Trinity Press International is an independent, ecumenical, and interreligious publisher whose goal is to create a strong and vigorous literature that will enlighten and quicken religious thought and action throughout the world. The press provides serious and accessible books, often interdisciplinary in character, for a broad range of readers, that address the questions people ask and that assist in the formation of intelligent, moral, and effective faith communities. Some of the categories in which they publish are religion, theology, and ethics, scripture studies, women's studies, religious education, and reference works. They do not want dissertations or essays. They do twenty to twenty-five titles a year, and they have 150 books in print. They will send out guidelines. Send a query letter, a proposal, and some sample chapters.

TRIUMPH BOOKS (See LIGUORI PUBLICATIONS)

XXIII PUBLICATIONS (See TWENTY-THIRD PUBLICATIONS)

TWENTY-THIRD PUBLICATIONS, INC.
P. O. Box 180, 185 Willow Street
Mystic, Connecticut 06355
203-536-2611
FAX 203-572-0788

Gwen Costello, Editorial Director
John Van Bemmel, Managing Editor

This is a Roman Catholic publishing firm specializing in religious education, catechetics, theology, spirituality, and creation spirituality. They mean their books to help lay people live the Gospel and to practice the teachings of the Second Vatican Council. They specifically do not want to see fiction, children's books, or manuscripts on Scripture from non-Catholic presuppositions. **Vision 23** and **XXIII Publications** are two other imprints used in their publishing program. They produce around forty books per year, and maintain 260 in print. Guidelines and catalog are available. On first contact, send a query letter and two sample chapters.

TYNDALE HOUSE PUBLISHERS, INC.
351 Executive Drive, Box 80
Wheaton, Illinois 60189-0080
708-668-8300
FAX 708-668-9092

Wendell Hawley, Senior Vice President, Editorial
Ronald Beers, Vice President, Editorial
Dan Elliot, Editorial Director
Kenneth Petersen, Acquisitions Editor
Carole Johnson, Editorial Manager

Tyndale House Publishers is a non-denominational religious house that publishes around 100 general interest books each year for the evangelical Christian market. Their books cover a wide range of categories, including Bibles, home and family, Christian living and Christian growth, devotional, motivational, children, youth, inspirational, theology, doctrine, fiction, general reference, and some miscellaneous selections like humor and puzzle books. They do not publish any secular books, and they have no demands for multi-culture viewpoints in their nonfiction books, although there is a limited demand for this in their fiction. No poetry or sermons are published. They do not hold a particular denominational or doctrinal view but publish books that minister to the spiritual needs of people and that express biblically supportable approaches to life in the tradition of orthodox Christianity. Other Tyndale imprints are **Living Books, Pocket Guides,** and **Windrider.** They have over 1,000 titles on their backlist. Guidelines for writers are available. Tyndale has changed its manuscript review procedures. Now, to get possible publishing projects into the hands of the Tyndale editors, they want writers to work through The Writer's Edge. This service is located at P. O. Box 1266, Wheaton, Illinois, 60189. However, they do consider manuscripts or proposals submitted by professional literary agents, Tyndale authors, or other previously published authors.

UNITED CHURCH PRESS (See THE PILGRIM PRESS)

THE UNITED CHURCH PUBLISHING HOUSE
85 St. Clair Avenue E.
Toronto, Ontario M4T 1M8
Canada
416-925-4850
FAX 416-925-9692

Peter Gordon White, Editor in Chief
Elizabeth Phinney, Managing Editor

The United Church of Canada operates this house, which publishes ten to fifteen titles per year by Canadian authors only. The books must be of interest to Canadians and must be tied to some aspect of Canadian living. Send a query letter.

THE UNITED METHODIST PUBLISHING HOUSE
201 Eighth Avenue South
Nashville, Tennessee 37203-3957
615-749-6000
FAX 615-749-6079

Neil M. Alexander, Editorial Director
Michael E. Lawrence, Managing Editor
Mary Catherine Dean, Editor
Sally Sharpe, Editor
Janice Grana, Publisher, Upper Room Books
George Donigian, Editor for Leadership Books and Resources, Upper Room Books
JoAnn E. Miller, Editor for General Inspirational and Devotional Books, Upper Room Books
Rita Bennett Collett, Associate Editor, Upper Room Books

The United Methodist Publishing House publishes resources for the Christian community to help readers know, love, and serve God and neighbor. This publishing program includes books for clergy, lay professional, paraprofessional, and lay readers. They do from twelve to fifteen books (150 titles per year are published including all UMPH imprints, with some 1,500 total books in print) per year in the areas of books, church school curriculum, inspiration, pastoral ministry, scholarship, United Methodist/Wesleyan studies, and official United Methodist resources. (See also the **Abingdon Press** listing.) Under the **Upper Room Books** imprint, they publish devotional and inspirational material for Christians. The general house is looking for ethnic books for African-Americans, Native Americans, and Asian-Americans, and also books on parenting, marriage, and the family. They do not want to see poetry, fiction, biography, autobiography, non-religious children's books, or sermon collections. No guidelines are available. A track record of previous publications is virtually necessary for serious consideration in the case of unsolicited proposals. Send a proposal and two sample chapters and include information on competitive books and what sets yours apart.

UNIVERSITY PRESS OF AMERICA
4720 Boston Way
Lanham, Maryland 20706
301-459-3366
FAX 301-459-2118

Julie Kirsch, Acquisitions Editor
Michelle R. Harris, Acquisitions Editor
Helen Hudson, Editor

This university press issues scholarly books in the social sciences and humanities, including religious books for non-denominational academic classroom use (about fifty such religiously oriented books appear each year). Among the interests of this house are books in biblical studies, philosophy of religion, history, comparative religions, world religions, religious psychology, theology, and language studies. They will not publish fiction, poetry, inspirational works, or non-academic projects. Most of their publishing is done via copublishing programs and the arrangement of research advances, guaranteeing a certain number of advance orders, and where the author supplies camera-ready pages. Guidelines are available. They will accept a query letter or synopsis, but they prefer getting a copy of the entire manuscript.

UNUSUAL PUBLICATIONS (See BOB JONES UNIVERSITY PRESS)

UPPER ROOM BOOKS (See THE UNITED METHODIST PUBLISHING HOUSE)

VICTOR BOOKS
4050 Lee Vance View
Colorado Springs, Colorado 80918
719-536-0100
FAX 719-536-3279

James Elwell, Vice President and Publisher, Victor Books
Arnold Berntsen, Vice President and Publisher, SP Publications
Greg Clouse, Editorial Director
Robert N. Hosack, Academic Resources Editor
David Horton, Senior Acquisitions Editor
Liz Duckworth, Managing Editor, Children's Books

Victor is a full-spectrum, ministry-oriented publishing house. It was until recently a division of SP Publications, the evangelical curriculum publisher. Now, both Victor and SP Publications are formally owned by Cook Communications Ministries. The Victor publishing philosophy is to create life-related Christian books of either a contemporary or traditional nature that challenge, inspire, inform, and entertain readers around the world, and to do this they publish in several genres, including fiction, personal growth, family, finance, Christian living, and academic/reference volumes. While they aim their books at the man and woman in the local church, primarily of mainline and evangelical Protestant denominations, they no longer publish adult church education products (personal Bible study and small group materials). They do, however, have an expanding line of toddler's and children's products. **Bridgepoint** is their imprint for academic books committed to serving college and seminary professors, students, pastors, and other more sophisticated readers. Other imprints under which this house publishes are **SonPower Youth Resources, SP Publications, Inc.** (formerly Scripture Press Publications, Inc.), and **Winner Books.** They publish 100 to 120 titles annually, and they have over 500 books in print. For unsolicited projects, they accept proposals and queries only, not manuscripts; send cover letter, curriculum vitae, project summary, and sample chapter.

VICTORY HOUSE, INC.
P. O. Box 700238
Tulsa, Oklahoma 74170
918-747-5009
FAX 918-747-1970

Lloyd B. Hildebrand, Managing Editor

Victory House publishes five to ten books each year, and seeks to encourage Christians to build bridges to each other based on the commonalities they share as believers. They want their books to edify the church and to develop fresh approaches that incorporate show-don't-tell techniques that create vivid images for the reader. They publish in diverse categories, including fiction, self-help, autobiography, books on Christian teaching, worship, family living, prayer, intercession,

American heritage, and so on. They have 25 titles in print, will provide guidelines, and prefer writers of both fiction and nonfiction to approach them with a complete manuscript.

VINE BOOKS (See SERVANT PUBLICATIONS)

VISION 23 (See TWENTY-THIRD PUBLICATIONS, INC.)

VISION HOUSE PUBLISHING, INC.
1217 N.E. Burnside Road
Gresham, Oregon 97030
503-492-0200

John Van Diest, President

This new publisher is not to be confused with the former Vision House Publishers that was a division of Gospel Light Publications in California (it is now no longer publishing). The new Vision House is a company committed to producing media for world-wide consumption with a focus on bringing people closer to God through Christ in order to edify and equip the church for service. They publish five to ten titles per year in Christian living, practical theology, and critical thinking. They are also starting to publish some fiction. Guidelines are available. They want a query and some sample chapters.

WADSWORTH PUBLISHING COMPANY
10 Davis Drive
Belmont, California 94002
415-595-2350
FAX 415-592-3342

Gary Carlson, Editor in Chief
Tammy Goldfeld, Editor

Wadsworth, a college text publisher, is a subdivision of International Thomson Publishing. They produce 175 textbooks per year in most of the academic areas and maintain over 925 titles on their backlist. Of the number of texts they publish, five to ten are devoted to religion textbooks—mostly in the area of world religions and anthologies of religion. Send a book proposal only.

WARNER PRESS
P. O. Box 2499
1200 East Fifth Street
Anderson, Indiana 46018
317-644-7721
FAX 317-649-3664

Robert Rist, Chairman
David C. Schultz, Editor in Chief
Dan Harman, Book Editor

Warner produces books and supplies and is the book and curriculum publishing arm of the Church of God—Anderson, Indiana. They develop, publish, and market ten to fifteen book titles each year, mostly of interest to members of their denomination. No guidelines are available. Query only.

THE WESTMINSTER PRESS/JOHN KNOX PRESS
100 Witherspoon Street
Louisville, Kentucky 40202-1396
502-569-5043
FAX 502-569-5018

Davis Perkins, Editorial Director
Stephanie Egnotovich, Editorial Manager
Cynthia L. Thompson, Academic Books Editor
Jeffries Hamilton, Academic Books Editor
Harold Twiss, General Books Editor

Westminster and John Knox, both official publishing arms of the Presbyterian Church, USA, have combined their publishing efforts into one house which is now a division of the Presbyterian Publishing Corporation. Under both imprints, they publish several kinds of books with a wide latitude on the interpretation of religious truth for the general audience, including academic titles, theology, philosophy, ethics and present-day ethical issues, archaeology, history, pastoral counseling, prayer books, and titles on personal growth. Westminster/John Knox seeks to contribute to the intellectual life of the church and the spiritual development of Christians by publishing serious works of high merit, representing first-rate thinking on a range of religious, social, and cultural concerns. They do eighty to 100 books per year, and they have 1,200 titles in print. They request that a query letter and synopsis with sample chapters be sent for the first contact.

WHEATON LITERARY SERIES (See HAROLD SHAW PUBLISHERS)

WHITAKER HOUSE
580 Pittsburgh Street
Springdale, Pennsylvania 15144
412-274-4440
FAX 412-274-4676

Robert E. Whitaker, President

This charismatic house produces ten or so books a year that reflect various aspects of life in Christ, as well as books on family life. Whitaker wants "how to" books that help average Christians grow in their faith. Their main area of interest is in popular pentecostalist literature, and they specialize in doing books with already-known charismatic leaders. There are about 80 Whitaker titles now in print. Query letter only.

WILD ONION (See LOYOLA PRESS)

WINDRIDER (See TYNDALE HOUSE PUBLISH-ERS, INC.)

WINNER BOOKS (See VICTOR BOOKS)

WINSTON-DEREK PUBLISHERS
P. O. Box 90883
Nashville, Tennessee 37209
615-321-0535
FAX 615-329-4824

Maggie Staton, Editor
James C. Winston, Editor, Religious Trade Division

Winston-Derek publishes fiction and nonfiction for the adult and juvenile readers, including books in religion, self-help, and human behavior and development. They are looking for things that are unique but theologically sound for both the Catholic and evangelical general interest markets. In fiction, they do not want occult, science fiction, or New Age fiction. They do seventy-five to 100 titles per year and have over 700 books in print. Imprints of this house include **Scythe Publications, Magpie Books,** and **One Horn Press.** For nonfiction, send a complete synopsis, along with the full manuscript and some author background information. For fiction, send a proposal or a complete manuscript.

WOMAN'S MISSIONARY UNION (See NEW HOPE)

WOOD LAKE BOOKS, INC.
10162 Newene Road
Winfield, British Columbia V4V 1R2
Canada
604-766-2778
FAX 604-766-2736

David Cleary, Editor

Wood Lake is an ecumenical/mainline press publishing ten titles per year related to the seasons of the church and to clergy resources. They also do fiction for children, teens, and adults. They publish only Canadian authors. Guidelines and a catalog are available. Send a book proposal and two or three sample chapters.

WORD PUBLISHING, INC.
1501 LBJ Freeway, Suite 650
Dallas, Texas 75234-6069
214-488-9673
FAX 214-488-1311

Byron Williamson, President, Nelson-Word Publishing Group
Kip Jordan, Executive Vice President and Publisher
Joey Paul, Vice President, Trade Publishing
David Moberg, Senior Vice President, Bibles

Word, now owned by **Thomas Nelson Publishing,** is part of the NelsonWord Publishing Group. (The two companies continue to operate as separate product development and marketing units and function autonomously within the group.) Word has traditionally published material having to do with personal growth in Christ, Bible studies, Christian counseling, theology, biblical commentaries, family life, life-application, juvenile and young adult books, and Christian lifestyles. They consider themselves a service company in the Christian communications business. The reading audience has predominately been adults of mainline Protestant as well as evangelical groups, and they have published around sixty books per year (with over 1,200 now in print). However, as they are no longer able to review or respond to individual manuscript submissions, Word is not encouraging unsolicited manuscripts, nor are they able to provide manuscript guidelines.

WORLD AFLAME PRESS (See PENTECOSTAL PUBLISHING HOUSE)

WORLD PUBLISHING CO., INC.
2976 Ivanrest Avenue
Grandville, Michigan 49418
616-531-9110
FAX 616-531-9120

Skip Knapp, President
Dan Penwell, Director of New Product Development

World is a subdivision of Riverside Book and Bible House, and they sometimes use the **Riverside** imprint. They do twenty-five titles per year, mostly Bibles and testaments, and have 335 such titles in print. On occasion they do publish some books that seek to make the Bible more understandable to the average person, mostly popular-level Bible reference tools. No guidelines. Send a book proposal with a well-developed outline and chapter summaries.

WRS PUPLISHING
701 North New Road
Waco, Texas 76702-1207
817-776-6461
FAX 817-757-1454

Ann Page, Acquisitions Director

WRS specializes in nonfiction books that focus mainly on social trends and issues, biographies and autobiographies (of normal people with special stories to tell), and children's books, and they are interested in doing materials for the African-American population. They do forty to forty-five books each year, with about 70 currently in print. Send a query letter with a book proposal.

WYNWOOD PRESS (See BAKER BOOK HOUSE)

YALE UNIVERSITY PRESS
92A Yale Station
New Haven, Connecticut 06520
203-432-0900
FAX 203-432-2394

Charles Grench, Executive Editor
Meryl Lanning, Managing Editor

Most of the religious books published by Yale are academic and scholarly books for members of academic communities, but some are done for the more general reading audience. They do scholarly books on all aspects of religion that make a first-rate contribution to scholarship in all aspects of religion available to scholars, students, and a wider readership. Their mix includes archaeology, biblical exposition, and history of early Christianity. They do not want to see fiction, proselytizing works, and unscholarly tracts. Yale publishes 150 books each year, and they have nearly 2,000 titles in print. Query first. Send a letter plus a prospectus and a curriculum vitae.

YOUTH SPECIALTIES (See ZONDERVAN PUB-LISHING HOUSE)

ZONDERVAN PUBLISHING HOUSE
5300 Patterson Avenue, S.E.
Grand Rapids, Michigan 49503
616-698-6900
FAX 616-698-3439

Scott W. Bolinder, Vice President and Publisher
Stanley N. Gundry, Vice President and Editor in Chief
Lyn Cryderman, Associate Publisher
Ed van der Maas, Senior Acquisitions Editor
John Sloan, Senior Acquisitions Editor
Ann Spangler, Senior Acquisitions Editor
Sandy Vander Zicht, Senior Acquisitions Editor
Jack Kuhatschek, David Lambert, Acquisition Editors
James E. Ruark, Senior Editor

Zondervan is a division of HarperCollins Publishers, Inc. They want to take a fresh approach to issues and problems for the nondenominational evangelical Protestant reading audience. The firm publishes general nonfiction, biographies, self-help books, some adult fiction (although they have a renewed interest in the fiction market), books for children and youth, books for ministry to children and youth, books on family life and marriage, Bible study resources, and devotional books. Zondervan is interested in widening its vision by acquiring books from high-profile figures in order to appeal to a broad core reading market and to cross Christian bookstore boundaries. They also produce a select number of academic and professional titles for classroom use in colleges and seminaries in various fields, such as biblical studies, theology, church history, preaching, counseling, and the humanities. Zondervan also has a copublishing and distribution partnership with Youth Specialties (of El Cajon, California) in the publishing of material for volunteer and professional youth workers. The firm also owns **Editorial Vida,** the publisher and distributor of Christian books and Bibles in Spanish, French, and Portuguese. Zondervan does 100+ books annually, and they have a backlist of about 1,000 titles currently in print. Submission guidelines are available. Send a book description, table of contents with a summary of each chapter of the writing project, author biographical information, and writing samples.

10

SELECTIVE BIBLIOGRAPHY:

Some of the Better Books on Writing, Editing, Publishing, Book Production, Research, and Usage

The following books are especially helpful and interesting. This is a subjective opinion, of course, but all opinions are subjective. There are hundreds and hundreds of specialized books and other sources of information on these subjects; here are some very useful books that have appeared in recent years. Many of these titles are out-of-print, so you will have to check your local library. But many are available, and may either be consulted in a good library or ordered from most any bookstore. If you are interested in finding and buying some of the out-of-print ones, ask a secondhand book dealer to find them for you. (This can be especially fruitful if you can locate a specialty used-book house that deals with titles for bibliophiles on books, writing, and publishing, for such a person may even have some of these in stock.) Nearly all such dealers offer a search service, and through their channels of communications with other dealers, they are able to find many titles that you may want that are out of print, even from publishing houses no longer in business.

Annotated Bibliography

Book Publishing

GENERAL

The Art and Science of Book Publishing, by Herbert S. Bailey, Jr. (Athens, Ohio: Ohio University Press, 1990). The former director of Princeton University Press offers a rigorous introduction to the editorial, production, and especially business aspects of publishing. Formulas, forms, and schedules are given for pricing, advertising, reprinting, and other issues.

At Random: The Reminiscences of Bennett Cerf, by Bennett Cerf (New York: Random House, 1977). The inside history of an important publishing house and the fascinating story of one of America's most famous publishers. He recalls with candid opinions the people he knew (such as Truman Capote, William Faulkner, Eugene O'Neill, James Joyce, George Gershwin, and many others) and also has delightful anecdotes of many of the authors he published and many of the people who worked for the house.

The Awful Truth About Publishing: Why They Always Reject Your Manuscript—and What You Can Do About It, by John Boswell (New York: Warner Books, 1986). The straight facts about the business and an honest but refreshing analysis of what it takes to get in print today.

The Bantam Story: Thirty Years of Paperback Publishing, 2nd edition, by Clarence Petersen (New York: Bantam Books, 1975). The history of the largest paperback house and the development of the paperback field.

Between Covers: The Rise and Transformation of American Book Publishing, by John W. Tebbel (New York: Oxford University Press, 1987). A colorful and well-researched single volume history of American publishing that uses anecdote and biography to get behind the famous imprints and people of the field. Traces the industry from its cottage roots to today's world of mergers and conglomerates.

The Blockbuster Complex, by Thomas Whiteside (Middletown, Conn.: Wesleyan University Press, 1981). The "big deals" side of publishing is here explored. Nearly all the material appeared originally in *The New Yorker*.

The Book About Books: The Anatomy of Bibliomania, by Holbrook Jackson (New York: Avenel Books, 1981). Jackson (d. 1948) was a quintessential bookman, one who loved books and considered them the spirit and force of life. This book is for all booklovers and bibliomaniacs who understand that addiction. It is written after the style of Robert Burton's 17th Century *The Anatomy of Melancholy*.

Book Publishers Directory (Detroit: Gale Research, annual). This is a listing of over 9,000 private, special-interest, government, association, and institutional publishers.

Books: From Writer to Reader, by Howard Greenfield (New York: Crown Publishers, 1976). Greenfield describes all the steps in general book publishing, from author to agent to publisher to bookseller to reader. Good for new authors and those new to publishing.

Books: Their History, Art, Power, Glory, Infamy and Suffering According to Their Creators, Friends and Enemies, by Gerald Donaldson (New York: Van Nostrand Reinhold Company, 1981). The author answers hundreds of questions in this spirited and breezy tour of books and book people. Full of facts on bookmaking, bookselling, and bookworms, this book is beautifully illustrated throughout.

Books and Book People in 19th Century America, by Madeleine B. Stern (New York: R. R. Bowker Company, 1978). Important events in the history of publishing are presented, including the history, from 1872 to 1947, of the trade journal *Publishers Weekly*.

Books in Print, 15 vols. (New Providence, N.J.: R. R. Bowker Company, updated annually). To check what is in print, who wrote it, and where it is available, consult this listing of all books currently in print, organized by author, title, and subject. Over 600,000 titles from more than 13,000 publishers.

Book Publishing: A Basic Introduction, expanded edition, by John P. Dessauer (New York: Continuum, 1989). An excellent look at the industry and how it works. Especially useful for those interested in a career in the field.

Book Publishing: Inside Views, compiled by Jean Spencer Kujoth (Metuchen, N.J.: Scarecrow Press, 1971). 50 articles by experts on trends in the book industry.

Book Publishing: What It Is, What It Does, 2nd edition, by John P. Dessauer (New York: R. R. Bowker, 1981). A complete survey of the industry, from the creation of books through the manufacturing, financing, planning, marketing, and delivery of them. The author is one of the publishing industry's best students, and has produced one of the best texts of the field.

Book Publishing Career Directory, 5th edition, edited by Bradley J. Morgan (Detroit: Gale Research, Inc., 1993). What does it mean to be part of the book publishing industry? This is a comprehensive yet practical, one-step guide to finding just the right spot in the field. Industry leaders give advice on what to expect in publishing, the preparation and background required, the various jobs in the field, typical career paths, specialty houses, the small press scene, and much more. Some of the contributors include Judith Appelbaum, Samuel Vaughn, Herbert J. Addison, and Anne E. Maitland. The unique segment that is religious publishing is handled in a chapter by Leonard George Goss entitled "Religious Book Publishing: The State of the Heart."

The Book Revolution, by Robert Escarpit (London: George G. Harrap & Company, Ltd., 1966). This was originally a study done for the United Nations Educational, Scientific, and Cultural Organization (Paris). The author was a professor at the University of Bordeaux. It covers the origins of book publishing, with recommendations (at least as of 1966) regarding its future.

Books: The Culture and Commerce of Publishing, by Lewis Coser, Charles Kadushin, and Walter Powell (New

York: Basic Books, 1982). The entire spectrum of book publishing is studied by three sociologists. Illuminating.

The Bowker Annual of Library and Book Trade Information (New Providence, N.J.: R. R. Bowker Company, updated annually). This almanac completely surveys the book industry.

The Business of Book Publishing: Papers by Practitioners, edited by Elizabeth A. Geiser and Arnold Dolin, with Gladys S. Topkis (Boulder, Colo.: Westview Press, 1985). A textbook for publishing courses and seminars covering all the phases and functions of the book publishing process. The many contributors represent the industry's leaders.

The Business of Publishing: A PW Anthology, edited by Arnold Ehrlich (New York: R. R. Bowker Company, 1976). A collection of 45 articles from *Publisher's Weekly*, the book industry journal.

A Candid Critique of Book Publishing, by Curtis G. Benjamin (New York: R. R. Bowker Company, 1977). The former president of the McGraw-Hill Book Company talks about the many important challenges facing the industry.

The Caxton Club 1895-1995, by Frank Piehl (New Castle, Del.: Oak Knoll Press, 1995). The Caxton Club was founded in Chicago in 1895 by fifteen bibliophiles for "the literary study and promotion of the arts pertaining to the production of books" and "the occasional publishing of books designed to illustrate, promote, and encourage these arts." This is a history of the now century-old club, along with a history of its sixty publications, all distinguished by their content and design.

Chronicles of Barabbas 1884-1934, 2nd edition, by George Doran (New York: Holt, Rinehart & Winston, 1952). A famous publisher tells many stories and ruminates about the achievements of his profession.

Communicating Ideas: The Crisis of Publishing in a Post-Industrial Society, by Irving Louis Horowitz (New York: Oxford University Press, 1986). A scholarly study of where the publishing industry is going.

Current Christian Books, 3 vols., an official publication of the Christian Booksellers Association (Colorado Springs, Colo.: Christian Booksellers Association, annual). The most complete listing of available Christian books. Organized into three volumes: Title, Author, and Subject. Over 50,000 titles are listed in 30-plus subject categories, with over 22,000 authors of Christian books listed alphabetically. Updated annually.

Endless Frontiers: The Story of McGraw-Hill, by Roger Burlingame (New York: McGraw-Hill Book Company, 1959). A history of the firm.

A Few Good Voices in My Head: Occasional Pieces on Writing, Editing, and Reading My Contemporaries, by Ted Solotaroff (New York: HarperCollins Publishers, 1987). Astute insights and criticism of the corporate mentality that has taken over book publishing.

The Financial Side of Book Publishing: A Correspondence Course in Business Analysis for the Non-Accountant, by Robert J. R. Follett (New York: Association of American Publishers, 1982). Nineteen self-study lessons in basic financial and accounting skills as they are related to the book publishing industry.

The First One Hundred and Fifty Years: A History of John Wiley and Sons, Inc., 1807-1957, Various contributors (New York: John Wiley & Sons, Inc., 1957). An informal institutional history of the Wiley firm that begins when Charles Wiley opened his small printing shop in 1807 (he became a publisher in 1814 with James Fenimore Cooper's *The Spy*), moves through the long life and contribution of Charles' son John Wiley and John's partner, George Palmer Putnam, and ends (the book, not the firm) in 1957 with Wiley a major, international publishing house. Mostly covers the books they published during this 150-year period. (Confer with *Wiley: One Hundred and Seventy-five Years of Publishing.*)

A Genius for Letters: Booksellers and Bookselling from the Sixteenth to the Twentieth Centuries, edited by Robin Myers and Michael Harris (New Castle, Del.: Oak Knoll Press, 1995). The contributors, including Anthony Hobson, Luigi Balsamo, Giles Mandlebrote, and Simon Eliot, unravel some of the complexities of the market place through the sale of books—a trade at the center of an interlocking range of business activities.

Getting Into Book Publishing, 3rd edition, by Chandler B. Grannis (New York: R. R. Bowker Company, 1983). A booklet from the Bowker publicity department presenting the variety of jobs in the book publishing field. For anyone wanting to get into the fray.

Getting Into Print: The Decision-Making Process in Scholarly Publishing, by Walter W. Powell (Chicago: University of Chicago Press, 1985). Case studies of "Apple Press" and "Plum Press" by a professor of sociology to show how academic editors choose the new titles they sponsor. Gives an insider's appreciation for the book publishing business and shows how it differs from other sorts of organizations.

Getting Published: The Acquisition Process at University Presses, by Paul Parsons (Knoxville, Tenn.: University of Tennessee Press, 1989). A serious analysis of the selection process inside the world of university press publishing. Traces the steps from manuscript acquisition all the way through final approval by the press's publishing committee.

Golden Multitudes, by Frank Luther Mott (New York: R.R. Bowker Company, 1947). A history of publishing but also a literary history of the bestsellers from 1662 to 1945.

Great Books and Book Collectors, by Alan G. Thomas (London: Spring Books, 1975). The jacket copy is accurate: A gloriously illustrated account of some of the world's greatest books, their creation and survival, and the men who were responsible for them.

A Guide to Book Publishing, revised edition, by Datus C. Smith, Jr. (Seattle, Wash.: University of Washington Press, 1989). An excellent, step-by-step handbook explaining the field.

A History of Book Publishing in the United States, 4 volumes, by John W. Tebbel (New York: R.R. Bowker Company, 1981). An impressive and massive chronicle of the entire industry, the most extensive one written. The first volume covers The Creation of an Industry, 1630-1865. The second volume is The Expansion of an Industry, 1865-1919. Volume three is The Golden Age Between Two Wars, 1920-1940. The last volume covers The Great Change, 1940-1980.

The House of Harper, by Eugene Exman (New York: Harper & Row, 1967). A history of Harper's first 150 years, with both the successes and the failures.

The House of Zondervan, by James E. Ruark and Ted W. Engstrom (Grand Rapids, Mich.: Zondervan Publishing House, 1981). Published to celebrate Zondervan's fifty years (in 1981) of book publishing. The firm has made an important contribution not only to religious trade publishing in particular but more broadly to the Christian world in general. Zondervan in large part carried the rapid growth of evangelical Christian publishing throughout the sixties and seventies. The company is now a division of HarperCollins Publishers.

How To Get the Right Job in Publishing, by William H. Scherman (Chicago: Contemporary Books, Inc., 1983). An in-depth look at book, magazine, and newspaper publishing, with a view to getting, keeping, and advancing in your chosen job. Discusses what jobs are available, what aptitudes are needed for them, how to approach publishers regarding the position you want, and how to advance after landing entry-level work.

How To Break Into Publishing, by Roberta Morgan (New York: Barnes & Noble Books, 1980). Publishing is a profession that attracts large numbers of bright people who are intellectually, literarily, and artistically inclined. This is a career guide to the many positions in the field.

The Huenefeld Guide to Book Publishing, 5th edition, by John Huenefeld (Bedford, Mass.: Mills & Sanderson,

Publishers, 1993). In a complete, readable, and practical way, this covers the small-to-medium-sized independent publishing operation from nuts-and-bolts to overall business strategy.

In Cold Type: Overcoming the Book Crisis, by Leonard Shatzkin (Boston: Houghton Mifflin Company, 1982). A controversial examination of the practices and problems of an industry still in crisis. Advocates the expanded use of computers for analysis and operational control to salvage publishing's appalling inefficiency. Everyone in the field should read Shatzkin's chapter on the economics of publishing.

Indecent Pleasures, by William Targ (New York: Macmillan Publishing Company, 1975). Reminiscences and observations from many celebrated writers who also have much to say about the state of publishing.

Inside Publishing, by Bill Adler (New York: Bobbs-Merrill, 1982). A chatty, "insiders" look at what publishing is all about. Adler is one of the big-name New York agents.

Inside Religious Publishing: A Look Behind the Scenes, edited by Leonard George Goss and Don M. Aycock (Grand Rapids, Mich.: Zondervan Publishing House, 1991). The publishing scene can be a mystery to people who want to write or otherwise be involved in the field. And religious publishing seems stranger yet. In this book, over 30 experts dispel the mysteries and show one how to get started.

In the Company of Writers: A Life in Publishing, by Charles Scribner, Jr. (New York: Charles Scribner's Sons/ Simon & Schuster, 1991). Memoirs from the son of the founder of Charles Scribner's Sons, and the editor, in his later years, of Ernest Hemingway. Scribner also started a line of reference books at his house that helped the firm move away from an almost total reliance on fiction.

In the Web of Ideas: The Education of a Publisher, by Charles Scribner, Jr. (New York: Charles Scribner's Sons/ Simon & Schuster, 1993). Reminiscences of the man who succeeded his father as head of the century-old Charles

Scribner's Sons in 1952, and ran it until after it was acquired by Macmillan in 1984 and ultimately thereafter by Simon & Schuster.

Irving to Irving: Author-Publisher Relations, 1800-1974, by Charles A. Madison (New York: R. R. Bowker Company, 1974). Specific cases that show the evolution of publishing contracts, copyright agreements, and other legal arrangements between writers and their publishers.

The Knowledge Context: Comparative Perspectives on the Distribution of Knowledge, by Philip G. Altbach (Albany: State University of New York Press, 1987). Scholarly study of publishing and the international distribution of knowledge. Examines international copyright, technological developments in publishing, textbooks, book distribution, and more.

Literary Market Place (New Providence, N.J.: R. R. Bowker Company, updated annually). An exhaustive directory of the entire publishing enterprise in this country, including all the houses, editors, agents, editorial services firms, etc. One of the most valuable references anyone interested in publishing can ever consult.

Literature in the Market Place, by Per Gedin; trans. George Bisset (Woodstock, N.Y.: The Overlook Press, 1977). A Swedish publisher takes a broad view of book publishing in its historical and social context and suggests that the progress of the book trade is related to the prosperity and decline of bourgeois society and culture.

Memoirs of a Dissident Publisher, by Henry Regnery (New York: Harcourt Brace Jovanovich, 1979). The publisher of John Dos Passos, Wyndham Lewis, Ezra Pound, Konrad Adenauer, and William F. Buckley gives his own intriguing personal reflections on the history of his publishing house. This will be of interest to those in book publishing and those concerned with the important issues of our times.

The Memoirs of a Publisher, by Frank Nelson Doubleday (New York: Doubleday, 1972). The publisher recounts his early days with Scribner's, and then the founding and success of his own house. Doubleday has many very interesting comments on the famous people he published.

The Money Side of Publishing: Fundamentals for Non-Financial People, by Jean V. Naggar (New York: Association of American Publishers, 1976). This is a report of a 1976 conference sponsored by the AAP, including topics such as working capital, cash flow, operating statements, production costs, contracts, etc.

Now Barabbas, by William Jovanovich (New York: Harper & Row, 1964). Provocative views from the leader of Harcourt Brace Jovanovich on the publisher and editor relationship to writers, booksellers, readers, and others.

Of Making Many Books: A Hundred Years of Writing and Publishing, by Roger Burlingame (New York: Charles Scribner's Sons, 1948). History of the first hundred years of the Charles Scribner firm.

On Writing, Editing, and Publishing: Essays Explicative and Hortatory, 2nd edition, by Jacques Barzun (Chicago: University of Chicago Press, 1986). A collection of fugitive essays and articles done over the years on the common theme of writing/editing/publishing. By one of the truly admired masters of English prose and university professor emeritus at Columbia on what makes good writing, efforts at desexing the language, the encroachment of copyeditors upon an author's meaning, and much more.

One Book/Five Ways: The Publishing Procedures of Five University Presses. (Los Altos, Calif.: William Kaufmann, 1978). A case study of a single manuscript at five scholarly houses—University of Chicago Press, MIT Press, University of North Carolina Press, University of Texas Press, and University of Toronto Press—covering the acquisitions, editorial, production, design, sales, and marketing steps.

Opportunities in Publishing Careers, by John Tebbel (Skokie, Ill.: National Textbook Company, 1975). On the nature of book publishing and how to get started in it.

Opportunities in Book Publishing, by John Tebbel (Skokie, Ill.: National Textbook Company, 1980). The making and marketing of books requires the talents of a great many people—editors, copyeditors, graphic designers, artists, typesetters, publicity and promotion experts, production personnel, business managers, marketing and salespersons, and more. Many writers have found that book publishing offers a creative career in an interesting field. This vocational guidance manual sets the stage.

The Oxford University Press: An Informal History, by Peter Sutliffe (Oxford and New York: Oxford University Press, 1978). A history of five hundred years of publishing that includes British publishing, the international trade, and the New York branch.

Paperback Parnassus, by Roger H. Smith (Boulder, Colo.: Westview Press, 1976). This covers the current (as of 1976) mass-market paperback industry and its relations with the rest of book publishing.

Paperbacks, U.S.A.: A Graphic History, 1939-1959, by Piet Schreuders, trans. Josh Pachter (San Diego, Calif.: Blue Dolphin Enterprises, Inc., 1981). An amusing and engrossing history of the first twenty years of paperback publishing history with an emphasis on the covers of the books. The author, a Dutch designer and editor, finds much commercially bred bad taste but also occasionally original and unique design and art. For those interested in the cultural phenomenon of the so-called "paperback revolution."

Perspectives On Publishing, edited by Philip G. Altbach and Sheila McVey (Lexington, Mass.: Lexington Books/D.C. Heath and Company, 1976). A study of the publishing industry, which the contributors see as the gatekeeper of ideas, the shaper of culture, and the protector of the intellectual system. The global intellectual community depends on publishers to select, produce, and distribute the material necessary to continued dialogue and knowledge dissemination.

The Popular Book: A History of America's Literary Taste, by James D. Hart (Berkeley, Calif.: University of California Press, 1961). Hart is a literary historian who originally published this in 1950. It is a critical review and cultural critique of popular authors and their books.

Publishers on Publishing, edited by Gerald Gross (New York: R. R. Bowker, 1961). 36 publishers offer self-portraits and insight into how publishing decisions are made.

Publishing and Bookselling, 5th edition, by F. A. Mumby and Ian Norrie (London: Jonathan Cape, 1974). A famous history that first appeared in 1930, now covering all the vital issues concerning the book trade from the earliest times to 1970. Records the history of 400 publishers during this period, along with 350 booksellers, all mostly from the British Isles.

Publishing: The Creative Business, by Harald Bohne and Harry van Ierssel (Toronto, Ont.: University of Toronto Press, 1973). This is particularly useful on the business aspects of the book publishing operation, including material on accounting and financial procedures.

Publishing Then & Now: 1912-1964, by Alfred A. Knopf (New York: New York Public Library, 1964). A Bowker Memorial Lecture, this pamphlet contains reminiscences and notes from an eminent career in publishing.

Religious Publishing and Communications, by Judith S. Duke (White Plains, N.Y.: Knowledge Industry Publications, Inc., 1981). This is a rather technical report on the state of the religious communications industry and an attempt to assess its future. Religious book publishing, which constitutes a small sector of the total book publishing industry, is the second largest sector of the religious communications market. Good information but needs to be updated.

Second Impression: Rural Life with a Rare Bookman, by Barbara Kaye (New Castle, Del.: Oak Knoll Press, 1995). Part three of a fascinating bookselling trilogy offering an interesting account of the antiquarian book world and how it survived the war years, as well as English village life in the post-war years. The other books in the trilogy are *Minding My Own Business,* by Percy Muir, and *The Company We Kept,* by Barbara Kaye (Mrs. Percy Muir).

The State of the Book World, by Alfred Kazin, Dan M. Lacy, and Ernest L. Boyer (Washington, D.C.: Library of Congress, Center for the Book, 1980). Papers delivered at a Library of Congress symposium.

The Textbook in American Society, by John Y. Cole and Thomas G. Sticht (Washington, D.C.: Library of Congress, Center for the Book, 1981). 18 papers from writers, critics, educators, and publishers from a Center for the Book symposium on textbooks, literacy, and publishing.

To Advance Knowledge: A Handbook on American University Press Publishing, by Gene R. Hawes (New York: American University Press Services for AAUP, 1967). A guide to the history, objectives, economics, authors, and reading audience of scholarly publishing.

To Be a Publisher: A Handbook on Some Principles and Programs of Book Publishing Education, prepared by the Association of American Publishers (New York: The Association of American Publishers, Inc., 1979). This information comes form the Education Committee of the AAP, and is used in course outlines for publishing training. It includes 30 job descriptions in the field.

The Truth About Publishing, 8th edition, by Sir Stanley Unwin, revised and partly rewritten by Philip Unwin (London: George Allen & Unwin, 1976). A British publisher's perspective on the industry that was originally offered more than eighty years ago.

Two-Bit Culture: The Paperbacking of America, by Kenneth C. Davis (Boston: Houghton Mifflin, 1984). A history of the paperback book, which has made an extraordinary contribution to our social, literary, educational, and cultural life. "The paperback revolution" simply means that more Americans read more books than ever before.

Two Park Street: A Publishing Memoir, by Paul Brooks (Boston: Houghton Mifflin, 1986). An intriguing institutional history of a major publishing house.

Under Cover: An Illustrated History of American Mass Market Paperbacks, by Thomas L. Bonn (New York: Penguin Books, 1982). An illustrated celebration and brief history of "the paperback revolution" focusing on the changing style of paperback covers. For students of culture and the history of ideas, editors, book designers, artists, book collectors, and others involved in the world of books.

What Happens in Book Publishing, 2nd edition, edited by Chandler B. Grannis (New York: Columbia University Press, 1967). More than 20 contributors offer essays in this well known survey of the American book publishing business. Covers creating and distributing the trade book, along with publishing in specialty areas (religious, technical, children's, etc.).

Where There Is a Vision: The Inspiring Story of God's Faithfulness Through Fifty Years of Publishing The Good News, by Muriel B. Dennis and Lane T. Dennis (Westchester, Ill.: Good News Publishers, 1988). An institutional history as well as an inspiring personal story of the founding of Good News Publishers/Crossway Books in 1938 by Clyde Harold Dennis. Today, the company is a major publisher of serious Christian books and a highly creative house that publishes many of the leading religious authors of the day.

Who Does What and Why in Book Publishing: Writers, Editors, and Money Men, by Clarkson N. Potter (New York: Carol Publishing, 1990). A look at the industry from three almost entirely different perspectives—the writer, the editor, and the financier.

Wiley: One Hundred and Seventy-five Years of Publishing, by John Hammond Moore (New York: John Wiley & Sons, 1982). A second interesting history of the Wiley house, one of the oldest publishing institutions in the country, that covers 1957 through 1982—the years many refer to as the golden age for English-language publishers. This one picks up where **The First One Hundred and Fifty Years** leaves off, but this time emphasizing the people in Wiley rather than the books they published. A very well-done institutional history of one of the most important professional, medical, educational, and international publishing houses in the country.

Words and Faces, by Hiram Haydn (New York: Harcourt Brace Jovanovich, 1974). Memoirs of a celebrated book editor.

Works of Genius, by Richard Marek (New York: Atheneum, 1987). A well-known editor writes about the publishing business.

Writing Was Everything, by Alfred Kazin (Cambridge, Mass.: Harvard University Press, 1995). These memoirs will interest all those who cannot explain the hold of books on them. They mix lively autobiography, feisty history, and serious literary criticism from one who has lived the life of the mind since 1934, when at the age of nineteen he became a book review editor for *The New Republic*. He thought then and he still thinks great writing matters. The slight book comprises the Harvard University Massey Lectures in the *History of American Civilization*—three major essays of the author's reminiscences before, during, and after the second world war. The pages are filled with anecdotes on the famous, including Saul Bellow, John Cheever, William Faulkner, Flannery O'Connor, George Orwell, Katherine Anne Porter, Evelyn Waugh, Simone Weil, Tennessee Williams, and Richard Wright.

BOOKMAKING, PRODUCTION, TYPOGRAPHY, SPECIMEN BOOKS, AND DESIGN

American Book Design and William Morris, by Susan Otis Thompson (New York: R. R. Bowker Company, 1977). Thompson covers design and typographic history for the first third of this century.

American Metal Typefaces of the Twentieth Century, by Mac McGrew (New Castle, Del.: Oak Knoll Press, 1993). This massive type specimen book covers every known typeface designed and cast in metal in America during this century.

Anthology, edited by Sir Francis Meynell and Herbert Simon (Boston: David R. Godine, 1980). 23 articles on the history of printing and the modern revival in typography.

The Art and History of Books, by Norma Levarie (New Castle, Del.: Oak Knoll Press, 1995). Lavishly illustrated history of fine books, with a panorama of book design from its earliest days to the present. 176 facsimile pages from books of unusual beauty or interest.

The Art of Book-Binding, by Edward Walker (New Castle, Del.: Oak Knoll Press, 1984). Originally published in 1850, this was the first book written by an American on the subject of bookbinding.

The Biography of Ottmar Mergenthaler, edited by Carl Schlesinger (New Castle, Del.: Oak Knoll Press, 1992). A tribute to the world-famous inventor of the Linotype machine.

The Book: The Story of Printing and Bookmaking, by Douglas C. McMurtrie (New York: Dorset Press, 1989). Originally published in 1943, McMurtrie's illustrated history of the printed book reveals how books came into being, how printing was invented, and how bookmaking came to be a craftsman's art. The author was a well-known typographer and book designer.

Bookbinding and Conservation by Hand: A Working Guide, by Laura S. Young (New Castle, Del.: Oak Knoll Press, 1995). A working guide to hand bookbinding and book conservation. Originally published in 1981, this edition has a revised bibliography and a new list of supply sources.

Book Design: Systematic Aspects, by Stanley Rice (New York: R. R. Bowker Comapny, 1978). This is a well-illustrated manual on all the elements of book design.

307

Book Design: Text Format Models, by Stanley Rice (New York: R. R. Bowker Company, 1978). This resource amounts to an "order catalog" of text typography for designers, editors, printers, and others who specify book typography. With a good range of visual models, this book helps to easily incorporate all the possible variations.

The Book in America, revised edition, by Hellmut Lehmann-Haupt, Lawrence C. Wroth, and Rollo G. Silver (New York: R. R. Bowker Company, 1951). The history of bookmaking in the United States.

Book Manufacturing Glossary, edited by Sharon McClellan (Ann Arbor, Mich.: Braun Brumfield, Inc., n.d.). Gathers from many different sources the definitions for terms commonly used in the graphic arts with a particular emphasis on book manufacturing.

Bookmaking: The Illustrated Guide to Design/ Production/Editing, 2nd edition revised and expanded, by Marshall Lee (New York: R. R. Bowker Company, 1980). This gives a very good introduction to exactly what needs to be known by those engaged in planning and producing books.

The Bookman's Glossary, 6th edition, by Jean Peters (New Providence, N.J.: R. R. Bowker Company, 1983). A guide for those interested in the terminology used by publishers, bookstores, librarians, and book collectors in the production and distribution of books.

Books and Printing: A Treasury for Typophiles, edited by Paul A. Bennett (New York: The World Publishing Company, 1951). Information on all matters typographic that will appeal to the curiosity of editors and writers, along with typographers and technicians.

Books for the Millions, by Frank Comparato (Harrisburg, Penn.: Stackpole Books, 1971). A history of book manufacturing.

A Brief Survey of Printing History and Practice, by Stanley Morison and Holbrook Jackson (New York: Alfred A. Knopf, 1923). Morison and Jackson are vastly important names in this field. This book is dated now, but well worth seeing as a good summary.

Designing with Type: A Basic Course in Typography, revised editon, by James Craig (New York, Watson-Guptill, 1980). Standard text on the five major type categories, with many good illustrations and a helpful bibliography.

Do-It-Yourself Graphic Design, edited by John Laing (New York: Macmillan Publishing Company, 1984). Good overall introduction to the many aspects of graphic design.

Doors of Perception: Essays in Book Typography, by Harry Duncan (New Castle, Del.: Oak Knoll Press, 1987). Insights on designing, printing, and publishing imaginative literature.

Early American Books and Printing, by John T. Winterich (New York: Dover Publications, Inc., 1981). Bibliographic Americana. A republication of the original 1935 edition of this book on books.

Editing by Design: A Guide to Effective Word and Picture Communication for Editors and Designers, 2nd edition, by Jan V. White (New York: R. R. Bowker Company, 1980). Expert textbook help in solving design problems in books and magazines.

Encyclopedia of the Book, 2nd Edition, by Geoffrey Ashall Glaister (New Castle, Del.: Oak Knoll Press, 1996). A new printing of this indispensable standard reference guide to the book, offset from the second edition of 1979. Contains over 3,000 definitions of terms in bookbinding, printing, papermaking, and the book trade.

An Essay on Typography, by Eric Gill (Boston: David R. Godine, 1988). Often splenetic but always fascinating advice on design and the typographer's craft.

Fine Bookbinding in the Twentieth Century, by Roy Harley Lewis (New York: Arco Publishing, Inc., 1985). Looks at the century's leading designer-bookbinders and the various ways they went about their artistic work. With 33 color and 82 monochrome illustrations.

Finer Points in the Spacing and Arrangement of Type, by Geoffrey Dowding (London: Wace, 1954). Fun but idiosyncratic approach to type aesthetics.

Five Hundred Years of Printing, revised edition, by S. H. Steinberg (New York: Penguin, 1974). One of the best single-volume histories of the subject.

Glaister's Glossary of the Book, by Geoffrey Glaister (Berkeley, Calif.: University of California Press, 1979). Good discussion of the various specialty areas that fall within bookmaking and publishing. Includes historical and biographical episodes.

Heritage of the Graphic Arts, edited by Chandler B. Grannis and arranged by Robert L. Leslie (New York: R. R. Bowker Company, 1972). Lectures on or delivered by 23 experts of typography and book design.

How a Book is Made, by Aliki Brandenberg (New York: Harper & Row, Publishers, 1988). This book was designed to introduce children to the world of books, illustrated by the author with colorful drawings of animal figures throughout—representing authors, editors, publishers, designers, production directors, color separators, etc. But if anyone is interested in the various steps that go into the making of a book, and a painless explanation of the technical processes leading to printed material, this is actually a surprisingly thorough introduction.

How Typography Works (and Why It Is Important), by Fernand Baudin (New York: Design Press, 1988). A practical but learned and enlightening book. Shows that while the technology of typography is very sophisticated, the education level in the field is quite low.

The Ideal Book, by William Morris, edited by William S. Peterson (Berkeley, Calif.: University of California Press, 1982). As a printer and founder of the Kelmscott Press (in 1891), William Morris produced many beautiful books. The craft of bookmaking owes much to Morris. This book contains all the known writings of Morris on the book arts, as well as photographs of books and medieval manuscripts he referred to, and four interviews on his work as a printer.

The Illustrated Book: Its Art and Craft, by Diana Klemin (New York: Clarkson N. Potter, 1970). A highly respected art director surveys and critiques the work and methods of 74 book artists.

In Print: Text and Type, by Alex Brown (New York: Watson-Guptill, 1989). Excellent analysis of typefaces and strong coverage on all the new technologies in the field of typography. This book would be particularly useful for writers and editors and other non-specialists who need to understand typography.

Introduction to Typography, by Oliver Simon (London: Faber and Faber, 1946). A classic introductory text on the essentials of book design and type that is appropriate for writers, editors, production specialists, designers, and all others who work with books.

James A. Michener's Writer's Handbook: Explorations in Writing and Publishing, by James A. Michener (New York: Random House, 1992). Michener describes the steps in creating a book—from the idea stage through self-editing through the editing and publishing process through production—and shares the secrets of his success.

Lettering Design: Form and Skill in the Design and Use of Letters, by Michael Harvey (New York: Bonanza Books, 1975). Analytical approach to letterforms, with practical teaching on the shapes of letters and how they should go together.

Letters of Credit: A View of Type Design, by Walter Tracy (Boston: David R. Godine, Publisher, Inc., 1986). Tracy helps one understand what makes type beautiful, aesthetic, and legible.

Of the Decorative Illustration of Books Old and New, by Walter Crane (London: Bracken Books, 1984). Originally published in 1896, this book is full of wonderful illustrations. Crane gives special attention to the decorative art actually designed for book pages, rather than photography or engravings, or other illustrations tipped in after being printed separately.

Photo Typesetting: A Design Manual, by James Craig (New York: Watson-Guptill, 1978). Companion volume to the author's Designing with Type.

Pocket Pal: A Graphic Arts Production Handbook, 13th edition (New York: International Paper Company, 1983). Brief but invaluable guide to all aspects of book production. This has been a favorite among artists, designers, advertisers, and buyers of printing since it first appeared in 1934.

Preparing Art and Camera Copy for Printing: Contemporary Procedures and Techniques for Mechanicals and Related Copy, by Henry C. Latimer (New York: McGraw-Hill Book Company, 1977). This book is a step-by-step manual for the working artist and book production manager on how to prepare art and copy for all the printing processes.

Printing and Promotion Handbook, 3rd edition, by Daniel Melcher and Mary Larrick (New York: McGraw Hill Book Company, 1966). Alphabetically arranged terminology in the book printing, production, and marketing fields.

Printing for Pleasure, by John Ryder (Chicago: Regnery Gateway, 1977). A great book for anyone interested in letterpress printing as a hobby.

Printing Types: Their History, Forms and Use, 2 vols., by Daniel Berkeley Updike (New York: Dover Publications, Inc., 1980). Originally published by Harvard University Press in 1922. With more than a thousand pages and with over 300 illustrations of types covering a 500-year span, Updike's volume is the definitive work on letterforms in printing.

Production for the Graphic Designer, by James Craig (New York: Watson-Guptill, 1974). This is a manual on all the different stages in print production, from typesetting and imposition to folding and binding.

Production Planning and Repro Mechanicals for Offset Printing, by Henry C. Latimer (New York: McGraw-Hill Book Company, 1980). A guide to the most effective use of printers, typographers, and other production services. Offers comprehensive and useable help on offset printing (a widely-used printing process in advertising and book publishing) to artists, editors, and others.

Rookledge's International Typefinder, by Christopher Perfect and Gordon Rookledge (New York: PBC International, 1986). Shows how to identify type by category, by letter, and by alphabetical listing. The Bible of specimen books.

A Short History of the Printed Word, by Warren Chappell (Boston: Nonpareil Books/David R. Godine, Publisher, Inc., 1980). A fast-moving and fully illustrated history of the development of the art of western calligraphy and printing.

The Smithsonian Book of Books: The Book Lover's Guide to the Craft, History and Mystery of Books and Bookmaking, by Michael Olmert (New York: Wings Books/Random House/by arrangement with the Smithsonian Institution Press, 1995). "The veneration of books is of great antiquity. . . . The world of books offers a truly wonderful showcase of human intelligence and ingenuity, craftsmanship and industry through the ages and around the globe." This thrilling volume is a total celebration of the world of writing, bookmaking, bookselling, intellectual creation, culture, and book lore. The Smithsonian Institution has produced a magnificent coffee-table book with text by Shakespearean scholar Olmert and over 350 photographs—most in beautiful full-color.

Tips on Type, by Bill Gray (New York: Van Nostrand Reinhold, 1983). Good tips for typography in ad copy and layout.

Twentieth Century Type Designers, by Sebastian Carter (New York: Taplinger, 1987). Many consider this to be the best biographical history of and general introduction to 20th century typography. Includes such figures as Goudy, Morison, Rogers, Wiggins, and Zapf.

Type Faces for Bookwork and Display, compiled by the Billing Group (London: Billing & Sons Limited, n.d.). A book of specimens for publishers and print-buyers that presents the full range and variety of type faces and sizes. Also a great volume for the student of typography.

Type Foundries of America and Their Catalogs, by Maurice Annenberg (New Castle, Del.: Oak Knoll Press, 1994). Originally published in 1975, this book contains historical information on each foundry, a list of their specimen books with size and number of pages, and interesting historical and typographical information.

Typography: How to Make It Most Legible, by Rolf F. Rehe (Carmel, Ind.: Design Research International, 1974). Introduces the scientific literature on type design, and proposes type rules based on some psychological studies.

Using Type Right, by Philip Brady (Cincinnati, Ohio: North Light Books, 1988). This book focuses mainly on practical solutions to type design, with entertaining examples of the dos and don'ts. Gives 121 basic rules of typography.

BOOK EDITING

The Art of Literary Publishing: Editors on Their Craft, edited by Bill Henderson (Wainscott, N.Y.: Pushcart Press, 1980). 24 articles from professional editors, many well-known in the field.

Author and Editor at Work: Making a Better Book, by Elsie Myers Stainton (Toronto: University of Toronto Press, 1982). The former managing editor at Cornell University Press gives advice first to authors and then to editors about how to better do their own work, and then get along most effectively with each other. Knowing what may cause problems for an editor is important information for authors, and vice versa.

The Complete Guide to Editorial Freelancing, by Carol L. O'Neill (New York: Harper & Row, Publishers, 1979). A thorough and useful survey of what it takes to be in the freelancing business.

Copyediting: A Practical Guide, 2nd edition, by Karen Judd (Los Altos, Calif.: Crisp Publications, 1990). A lively manual full of professional advice and examples for editors at all stages. Goes from the basics through the bibliography and gives a good overview of the copy editors role in the publishing process.

Copy-editing: The Cambridge Handbook Desk Edition, 3rd edition, by Judith M. Butcher (New York: Cambridge University Press, 1991). Handles the whole range of editorial processes necessary to move from the text or disk to the printed page. Many excellent checklists and examples.

Directory of Editorial Resources, compiled by the Staff of Editorial Experts (Alexandria, Va.: Editorial Experts, Inc., current edition). A compendium of information for professional editors.

Editing Fact and Fiction, by Leslie T. Sharpe and Irene Gunther (New York: Cambridge University Press, 1994). A lively and concise overview of the many opportunities in and the different kinds of book editing, meant both for those who think they want to get into editing and those already working in it.

The Editor and Author Relationship, by Warren G. Bovee (Marquette, Wis.: The Center for the Study of the American Press, 1965). Initially, this was a report submitted to The Magazine Publishers Association, but this is of interest to all editors and writers, whose destinies after all are intertwined. Candid recommendations follow the results of a survey to 100 editors.

Editors On Editing: What Writers Need to Know About What Editors Do, 3rd edition, edited by Gerald Gross (New York: Grove Press, 1993). A superb collection of essays from industry insiders to help writers (as well as editors) understand editing at its best. All writers, editors, publishers, and agents should have this. The chapter on "Editing for the Christian Marketplace" was done by Janet Hoover Thoma.

Editor to Author: The Letters of Maxwell E. Perkins, edited by John Hall Wheelock (New York: Charles Scribner's

315

Sons, 1950). Letters to his authors from one of the greatest literary editors of all time. Instructive for all editors.

The Elements of Editing: A Modern Guide for Editors and Journalists, by Arthur Plotnik (New York: Macmillan Publishing Company, 1982). A fun-to-read, informal guide in the tradition of Strunk and White's *The Elements of Style,* and also an inside look at editing and editorial advice. Writers and editors should have this.

The Expert Editor: Tips, Advice, Insights, and Solutions, edited by Ann R. Molpus (Alexandria, Va.: Editorial Experts, Inc., 1990). The staff of Editorial Experts, an editorial consulting firm, cover many different areas, including setting productivity standards, maintaining editorial integrity, editing "prima donna" authors, and developing writers' guidelines.

The Fiction Editor, by Thomas McCormack (New York: St. Martin's Press, 1988). A superb essay on the art and craft of editing fiction.

Language On a Leash, by Bruce O. Boston (Alexandria, Va.: Editorial Experts, Inc., 1988). Interesting collection of essays examining the nuances of writing, editing, usage, and the English language.

The Levels of Edit, 2nd edition, by Robert Van Buren and Mary Fran Buehler (Pasadena, Calif.: Jet Propulsion Laboratory, California Institute of Technology, 1980). Very useful in the field of technical communication. This brief book analyzes the editorial process and identifies five levels of edit that are cumulative combinations of nine types of edit: coordination, policy, integrity, screening, copy clarification, format, mechanical style, language, and substantive.

Max Perkins: Editor of Genius, by Scott Berg (New York: E. P. Dutton & Company, 1978). A moving biography of a truly great editor, full of interesting background on the book trade. Some of the literary careers Perkins nourished were those of Fitzgerald, Hemingway, Thomas Wolfe, Sherwood Anderson, and Taylor Caldwell.

Scholarly Editing in the Computer Age: Theory and Practice, by Peter L. Shillingsburg (Athens, Ga.: University of Georgia Press, 1986). Looks at the theoretical foundations of scholarly editions, explores the needs of scholars and critics, and suggests ways that computer technology can make it easier and economically more feasible to do scholarly books.

STET! Tricks of the Trade for Writers and Editors, edited by Bruce O. Boston (Alexandria, Va.: Editorial Experts, Inc., 1986). This book collects invaluable articles from *The Editorial Eye,* a magazine focusing on publications standards and practices. The material falls into separate topics—editing (on being an editor, special editorial problems, the levels of edit), writing (tools for writers, the writers' craft, plain English), publications management (running the shop, productivity standards, production), indexing, proofreading, lexicography, and the finer points of spelling, punctuation, and usage.

Substance and Style: Instruction and Practice in Copyediting, by Mary Stoughton (Alexandria, Va.: Editorial Experts, Inc., 1989). A self-teaching manual full of exercises and examples.

The Thesis and the Book, edited by Eleanor Harman and Ian Montagnes (Toronto: University of Toronto Press, 1983). The real differences between a thesis or dissertation and a publishable book are explored by six contributors who are editors, publishers, and scholars. Careful attention to this book will result in improved academic writing.

What Is An Editor? Saxe Commins At Work, by Dorothy Commins (Chicago: University of Chicago Press, 1978). An unusually good survey of the publishing process by looking at one of the outstanding literary editors of Random House who influenced such personalities as Dreiser, Faulkner, O'Neill, Michener, and many others.

BOOK REVIEWING

Best Books in Print: 800 In-Depth Christian Book Reviews from "The Christian Literature World," edited by

Jay P. Green, Sr. (Lafayette, Ind.: Sovereign Grace Trust Fund, annual). A reference volume intended to be used as a guide to book purchases, these reviews all appear originally in the magazine *The Christian Literature World*, and are written by Jay P. Green, Robert H. DuVall, and other guest reviewers. Every year the editors choose 800 of the 25,000 or so volumes in print that claim to be Christian in content and give specific information to help separate the good from the bad. There are 300 categories ranging from abiding and abortion to worship and writing.

Book Reviewing, edited by Sylvia E. Kammerman (Boston: The Writer, Inc., 1978). Twenty book editors, critics, and reviewers offer this comprehensive guide to writing proper book reviews for newspapers, magazines, radio, and television. From short descriptions to the critical essay, everything about reviewing is covered here.

Panic Among the Philistines, by Bryan F. Griffin (Chicago: Regnery Gateway, 1983). A scathing and devastating attack, often with hilarious examples, on the present state of book reviewing and publishing.

Reviews and Reviewing: A Guide, edited by A. J. Walford (Phoenix, Ariz.: The Oryx Press, 1986). This is a collection of essays from 9 contributors providing guidelines for the reviewing of books and other materials from many different disciplines. Covers the art of reviewing, the role of the book-review editor, and has chapters on reviewing in specialized areas (religion, philosophy, social sciences, life and earth sciences, medicine, etc.).

Rotten Reviews: A Literary Companion, edited by Bill Henderson (New York: Barnes & Noble Books, 1995). Consists of insensitive and superficial reviews of books that went on to become justly famous. For all writers who have been dismissed by uninformed, incompetent, and basically rotten reviews.

CENSORSHIP AND THE FREEDOM TO READ AND PUBLISH

Banned Books, 4th edition, by Anne Lyon Haight and revised and enlarged by Chandler B. Grannis (New York: R. R. Bowker Company, 1978). Examines the types of censorship and gives a chronology of censorship from 387 B.C. to A.D. 1978.

Book Burning, by Cal Thomas (Wheaton, Ill.: Crossway Books, 1987). Exposes the hypocrisy of political and religious liberals and secularists who systematically suppress theistic points of view (particularly Christian). They censor conservative ideas out of the media and ban conservative books from the academy, all the time masquerading as pluralists.

Censorship Landmarks, compiled by Edward DeGrazia (New York: R. R. Bowker Company, 1969). A lawyer active in many important defense cases traces the history of censorship adjudication.

Dr. Bowdler's Legacy: A History of Expurgated Books in England and America, by Noel Perrin (Hanover, N.H.: University Press of New England, 1969). Dr. Bowdler once expurgated, or "Bowdlerized," some of Shakespeare's more bawdy passages. This is an entertaining account of how others have tried such things over the years.

The End of Obscenity, by Charles Rembar (New York: Random House, 1968). The defense lawyer in the cases of *Fanny Hill, Lady Chatterley,* and *Tropic of Cancer* describes the trials.

The Flight from Reason: Essays on Intellectual Freedom in the Academy, the Press and the Library, by David K. Berninghausen (Chicago: American Library Association, 1975). Addressed mainly to library concerns for intellectual freedom.

INDEXING

Indexing Books, revised edition, by Robert L. Collision (Tuckahoe, N.Y.: John de Graff, 1967). An overview of the concepts that have to be mastered in preparing a comprehensive index.

Indexing From A to Z, by Hans Wellisch (New York: H. H. Wilson, 1991). Wonderful resource for anyone, at any stage, in the preparing of indexes. Arranged by topics.

Indexing Your Book: A Practical Guide for Authors, by Sina Spiker (Madison, Wis.: The University of Wisconsin Press, 1987). A small manual full of excellent help on assembling index items, analyzing those items, arranging the index, and preparing the copy. Additional material on indexing with computers.

Register of Indexers, by the American Society of Indexers (Washington, D.C.; American Society of Indexers, Inc., n.d.). A list of freelance indexers seeking index assignments.

PROOFREADING

Mark My Words: Instruction and Practice in Proofreading, by Peggy Smith (Alexandria, Va.: Editorial Experts, Inc., 1987). The author offers many exercises in this self-teaching manual on proofreading techniques.

Proofreading Manual and Reference Guide, by Peggy Smith (Alexandria, Va.: Editorial Experts, Inc., 1981). This is a course textbook and individual instructional manual or refresher course on the techniques of proofreading. It covers all the standard editorial marks and how and when to use them, and also provides the important background that proofreaders need to know to understand their role in the publishing process.

COPYRIGHT AND LITERARY LAW

Answers to Common Questions of Publishers on U.S. Copyright Law, by George B. Newitt and Janet M.

McNicholas (Chicago: Allegretti & Witcoff, Ltd., n.d.). Handles questions related to registration and ownership, the scope of copyright protection, and international protection, as well as copyright notice questions, copying and fair use matters, and questions related to dispute resolution.

Author Law & Strategies, by Brad Bunnin and Peter Beren (Berkeley, Calif.: Nolo Press, 1983). An outstanding guide for the working writer. All areas of literary law are covered.

Book Publishers' Legal Guide, by Leonard D. Du Boff (Redmond, Wash.: Butterworth Legal Publishers, 1987). The business, accounting, copyright, contracts, censorship, rights, suppliers, and trade practices side of publishing.

Book Publishing and Distribution: Legal and Business Aspects, by E. Gabriel Perle (New York: Practicing Law Institute, 1974). This is course handbook G4-2673 for the Practicing Law Institute, and has been prepared for their Book Publishing and Distribution Workshop. It is a valuable reference manual for attorneys and related professionals on copyright problems, relations between authors and publishers and publishers and manufacturers, contracts, tax considerations, book distribution and marketing questions, pricing and antitrust considerations, and more.

Copyright: How to Register Your Copyright and Introduction to New and Historical Copyright Law, by Walter E. Hurst (Hollywood, Calif.: Seven Arts Press, Inc., 1977). This book informs authors, songwriters, photographers, artists, and others how to do many practical things concerning copyright notice, and how not to lose their rights and economic opportunities through ignorance of the copyright laws. The book, however, is quite dated on new copyright interpretations.

Copyright Handbook, 2nd edition, by Donald F. Johnston (New York: R. R. Bowker Company, 1982). Thoroughly explaining the new copyright law of 1976 and its complexities, this is designed to offer a general understanding of the law and to provide an accessible format where specific information can be easily found.

Copyright Law of the United States of America (Washington, D.C.: United States Copyright Office of the Library of Congress, 1991) "The copyright law of the United States of America printed herein is the Act for the General Revision of the Copyright Law, Chapters 1 through 8 of Title 17 of the United States Code, together with Transitional and Supplementary Provisions, enacted as Pub. L. 94-553, 90 Stat. 2451, on October 19, 1976." Circular 92 from the Copyright Office, and revised to March 1, 1989.

Copyright Not Copycat: A Writer's Guide to Copyright, by Sally E. Stuart and Woody Young (San Juan Capistrano, Calif.: Joy Publishing, 1987). All writers have copyright questions, and this is a good general introduction to the concept of idea protection, copyright ownership, and so on. But beware, this book is very dated. Since the Berne Convention Implementation Act, which became effective in 1989, the copyright law of the U.S. has been fundamentally changed.

How To Use the Federal FOI Act (Washington, D.C.: FOI Service Center, 1125 15th Street, N.W., 20005). Have you ever wondered how to take advantage of the Freedom of Information Act? This book will tell you how.

Kirsch's Handbook of Publishing Law, by Jonathan Kirsch (Los Angeles: Acrobat Books, 1995). Written by a lawyer and an expert in literary law, intellectual property matters, and the publishing industry. Uses examples from leading publishing cases. This book is an indispensable quick access yet comprehensive resource book covering the full range of legal issues in publishing—idea protection, book development, contracts, electronic rights, multimedia rights, avoiding lawsuits, etc., and legal definitions of such things as defamation, invasion of privacy, copyright, and trademark.

Law and the Writer, edited by Kirk Polking and Leonard S. Meranus (Cincinnati, Ohio: Writer's Digest Books, 1978). Addresses all the questions for the legal problems writers encounter.

The Nature of Copyright: A Law of Users' Rights, by L. Ray Patterson and Stanley W. Lindberg (Athens, Ga.: The University of Georgia Press, 1991). Offers a new perspective on copyright law and the legal rights of copyrighted material. The authors warn against accepting inflated claims for copyright protection that are based on misunderstandings of the origin, the purpose, and the meaning of the nature of copyright.

Photocopying by Academic, Public, and Nonprofit Research Libraries, jointly prepared by the AAP and the Authors League (New York: Association of American Publishers, 1978). This material describes policies on fair use, photocopying, etc., and offers advice on questions often directed to librarians.

A Primer for Book Editors on U.S. Copyright Law, by George B. Newitt and Janet M. McNicholas (Chicago: Allegretti & Witcoff, Ltd., n.d.). Outline notes that cover the subject matter and scope of copyright, the Berne Convention Implementation Act of 1988, and the Visual Artists Rights Act of 1990.

Publishing Agreements: A Book of Precedents, 2nd edition, by Charles Clark (Boston: George Allen & Unwin, 1984). An authoritative and practical guide through copyright matters. Valuable new precedents have been added—for film, television, packaging rights, reprographic reproduction, electronic publishing, and more. The author has worked as an attorney and legal editor.

A Writer's Guide to Contract Negotiations, by Richard Balkin (Cincinnati, Ohio: Writer's Digest Books, 1985). A guide to negotiating specific processes for book and magazine contracts. Good advice from a literary agent on understanding what all the contract clauses really mean, and which are negotiable and which are not.

The Writer's Law Primer, by Linda F. Pinkerton (New York: Lyons & Burford, Publishers, 1990). A good guide to "preventive law" for writers who encounter legal issues,

323

whether they be writers of books, novels, screenplays, texts, articles, or computer programs. The author, an attorney, covers copyright law, author's rights, First Amendment issues, contracts, business considerations (taxes, insurance, noms de plume, etc.), lawsuits, and more.

Writer's Legal Companion, by Brad Bunnin and Peter Beren (Reading, Mass.: Addison-Wesley Publishing Company, Inc., 1988). A practical nonjargony guide to contracts, copyright, libel, and much more.

The Writer's Legal Guide, by Ted Crawford (New York: Hawthorne Books, 1977). Easy-to-use guide for understanding the legal aspects of publishing, negotiating contracts and more.

SELF-PUBLISHING

The Complete Guide to Self-Publishing, 3rd edition, by Tom and Marilyn Ross (Cincinnati, Ohio: Writer's Digest Books, 1994). All the information one needs to research, write, print, and promote one's own book. Appropriate for newcomers as well as professionals who wish to shape their own publishing destiny.

How To Publish Your Own Book: A Guide for Authors Who Wish to Publish a Book at Their Own Expense, by L. W. Mueller (Detroit: Harlo Press, 1976). The whole mystery of self publishing (most call it "vanity publishing") is but one fact: the author pays. The author, who is himself the director of a vanity press, answers the questions most frequently asked by writers who want to publish their own work.

Publishing Short-Run Books: How to Paste Up and Reproduce Books Instantly Using Your Quick Print Shop, 4th revised edition, by Dan Poynter (Santa Barbara, Calif.: Para Publishing, 1987). Going from typesetting to a finished book, this shows the self-publisher how to set type, paste up camera-ready copy, print economically, and bind books for "instant book production."

The Publish-It-Yourself Handbook: Literary Tradition and How-To, revised edition, edited by Bill Henderson (Wainscott, N.Y.: Pushcart Press, 1980). Anthology of articles, all by self publishers, describing the process of publishing your own work—when to do it, when not to do it, and how to do it—without commercial or vanity publishers. The hazards and rewards are spelled out.

BOOK MARKETING, DISTRIBUTION, DIRECT MAIL/MARKETING, AND ADVERTISING

The American Book Trade Directory (New York: R. R. Bowker Company, annual). Complete listing of the retail and wholesale book outlets in the United States and Canada. Contains invaluable information on specialty booksellers, size of outlet, paperback and remainder distributors, publishers and imprints, and much more.

The Basics of Book Marketing for Professional and Scholarly Publishing, prepared by the Marketing Committee, Professional and Scholarly Division, The Association of American Publishers (New York: The Association of American Publishers, Inc., 1988). A brief overview of the book marketplace and the elements of book marketing.

Book Buyers Handbook (New York: American Booksellers Association, annual). Directory of American publishers, with all their dealer terms and arrangements. Produced by the ABA for ABA booksellers.

Book Distribution in the United States: Issues and Perspectives, by Arthur Anderson & Company (New York: Book Industry Study Group, 1982). Covers the whole field, from the physical movement of books through inventory control and returns.

The Book Industry in Transition: An Economic Study of Book Distribution and Marketing, by Benjamin Compaigne (White Plains, N.Y.: Knowledge Industry Publications, Inc., 1978). A good though now somewhat dated compendium of the important statistics.

Book Marketing: A Guide to Intelligent Distribution, by Michael Scott Cain (Paradise, Calif.: Dustbooks, 1981). A concise survey of book marketing, with an interesting "revisionist history" of bookselling in the United States.

Book Marketing Handbook, 2 vols., by Nat G. Bodian (New York: R. R. Bowker Company, 1980 [vol 1] and 1983 [vol 2]). Over 500 numbered topics in the first volume and hundreds of studies and case histories in volume two provide a wealth of information on the sale and promotion of academic and professional books. All types of professional and scholarly publishing is included, while showing how various book and journal markets differ.

Book Marketing Made Easier, by John Kremer (Fairfield, Ia.: Ad-Lib Publications, 1986). Provides over 70 forms and records needed to carry out an effective marketing program for books.

Book Marketing Opportunities: A Directory of Book Wholesalers, Distributors, Chain Stores, Clubs, Catalogs, Reviewers, and Other Book Marketing Channels, by John Kremer, Marie Kiefer, and Bob McIlvride (Fairfield, Ia.: Ad-Lib Publications, 1986). Lists over 3,000 key contacts for the major new and used book marketing channels.

Bookselling in America and the World, by Charles Anderson (New York: Times Books, 1975). This book was prepared for the American Booksellers Association (75 years old in 1975) and presents the history of the American Booksellers Association and bookselling generally.

The Complete Direct Mail List Handbook: Everything You Need to Know About Lists and How to Use Them for Greater Profit, by Ed Burnett (Englewood Cliffs, N.J.: Prentice-Hall , Inc., 1988). The mailing list—not the copy and not the graphics—is the most important thing when it comes to getting a strong response in a direct mail campaign. This massive book is a guide to mastering the mathematics of testing mailing lists.

Complete Handbook of Profitable Marketing Research Techniques, by Robert P. Vichas (Englewood Cliffs, N.J.:

Prentice-Hall, Inc., 1982). A handbook on scientific market research, corporate policy, and strategy formulation. Many tips for decision-making, including 150 specific sources of information, statistics, and marketing data, and where to find hundreds of additional sources on competitors, markets, and customers.

Copywriter's Handbook: A Practical Guide for Advertising and Promotion of Specialized and Scholarly Books and Journals, by Nat G. Bodian (Philadelphia: Institute for Scientific Information Press, 1984). Hundreds of usable tips on successful copywriting for all involved in any aspect of specialized publishing.

Direct Mail Copy that Sells!, by Herschell Gordon Lewis (Englewood Cliffs, N.J., 1984). A well-respected direct mail and mass communications specialist teaches how to write effective sales copy. Very applicable for selling books via direct mail.

Direct Mail/Marketing Manual, 2 vols, assembled by the Manual Advisory Committee for Members of the DMMA (New York: Direct Mail/Marketing Association, Inc., 1984). A definitive source of direct marketing information containing practical instructional material for every department or operational function within a company's marketing structure.

Direct Mail Strategies for Sales and Marketing Executives, by Ed McLean (New York: Sales and Marketing Management Publications, 1978). An excellent resource for those in publishing responsible for the marketing and sale of books. Presents in a programmed learning format what direct mail can do for you, how to get a direct mail program started, how to learn about your market and your customers, what you should know about lists and tests, and how to evaluate results.

Formaides for Direct Response Marketing, compiled by the Ad-Lib Consultants (Fairfield, Ia.: Ad-Lib Publications,1983). Forms, sample letters, charts, formulas, and procedures to make book sales through mail order easy and effective.

The Greatest Direct Mail Sales Letters of All Time, by Richard S. Hodgson (Chicago: The Dartnell Corporation, 1986). Direct mail marketers from all over the country have provided samples of what they consider the all-time best direct mail letters done by the best direct response copywriters of today. Also contains samples (of the good and the bad) from the author's personal files of over 50 years.

Guts: Advertising From the Inside Out, by John Lyons (New York: AMACOM/American Management Association, 1987). A "street-smart" primer on what works and what doesn't work in advertising from one who has helped create some of the country's great ad campaigns.

How To Be Your Own Advertising Agency, by Bert Holtje (New York: McGraw-Hill Book Company, 1981). Instruction on how to set up, staff, and run your own in-house agency. Creating your own advertising agency is more practical than it may seem, and can lead to increased profit, reduced expenses, and more control over creative input.

How to Make Money Publishing Books, by John Huenefeld (Bedford, Mass.: Vinebrook Productions, Inc., 1974). A reference guide mainly for managers of small book publishing houses.

How to Make Your Advertising Twice as Effective at Half the Cost, by Herschell Gordon Lewis (Englewood Cliffs, N.J.: Prentice-Hall, Inc., 1986). A well-known and respected copywriter gives specific strategies for boosting the impact of ads while cutting their cost.

Marketing Books and Journals, by Pamela Spence Richards (Phoenix, Ariz.: Oryx Press, 1985). Excellent small volume for those involved especially in specialized publishing seeking overseas markets.

The Marketing Imagination, by Theodore Levitt (New York: The Free Press/Macmillan, Inc., 1983). The author, a professor at the Harvard Business School, is a widely respected figure in the marketing field. His book is full of expert advice on developing a clearly focused marketing strategy that is firm, intelligent, and creative.

The Marketing Plan: How to Prepare and Implement It, by William M. Luther (New York: AMACOM/American Management Association Book Division, 1982). A valuable tool to help clarify goals, pinpoint concrete objectives, develop a practical marketing plan, and produce ads that sell.

Olgilvy On Advertising, by David Olgilvy (New York: Vintage Books/Random House, Inc., 1985). From the author of *Confessions of an Advertising Man,* who *Time* magazine calls "the most sought-after wizard in the advertising business," this book is for people who know very little about advertising but need to know something.

101 Ways to Market Your Books: For Publishers and Authors, by John Kremer (Fairfield, Ia.: Ad-Lib Publications, 1986). From planning to design to advertising, this book gives 101 ideas, tips, and suggestions on how to market your book titles—with real examples showing how other publishing houses have done it.

1001 Ways to Market Your Books: For Authors and Publishers, by John Kremer (Fairfield, IA.: Ad-Lib Publications, 1989). 900 more ideas for marketing books, illustrated with real-life examples.

The Publisher's Direct Mail Handbook, by Nat G. Bodian (Philadelphia: ISI Press, 1987). This book presents great ideas for all those involved in publishing on the ways to approach specific markets through direct mail promotion, how to do testing, how to assemble the best formats and mailing lists, how to plan catalogs, etc.

Successful Direct Marketing Methods, 2nd edition, by Bob Stone, (Chicago: Crain Books, 1979). Many publishing houses have found direct marketing a complement to their normal marketing methods. This is a practical and comprehensive introduction to the direct marketing industry.

Systematic Approach to Advertising Creativity, by Stephen Baker (New York: McGraw-Hill Book Company, 1979). Advice on reaching creative solutions to advertising problems. Excellent ideas not only for advertising managers, but book artists, editors, and writers.

Tested Advertising Methods, 4th edition, by John Caples (Englewood Cliffs, N.J.: Prentice-Hall, Inc., 1979). The cover copy for this book reads, "Here are all the proven selling techniques that remove guesswork from advertising, making it a science of sure results." Not quite, but this standard guide on tested advertising methods gets close.

Trade Book Marketing: A Practical Guide, edited by Robert A. Carter (New York: R. R. Bowker Company, 1983). A helpful overview of current marketing practices and procedures, and a must for anyone concerned with selling books—editors as much as marketers and sales personnel.

The Writer's Guide to Self-Promotion and Publicity, by Elane Feldman (Cincinnati, Ohio: Writer's Digest Books, 1990). How to get attention for your writing.

Zondervan Author Guide to Book Promotion, compiled by the Media Relations Department of Zondervan Publishing House (Grand Rapids, Mich., 1994). A booklet meant primarily for Zondervan authors wanting to help coordinate publicity efforts in the promotion of their book. But this is a good introduction to the publicity process as team effort.

BOOKS ON WRITING OR FOR WRITERS

Acts: A Writer's Reflections on the Church, Writing, and His Own Life, by Larry Woiwode (San Francisco: HarperSanFrancisco, 1993). A narrative tour of the New Testament book of Acts with reflections on how far the Church has moved from the original infant Church recorded there. Woiwode uses Acts as a window through which he views writing and storytelling generally (as forms of teaching).

The Art of Fiction: Notes on Craft for Young Writers, by John Gardner (New York: Random House, 1991). The author breaks fiction down into its basic components: plot, character, sentence structure, and diction. He then shows how these are assembled to produce a novel.

The Art of Persuasion, by Steward LaCasce and Terry Belanger (New York: Charles Scribner's Sons, 1972). The authors show speakers and writers how to use the psychological techniques of persuasion.

The Associated Press Guide to Good Writing, by Rene J. Cappon (Reading, Mass.: Addison-Wesley Publishing Company, 1982). The how-to on reports, stories, articles, and presentations from the world's largest newsgathering organization.

The Author and His Publisher, by Siegfried Unseld; trans. Hunter Hannum and Hildegarde Hannum (Chicago: The University of Chicago Press, 1980). The author, who directs the major German literary publishing house Suhrkamp Verlag, writes about the author-publisher relationship. He closely examines four writers (Hermann Hesse, Bertolt Brecht, Rainer Maria Rilke, and Robert Walser) and their publishers and shows that the author's personality can affect the publisher's reaction.

Authors by Profession, 2 vols, by Victor Bonham-Carter (Los Altos, Calif.: William Kaufmann, Inc., 1978 [vol 1] and 1984 [vol 2]). This work is a history of how authors have practiced their profession, how they have related to their publishers, what professional organizations they have belonged to, their standing in public, etc. The first volume goes from the introduction of printing (about the year 1500) until the Copyright Act of 1911; the second picks up after the Copyright Act of 1911 and goes until the end of 1981.

An Author's Primer to Word Processing, by the Association of American Publishing (New York: AAP, 1983). A valuable overview of information that will help in preparing your manuscript electronically. A painless way to find out what the machines can do.

Becoming a Writer, by Dorothea Brande (Los Angeles: J. P. Tarcher, Inc., 1981 reissue). Here is an excellent look at the process of becoming a writer. One becomes a writer through work, but as Brande points out, the journey is worth the effort. The sections on creativity are especially good.

The Beginning Writer's Answer Book, revised and updated edition, edited by Kirk Polking, Jean Chimsky, and Rose Adkins (Cincinnati, Ohio: Writer's Digest Books, 1993). Written in a question and answer format, this book contains various pointers and answers all the questions beginning writers have about writing and being published. It covers both the book and magazine marketplaces, detailing information about on-line networks, databases, and computers.

The Best Writing On Writing, edited by Jack Heffron (Cincinnati, Ohio: Story Press, 1994). A collection of provocative views on fiction, nonfiction, poetry, the writing life, scriptwriting, etc., and observations on the art, craft, and profession of writing.

Breaking Into Print, by Philip J. Gearing and Evelyn V. Brunson (Englewood Cliffs, N.J.: Prentice-Hall, 1977). This is an excellent "how-to" guide for beginning writers of books.

The Business of Being a Writer, by Stephen Goldin and Kathleen Sky (New York: Harper & Row Publishers, 1982). The authors dish up a "meat-and-potatoes" book, basic and essential. As the title indicates, this work is about the business side of writing, things such as copywriting, contracts, agents, record keeping, taxes and so on.

Career Opportunities for Writers, by Rosemary Guiley (New York: Facts On File, Inc., 1985). Comprehensive guide to jobs in the writing, editing, and publishing fields. Excellent material on trade associations, as well as colleges offering studies in publishing communications.

Celebrating Children's Books, edited by Betsy Hearne and Marilyn Kaye (New York: Lathrop, Lee & Shepard Books, 1981). Good criticism of children's literature, for all who care about the books that children read. For the people who create, produce, and use them.

Chicago Guide to Preparing Electronic Manuscripts for Authors and Publishers. (Chicago: University of Chicago Press, 1987). An excellent reference tool for writers and editors covering all the aspects of preparing manuscripts in electronic form for submission to a publisher.

The Christian Writer's Book: A Practical Guide to Writing, by Don M. Aycock and Leonard George Goss (North Brunswick, N.J.: Bridge-Logos Publishers, Inc., 1996). A practical, easy-to-read, common sense manual, resource guide, and reference book, designed to help Christian writers through the research, writing, submissions, and publishing process. Of use mostly in the nonfiction area.

The Christian Writer's Handbook, by Margaret J. Anderson (San Francisco: Harper & Row Publishers, 1983). Beneficial for all who write articles in general, and for the Christian markets in particular. It goes from style to author's rights.

Christian Writers' Market Guide, by Sally E. Stuart (Wheaton, Ill.: Harold Shaw Publishers, updated annually). A very valuable and highly useful listing of over 850 Christian book houses as well as periodicals, what they publish, how many books or issues per year they produce, what they pay, their publishing guidelines, and how to submit manuscripts to them. Includes writer's groups and clubs, editorial service companies, writer's conferences, specialty markets, information on agents, and more. Good inside knowledge of the Christian writers' market.

Communication Theory for Christian Writers, by Charles H. Kraft (Nashville, Tenn.: Abingdon Press, 1983). Introduces the reader to modern communication theory through the skillful use examples drawn from modern living and the Bible. Helps in overcoming barriers to communication and in moving toward a more effective Christian witness.

The Complete Guide to Christian Writing and Speaking, edited by Susan Titus Osborn (Orange, Calif.: Promise Publishing Company, 1994). 20 contributors help and encourage writers at the beginning and intermediate stages by answering such questions as How do I start? and How can I improve my craft? A summary guide on topics ranging from writing picture books for children to book contracts.

The Complete Guide to Writing Nonfiction, edited by Glen Evans for the American Society of Journalists and Authors (Cincinnati, Ohio: Writer's Digest Books, 1983). One hundred and eight professional writers give a total guide to today's world of nonfiction, including a chapter on writing religion. Massive and worthwhile.

Confessions of a Moonlight Writer, by James H. Cox (Brentwood, Tenn,: J. M. Productions, 1981). If you are a novice and your interest is in writing for the church market, this book is a practical road map and will be valuable for you.

The Courage to Create, by Rollo May (New York: W. W. Norton and Company, Inc., 1975). A famous therapist observes the process of creativity and helps us in our search for creative possibilities. May finds that people express their being by creating and that the apprehension of beauty is a road to truth.

The Craft of Interviewing, by John Brady (Cincinnati, Ohio: Writer's Digest Books, 1976). A very comprehensive guide to getting interviews, doing your homework, and going face-to-face.

The Craft of Non-Fiction, by William C. Knott (Reston, Va.: Reston Publishing Company, 1974). This little book is an introduction to the craft of writing nonfiction material.

Creative Process, edited by Brewster Ghiselin (New York: New American Library, 1955). An older but still marvelous and inspiring collection of essays from some of history's most prolific writers on the theme of the joy of writing.

The Creative Writer, edited by Aron Mathieu (Cincinnati, Ohio: Writer's Digest Books, 1961). This book is a collection of articles from masters of writing on everything from plotting a novel to writing for the theater. Other sections treat the topics of working with editors, writing articles, and practical issues.

Creative Writing: For People Who Can't Not Write, by Kathryn Lindskoog (Grand Rapids, Mich.: Zondervan Publishing House, 1989). Fine insight into the writing life that blends advice, inspiration, and scholarly wit. Covers such things as the wonder of creativity, avoiding looking foolish in print, the writer-type temperaments, a brief history of the English language, and getting published, paid, and read.

Dakota: A Spiritual Geography, by Kathleen Norris (Boston: Ticknor & Fields/Houghton Mifflin Company, 1993). A sensitive, spiritual, and deeply moving book of "good telling stories" occasioned when a writer from New York and her poet-husband return to her family tradition on the Great Plains (in Lemmon, South Dakota) to find her geographical and cultural identity and to build her own traditions and pursue her vocation as a writer. Dakota shows the meaning of inheritance and how the power of words can effect change in the human heart.

First Paragraphs: Inspired Openings for Writers and Readers, by Donald Newlove (New York: Henry Holt and Company, 1993). The right opening can create a work of genius. These 75 selections (from the writing of Tolstoy, Joyce, Welty, Twain, Plath, et al.) prove this is true.

Freelance Writing: Advice From the Pros, by Curtis W. Casewit (New York: Collier Books, 1974). Many successful writers, through the author, give advice on the marketing of all types of writing. Covers research aids, book and article writing, specialty writing, interview techniques, finances, royalties and subsidiary rights, and much more.

The Freelancer: The Writer's Guide to Success, by Dennis E. Hensley (Indianapolis, Ind.: Poetic Press, 1984). An overview of freelancing in the religious market.

Getting Into Print, by Sherwood E. Wirt (Nashville, Tenn.: Thomas Nelson, Inc., 1977). For 15 years Wirt was associated with the Decision School of Christian Writing, and this book evolved out of that experience. Excellent insights on Christian writing from a veteran editor, prolific author, and teacher of writing.

Getting Published: A Guide for Businesspeople and Other Professionals, by Gary Belkin (New York: John Wiley & Sons, 1993). The author-editor relations side of getting into print.

Getting Published: The Writer in the Combat Zone, by Leonard S. Bernstein (New York: William Morrow and Company, Inc., 1986). Shows writers how to deal with the whole spectrum of writers' problems, from writer's block to knowing the right markets to negotiating with editors. Real help for survival in the publishing world.

Getting Published, by David St. John Thomas and Hubert Bermont (New York: Harper & Row Publishers, 1973). This book is a frank and realistic view of what getting published takes. It is not discouraging but it is honest in pointing out that not every writer will get published.

Getting the Words Right: How to Rewrite, Edit & Revise, by Theodore A. Rees Cheney (Cincinnati, Ohio: Writer's Digest Books, 1983). The secret to all good writing is revision. This book shows how one can improve anything one writes by three revision techniques: reduction, rearranging, and rewording.

Getting Your Foot in the Editorial Door, by Thomas A. Noton (Lakeland, Fla.: TCW Marketing Group, 1983). Step-by-step advice on understanding and approaching editors and publishers, valuable especially for beginning writers. The book takes much of the mythology out of the publishing process.

Grace is Where I Live: Writing as a Christian Vocation, by John Leax (Grand Rapids, Mich.: Baker Books, 1993). A poet's reflections on life lived as a writer, and the serious questions Christians must ask who chose the vocation of writing.

Guidebook to Successful Christian Writing, edited by June Eaton and Robert W. Walker (Wheaton, Ill.: Christian Writers Institute, 1990). Complete coverage on the art, craft, and inspiration of communicating the Christian message through the print media. Includes names, addresses, and statements by publishers serving the religious marketplace, terms writers and editors should know, and a checklist to avoid rejections.

Handbook for Academic Authors, by Beth Luey (New York: Cambridge University Press, 1988). Arizona State

University professor Luey takes academicians in hand to show them the business of publishing. Includes how to choose and approach a publishing house with solid guidance on preparing scholarly manuscripts, revising and submitting dissertations, contributing to the scholarly journals, book contracts, seeking permissions, the electronic formats, textbook writing, etc.

Handbook for Christian Writers, 3rd edition, compiled by the Christian Writers Institute (Carol Stream, Ill.: Creation House, 1973). This book is a collection of tips, ideas, and markets for the beginning writer of Christian literature.

How I Write, by Robert J. Hastings (Nashville, Tenn.: Broadman Press, 1973). This is an amusing and inspiring "how to" guide, mostly for neophytes. It is full of illustrations and ideas.

How To Be An Author, by Denys Val Baker (London: Harvill Press, 1952). An older but still very worthwhile slightly tongue-in-cheek guide telling exactly how not to do it.

How To Be Your Own Literary Agent, by Richard Curtis (Boston: Houghton Mifflin, 1983). Written by a literary agent who offers very practical advice for writers wishing to enhance the value of their work by acting as their own agent.

How To Get Happily Published, 4th edition, by Judith Appelbaum and Nancy Evans, (New York: HarperCollins Publishers, 1992). The title describes exactly what the authors attempt in this volume. Writers are told what they need to know about editors, agents, the markets, and much more. Written by two professional editors, the style is lively and interesting, and the information is invaluable.

How To Get Started in Writing, by Peggy Teeters (Cincinnati, Ohio: Writer's Digest Books, 1982). Step-by-step through the writing and publishing process, starting with small projects to help you build confidence as a writer.

How to Get Your Book Published, by Herbert W. Bell (Cincinnati, Ohio: Writer's Digest Books, 1985). Insider advice on how writers should work in partnership with their publishers.

How to Make Money Writing Little Articles, Anecdotes, Hints, Recipes, Light Verse, and Other Fillers, by Connie Emerson (Cincinnati, Ohio: Writer's Digest books, 1983). Shows how various short articles can be a profitable source of income. There is good instruction covering both writing and marketing angles.

How to Prepare Your Manuscript for a Publisher, by David L. Carroll (New York: Paragon House Publishers, 1988). The basics are handled here: spacing, margins, front matter, notes, capitalization, pagination, punctuation, illustrations, etc.

How To Read Slowly: A Christian Guide to Reading with the Mind, by James W. Sire (Downers Grove, Ill.: InterVarsity Press, 1979). Through practical chapters on reading fiction, nonfiction, poetry, and other material, readers are offered counsel on understanding not only what writers say but what lies behind what they say. (Reprinted by Multnomah Press as *The Joy of Writing: A Guide to Becoming a Better Reader.*)

How to Sell Your Book Before You Write It: Writing Book Proposals, Chapter Outlines, Synopses, by Edward F. Dolan, Jr. (San Rafael, Calif.: A Writer's Press, 1985). A good manual mostly for inexperienced writers.

How To Write a Book Proposal, by Michael Larsen (Cincinnati, Ohio: Writer's Digest Books, 1990). Written by a literary agent, this book is an effective guide through each step of writing a nonfiction book proposal to help writers create a professional-looking proposal that will convince a publisher to make an offer.

How To Write and Illustrate Children's Books and Get Them Published, consultant editors Treld Pelky Bicknell and Felicity Trotman (Cincinnati, Ohio: Writer's Digest Books, 1988). What makes a children's book a winner? Why are some classics? The contributors present valuable ideas on constructing stories (getting ideas, beginning a story, planning, and plotting), art instruction (taking a brief, interpreting a text), and getting published (approaching a publisher, presenting your work). All the contributors are experts who have had successful careers in children's books.

How To Write Irresistible Query Letters, by Lisa Collier Cool (Cincinnati, Ohio: Writer's Digest Books, 1987). Practical, easy-to-follow advice on writing professional queries that produce sales for articles and nonfiction books. Written by an author and literary agent, this is practical advice on how to craft persuasive letters that connect with an editor's imagination.

How To Write Non-Ficton That Sells, by F. A. Rockwell (Chicago: Henry Regnery Company, 1975). The title is the gist.

How You Can Make $20,000 A Year Writing, by Nancy Edmonds Hanson (Cincinnati, Ohio: Writer's Digest Books, 1980). Hanson offers a variety of ways to make income at writing.

If I Can Write, You Can Write, by Charlie Shedd (Cincinnati, Ohio: Writer's Digest Books, 1984). Shedd takes would-be writers over the hurdles of discouragement to the conviction that they, too, can be writers. He paints no rosy pictures, but gives a unique blend of instruction and inspiration.

If You Want to Write, by Brenda Ueland (St. Paul, Minn.: Graywolf Press, 1987). A wonderful book about the creative process that speaks to imagination and the great destroyer of the imagination—criticism.

In the Minister's Workshop, by Halford E. Luccock (Nashville, Tenn.: Abingdon Press, 1944). This is actually a guide to preaching, but Luccock has several helpful chapters on writing. His style is well worth studying. Reprinted by Baker Book House.

In the World: Reading and Writing as a Christian, by John H. Timmerman and Donald R. Hettinga (Grand Rapids, Mich.: Baker Book House, 1987). A Christian rhetoric and reader that presumes ethical, moral, and philosophical significance to the art of writing.

Into Print: Guides to the Writing Life, by the staff of Poets & Writers Magazine (New York: National Endowment for the Arts/QPBC, 1995). An excellent and practical resource for writers at all levels offering basic but important information about virtually all aspects of the writing craft, from editorial and contractual matters to how to buy health insurance designed for writers. A collection of the best articles from Poets & Writers Magazine.

Into Print: A Practical Guide to Writing, Illustrating and Publishing, by Mary Hill and Wendell Cochran (Los Angeles, Calif.: William Kaufmann, 1977). How to create a successful publishing project.

An Introduction to Christian Writing, by Ethel Herr (Wheaton, Ill.: Tyndale House Publishers, 1983). A helpful do-it-yourself introductory writing text for those asking the question, "Do I want to be a writer?" Emphasizes writing as a ministry.

Is There a Book Inside You? How to Successfully Author a Book Alone or Through Collaboration, by Dan Poynter and Mindy Bingham (Santa Barbara, Calif.: Para Publishing, 1985). Covers picking topics, how and where to do research, managing writing partnerships, evaluating publishing options, developing workable writing plans, ghostwriting, contracts, editors, etc.

It Won't Fly If You Don't Try, or How to Let Your Creative Genius Take Flight, by Richard Allen Farmer (Portland, Ore.: Multnomah Press, 1992). Because we were all created by a creative God and made in his image, we cannot be uncreative. Farmer offers techniques for harnessing our God-given creative juices by suggestion and exercise.

Jobs for Writers, by Kirk Polking (Cincinnati, Ohio: Writer's Digest Books, 1980). From advertising and book reviewing to public relations and speech writing, over forty different writing positions.

The Joy of Writing, by T. A. Noton (North Brunswick, N.J.: Bridge-Logos Publishers, 1981). Provides principles and illustrations of good writing and applies them to the writing of Christian fiction.

Literary Agents, by Michael Larsen (Cincinnati, Ohio: Writer's Digest Books, 1986). How to get and work with an agent.

Literature Through the Eyes of Faith, by Susan V. Gallagher and Roger Lundin (San Francisco: Harper & Row, 1989). Help in considering a work's purpose and its point of view.

Make Your Words Work: Proven Techniques for Effective Writing—For Fiction and Nonfiction, by Gary Provost (Cincinnati, Ohio: Writer's Digest Books, 1990). Help on refining style, writing description, being subtle, bringing music to words, handling characterization, finding viewpoint, tightening tension, developing credibility, and more.

The Making of a Writer: A Christian Writer's Guide, by Sherwood Eliot Wirt (Minneapolis, Minn.: Augsburg Publishing House, 1987). Where are the gifted writers who will share the truth about good and evil in today's culture? The purpose of this book is to find them, to guide them, and to help them improve their writing by learning how to use words, using the light touch, being their own editors, and learning from their rejections.

Maybe You Should Write a Book, by Ralph Daigh (Englewood Cliffs, N.J.: Prentice-Hall, Inc., 1977). This book has contributions from many now famous authors, such as Isaac Asimov, Saul Bellow, Taylor Caldwell, Louis L'Amour, Joyce Carol Oates, and Norman Vincent Peale. If you want to write a book, here is great encouragement, inspiration, and some basic help.

New England Writers and Writing, by Malcolm Cowley, edited by Donald W. Faulkner (Hanover, N.H.: University Press of New England, 1996). A collection of 25 examinations and appreciations ranging chronologically from Nathaniel Hawthorne to John Cheever, from the former literary editor of *The New Republic* and a lifelong student of American literature. These chapters—on such writers as Eugene O'Neill, Hart Crane, and Robert Frost—are both memoir and criticism. Cowley examines the writer's life and work in the context of community.

The Non-Fiction Book: How to Write and Sell It, by Paul R. Reynolds (New York: William Morrow & Company, 1970). Here is a broad discussion of how to research, organize, write, and revise the original draft of a manuscript. Many good illustrations are used to explain the specific advice given in the first section. The second section describes how the author should approach publishers and agents.

Nonfiction: From Idea to Published Book, by Harry Edward Neal (New York: Wilfred Funk, Inc., 1964). Neal gives the beginner an idea of what he or she is up against in the writing business. An older book for this discussion, but still valuable.

Nuts & Bolts Writer's Manual, by Loma Davies (Fort Lauderdale, Fla.: Cassell Publications, 1991). Presents tools for the writing trade and reviews the basic rules of writing, ways to increase creativity, methods to hook readers, the elements of style, and more.

On Being a Writer, edited by Bill Strickland (Cincinnati, Ohio: Writer's Digest Books, 1989). These intimate interviews with famous writers offer both inspiration and advice. They were taken from *Writer's Digest* magazine and reveal not only technical advice on writing but also delve into the writers personal moments. Some of the writers included are Hemingway, Faulkner, Dickey, L'Engle, Mailer, Steinbeck, and Wambaugh.

On Writers and Writing, by John Gardner, edited by Stewart O'Nan (Reading, Mass.: Addison Wesley Publishing Company, 1994). Gardner was the editor of the literary magazine *MSS*, and was an advocate for higher artistic and moral standards in our fiction. This is a posthumous collection of his reviews and essays on many literary figures, including John Cheever, Lewis Carroll, John Steinbeck, John Fowles, Italo Calvino, J. R. R. Tolkien, and Joyce Carol Oates. Gardner divided writers into five groups: Religious liberals and liberal agnostics, orthodox or troubled-orthodox Christians, Christians who have lost their faith and cannot stand it, diabolists, and heretics.

On Writing Well: An Informal Guide to Writing Nonfiction, 4th edition, by William Zinsser (New York: Harper & Row Publishers, 1990). If you need to brush up on your writing skills, this book is perhaps the first one to turn to. The lively advice is appropriate for fiction as well as nonfiction.

Opportunities in Free-Lance Writing, by Hazel Carter Maxon (Louisville, Ky.: Data Courier, Inc., 1977). Do you have in mind earning a living as a free-lance writer? How do you find and maintain markets for your work? This is a compact guide to opportunities in full-time or part-time freelancing. Much of practical use for both the fiction and the factual writer, particularly the newcomer.

Opportunities in Writing Careers, by Elizabeth Foote-Smith (Skokie, Ill.: National Textbook Company, 1982). An entertaining how-to book filled with anecdotes about famous writers.

People, Books and Book People, by David W. McCullough (New York: Harmony Books, 1980). This is an anthology of interviews McCullough conducted with 90 authors. It is intimate and revealing about what it takes to succeed in the writing field.

Practical Guide for the Christian Writer, by David S. McCarthy (Valley Forge, Penn.: Judson Press, 1983). The author takes you through each step of the writing process from basic planning to hints for getting your manuscript accepted. A positive-attitude approach to writing as ministry.

Reading Between the Lines: A Christian Guide to Literature, by Gene Edward Veith, Jr. (Wheaton, Ill.: Crossway Books, 1990). This is a wonderful guidebook for all lovers of books and reading. Veith shows how to recognize books that cultivate good literary taste, i.e., books that are spiritually and aesthetically satisfying.

Reality and the Vision: 18 Contemporary Writers Tell Who They Read and Why, edited by Philip Yancey (Dallas: Word Publishing, 1990). Contemporary writers the likes of Walter Wangerin, Calvin Miller, Larry Woiwode, and Virginia Stem Owens discuss their craft and pay tribute to their literary mentors.

The Religious Writers Marketplace, 4th edition, by William H. Gentz and Sandra H. Brooks (Philadelphia: Running Press, 1993). The previous edition of this comprehensive guide to the religious markets was full of typos and factual errors, but it did give some good general information on writing opportunities and resources. This is the revised and updated edition with over 1,500 main market areas listed. Also includes short articles offering advice to writers on particular topics.

Right Brain . . . Write On! Overcoming Writer's Block and Achieving Your Creative Potential, by Bill Downey (Englewood Cliffs, N.J.: Prentice-Hall, 1984). The subtitle tells the story on this very helpful book.

Sell Copy, by Webster Kuswa (Cincinnati, Ohio: Writer's Digest Books, 1979). Kuswa offers advice and strategies on writing material that sells.

Spiritual Quests: The Art and Craft of Religious Writing, edited by William Zinsser (Boston: Houghton Mifflin, 1988). This small volume is a great inspiration and treasure trove for writers.

The Successful Writers & Editors Guidebook: Guide to Writing for the Growing Religious Market, edited by Robert W. Walker, Janice Gosnell Franzen, and Helen Kidd (Carol Stream, Ill.: Creation House, 1977). 64 writing and publishing professionals offer a guide that is chock-full of writing and selling tips. (The material that looks at over 300 religious markets for books and articles really is quite dated, but the market listings are occasionally updated in various editions of *The Successful Writers & Editors Guidebook Market Guide,* produced every few years by the same publisher.)

Successful Writers and How They Work, by Larsten D. Farrar (New York: Hawthorne Books, 1959). This older title pulls together advice and tips from many established writers from many fields, including Norman Vincent Peale, Sloan Wilson, Abigail Van Buren, and Jesse Stuart.

This Business of Writing, by Gregg Levoy (Cincinnati, Ohio: Writer's Digest Books, 1992). The cover tagline for this book is accurate: A fun-to-read guide filled with practical advice on building a successful writing career that shows how business can be engaging and satisfying. According to this book, "the writing business" is not an oxymoron.

30 Steps to Becoming a Writer and Getting Published, by Scott Edelstein (Cincinnati, Ohio: Writer's Digest Books, 1993). Covers all the ground between getting started in publishing to getting published. A good "starter kit" and step-by-step program for writing and getting your material accepted by publishers.

Trying To Save Piggy Sneed, by John Irving (New York: Arcade Publishing, 1996). This collection contains twelve previously published short works by Irving, the author of *A Prayer for Owen Meany* and *The World According to Garp.* There are six short stories and three homages. The first three pieces, however, are memoirs and author's notes that offer some interesting insight into the creative writing imagination and the traditional writer's task of self-invention. ("I was in the process of inventing myself. Before I could invent anything else, I needed some practice.") The collection relates in an effective way the author's discovery of the powers of fiction-making. There is a heavy emphasis on the mentors and rivals who shaped Irving's defining obsessions—wrestling and writing. (He compares good writing to good wrestling a lot; "good writing means rewriting, and good wrestling is a matter of redoing—repetition without cease is obligatory, until the moves become second nature.")

The 28 Biggest Writing Blunders (and How to Avoid Them), by William Noble (Cincinnati, Ohio: Writer's Digest

Books, 1992). Written by a lawyer who is also the author of several books on the writers art, this will help writers create fiction and nonfiction that breaks free of mistakes that weigh one down. Noble shows that some of the worst mistakes involve sticking too strictly to the "rules."

The 29 Most Common Writing Mistakes (and How to Avoid Them), by Judy Delton (Cincinnati, Ohio: Writer's Digest Books, 1985). Delton goes into the writing pitfalls that turn editors off, all illustrated by good examples. Includes ample instruction in how to correct the problem to increase your chance of publication.

Wanted: Writers for the Christian Market, by Mildred Schell (Valley Forge, Penn.: Judson Press, 1975). This book has two main sections: The first deals with the writer; the second deals with different kinds of writing. There is a bibliography which is still useful, although it is now dated.

What's Really Involved in Writing and Selling Your Book, by Robert Aldleman (Los Angeles: Nash Publishing Corporation, 1972). This is a step-by-step guide in coming up with an initial idea for a book all the way to seeing it in print. The style is question and answer, and the author knows what he is talking about.

When People Publish: Essays on Writers and Writing, by Frederick Busch (Iowa City, Iowa: University of Iowa Press, 1986). Reflections on the working conditions and frustrations of authors.

The Word at Work from A to Z: A Handbook for Writers and Editors (Elgin, Ill.: The Publishing Center, David C. Cook Foundation, 1993). A compilation of the best material for writers from the quarterly publication *The Word at Work.* Includes dozens of issues, from cultivating awareness to writing with zest.

Write for the Religion Market, by John A. Moore (Palm Springs, Calif.: ETC Publications, 1981). Moore tells how to write specifically for religious periodical and news markets. He demonstrates various way to write a news story, a feature article, how to conduct an interview, and how to develop a personal style.

Write His Answer: Encouragement for Christian Writers, by Marlene Bagnull (San Juan Capistrano, Calif.: Joy Publishing, 1990). An introduction to successful Christian writing full of encouraging devotionals for "literature missionaries" called to write God's answer to the urgent needs of the world.

Write On Target, by Sue Spencer (Waco, Tex.: Word Books, Inc., 1976). Want to read a fun book on writing? This is it. Spencer spins a web of good writing about good writing.

Write The Word, by William Folprecht (Milford, Mich.: Mott Publications, 1976). A guide for the author including information on marketing, writer's clubs and conferences, and agents. Offers advice about word awareness, vocabulary development, finding ideas, and submitting manuscripts.

Write Tight: How to Keep Your Prose Sharp, Focused, and Concise, by William Brohaugh (Cincinnati, Ohio: Writer's Digest Books, 1993). Advice on how to say exactly what one needs to say, using the right word, and providing specific tests for writing so one can begin to check on wordiness.

Write to the Point—and Feel Better About Your Writing, by Bill Stott (New York: Columbia University Press, 1991). The author says, "Have something to say, and say what you mean to say as simply as you can." Wise and practical guide to the effective writing of nonfiction.

Writer to Writer: A Practical Handbook on the Craft of Writing From Idea to Contract, by Bodie and Brock Thoene (Minneapolis, Minn.: Bethany House Publishers, 1990). A very successful writing team explore "the whys and hows of writing." Covers writers tools, building a resource file, contacting editors, self-editing, packaging your material, and more. Includes good anecdotes and humor.

Writers and Writing, by Robert Van Gelder (New York: Charles Scribner's Sons, 1946). This book is a compilation of interviews the author had with many of the best known writers of the first half of this century.

Writers Dreaming, by Naomi Epel (New York: Carol Southern Books, 1993). A fascinating book that shows the deep connection between the subconscious and the imagination. The author, a dream researcher, has elicited from famous writers the details of their private dreams and in doing so reveals not only a glimpse into their minds but insight into the creative process of writing. Interviews compiled with William Styron, Anne Rice, Stephen King, Amy Tan, Maya Angelou, Clive Barker, John Barth, and others.

Writers In Residence: American Authors at Home, text and photographs by Glynne Robinson Betts (New York: The Viking Press, 1981). Photojournalist Betts takes readers on a picturesque journey throughout the nation into the homes of famous writers past and present. Longfellow, Poe, Twain, Faulkner, Sandburg, Bradbury, and Dillard are included, among many others.

Writers, My Friends, by Joyce Chaplin (Elgin, Ill.: David C. Cook Foundation, 1984). This monograph challenges editors and publishers to be active in the encouraging and training of Christian writers in the developing world. Caring for writers (in Africa and Asia) is Chaplin's Macedonian call, and the personal and editorial advice she shares in this material will help all who counsel new writers.

The Writer's Arena: An Anthology for Christian Writers, by Marion B. Forschler, Fannie L. Houck, and Maylan Schurch (Port Townsend, Wash.: Five Star Publications, 1994). 100 how-to articles to get (mostly) beginning writers on the road to publication. Full of tips and insights.

The Writer's Book, by Helen Hull (New York: Barnes & Noble, 1956). The Authors Guild presents this book as a helping hand to fledgling writers. Pearl Buck, Thomas Mann, James A. Michener, and W. H. Auden are some of the 40 people who have contributed to this well-rounded book.

A Writer's Capital, by Louis Auchincloss (Boston: Houghton Mifflin Company, 1974). This is the memoir of a well-known author giving his origin and development as a writer. The title is from the saying, "It has been said that his childhood is a writer's entire capital."

The Writer's Craft, edited by John Hersey (New York: Alfred A. Knopf, 1974). A distinguished writer and teacher offers insights into what it means to live by and for the craft of writing. A galaxy of writing stars give an accounting of the work they do and how they do it.

The Writer's Digest Guide to Good Writing, edited by Thomas Clark, Bruce Woods, Peter Blocksom, and Angela Terez (Cincinnati, Ohio: Writer's Digest Books, 1994). Advice and instruction and inspiration on writing, collected from the pages of *Writer's Digest* magazine (which has been published for the last 75 years). The advice comes from many contributors to the magazine, including Michael Crichton, Joyce Carol Oates, Kurt Vonnegut, Ray Bradbury, John Grisham, Robert Ludlum, Tom Clancy, et al.

The Writer's Digest Guide to Manuscript Formats, by Dian Dincin Buchman and Sell Groves (Cincinnati, Ohio: Writer's Digest Books, 1987). Solid help on understanding the standard formats that editors look for in book manuscripts, magazine articles, short stories, queries, book proposals, scripts, poems, plays, and more.

Writer's Encyclopedia, edited by Kirk Polking (Cincinnati, Ohio: Writer's Digest Books, 1983). 1,200 alphabetical entries to explain writing terms. Has much information or tells you where to get it. Comprehensive reference for all who edit or write, with good instruction on different writing techniques.

A Writer's Guide to Book Publishing, revised and expanded edition, by Richard Balkin (New York: Hawthorne/ Dutton, 1981). Written by a literary agent, this book is a solid introduction to the various facets of book publishing, and includes sections on manuscript preparation, contracts, and so on. Covers every phase of the editor-author relationship. A lucid survey and a popular textbook in publishing courses.

349

The Writer's Handbook, edited by S. K. Burack (Boston: The Writer, Inc., annual). A standard in the field, this annually revised handbook offers about two-thirds of its 700+ pages to articles on writing, and about one-third to markets. You cannot go wrong buying this one.

Writer's Market, edited by the editors of Writer's Digest (Cincinnati, Ohio: Writer's Digest Books, annual). How and where to sell books, articles, short stories, novels, plays, scripts, greeting cards and fillers. This invaluable volume tells you who and where the players are and is a guide to getting your work right in the editor's hands. Many writers regard this as the guide for all of the most used markets for all genres. It is updated annually.

Writer's Resource Guide, 2nd edition, edited by Bernadine Clark (Cincinnati, Ohio: Writer's Digest Books, 1983). Are you looking for time-saving information on zoos, embassies, museums, libraries, government information agencies? If so, this guide is for you. Over 1,600 sources of research information on almost all subjects.

Writer's Roundtable, edited by Helen Hull and Michael Drury (New York: Harper & Brothers, 1959). This is a still useful potpourri of information on writing, writers, and more technical matters.

A Writer's Story: From Life to Fiction, by Marion Dane Bauer (New York: Clarion Books/Houghton Mifflin Company, 1995). A companion to her *What's Your Story? A Young Person's Guide to Writing Fiction,* this book analyzes the artistic imagination and examines the origins of inspiration and the subconscious drives that compel authors to write.

The Writer's Survival Guide, by Jean Rosenbaum and Veryl Rausenbaum (Cincinnati, Ohio: Writer's Digest Books, 1982). This is one of the finest books on the more personal side of writing. The authors, one a psychiatrist and the other a psychoanalyst, deal with the author's personal and psychic life. Creativity, competitiveness, how rejections should be handled, developing a support system, and dealing with success are some of the topics covered in this excellent book.

A Writer's Time: A Guide to the Creative Process, from Vision through Revision, by Kenneth Atchity (New York: W. W. Norton and Company, 1986). A professor of writing and coeditor of the journal *Dreamworks* applies management principles to the specific needs of writers, especially beginning the creative process, using anxiety as a motivating force to creativity—and preparing a writing agenda.

Writing and Selling a Nonfiction Book, by Max Gunther (Boston: The Writer, Inc., 1973). Step-by-step, practical guide to writing successfully for one of today's most receptive markets. Chapters include scope, technique, and style in book writing.

Writing a Novel, by John Braine (New York: McGraw-Hill Book Company, 1975). Braine conducts a tour of his workshop and talks of the tools he uses in his fiction writing. Excellent for aspiring writers.

Writing: Craft and Art, by William L. Rivers (Englewood Cliffs, N.J.: Prentice-Hall, 1975). Rivers's book is a more generalized look at the craft of writing. Although an introduction, it is nevertheless helpful.

Writing for Publication, by Donald MacCampbell (New York: World Publishing Company, 1966). An inside look at the world of book publishing from one of New York's successful agents.

Writing for Religious and Other Specialty Markets, by Dennis E. Hensley and Rose A. Adkins (Nashville, Tenn.: Broadman Press, 1987). Specialty markets for religious and inspirational writers are far-reaching and plentiful. This book details information to help writers produce saleable manuscripts for these markets. Shows how to understand the unique needs of targeted groups, how to query editors, what are the proper formats for presenting various kinds of writing, and more.

Writing for the Joy of It: A Guide for Amateurs, by Leonard L. Knott (Cincinnati, Ohio: Writer's Digest Books, 1983). Knott says that writing for fun, not just for profit, is a worthy goal. He helps readers develop and evaluate their progress as writers through poetry, letters, journals, and autobiography.

Writing for the Religious Market, by Marvin E. Ceynar (Lima, Ohio: CSS Publishing Company, 1986). Good information for the beginner breaking into the field of religious writing and publishing.

Writing in America, by Erskin Caldwell (New York: Phaedra Publishers, 1976). Written slightly tongue-in-cheek, this book will tell one how to be a writer in this country and live!

The Writing Life, by Annie Dillard (New York: HarperCollins Publishers, 1990). A wonderful window through which the writing process is viewed. This will benefit any writer, but it will also help editors understand their writers.

Writing On Both Sides of the Brain: Breakthrough Techniques for People Who Write, by Henriette Anne Klauser (San Francisco: HarperSanFrancisco, 1987). The founder-owner of the "Writing Resource Workshops" helps writers tap into their own creative powers. She says, "It will show you how to make procrastination work for you instead of against you, how to capitalize on times of incubation when your inspiration is at a peak."

Writing Religiously: A Guide to Writing Nonfiction Religious Books, by Don M. Aycock and Leonard George Goss (Grand Rapids, Mich.: Baker Book House, 1984). Here is a full set of tools helping writers at all stages translate the creative imagination into written words. Shares the excitement of the religious book field on an intimate, personal basis with the reader, and offers much good advice about writing and being published.

Writing to Inspire: A Guide to Writing and Publishing for the Expanding Religious Market, edited by William Gentz (Cincinnati, Ohio: Writer's Digest Books, 1982). The subtitle gives the story. From 30 leading inspirational writers comes sometimes essential advice. Covers all types of religious writing.

Writing to Learn, by William Zinsser (New York: Harper & Row, Publishers, 1988). The author of *On Writing Well* shows how to think and write clearly on a wide variety of subjects—and how we can learn those subjects by writing about them.

Writing to Sell, 2nd edition, by Scott Meredith (New York: Harper & Row Publishers, 1974). Meredith is one of publishing's most successful literary agents. His advice to those interested in making their living in writing is directed mostly to fiction writers, but there is much helpful material for the nonfiction specialist as well. Good information on marketing practices, working habits, manuscript preparation, etc.

Writing With Power, by Peter Elbow (New York: Oxford University Press, 1981). This is a manual on the techniques of writing. Even the most experienced writer could benefit from this book.

You Can Tell the World, by Sherwood E. Wirt, with Ruth McKinney (Minneapolis, Minn.: Augsburg Publishing House, 1975). This book is aimed especially at the Christian writer. It is practical and inspirational, offering general guidelines for writing and publishing.

GRAMMAR, STYLE, AND USAGE

The Associated Press Stylebook and Libel Manual, edited by C. W. French, E. A. Powell, and H. Angione (Reading, Mass.: Addison-Wesley Publishing Company, 1982). Authoritative word on the rules of grammar, punctuation, and the general meaning and usage of over 3,000 terms. Extensive bibliography full of research sources.

The Careful Writer: A Modern Guide to English Usage, 3rd edition, by Theodore M. Bernstein (New York: Atheneum, 1984). Written by a long-time editor with *The New York Times*. A concise handbook that handles over 2,000 alphabetical listings of words and concepts that usually give writers pause, covering questions of use, grammar, punctuation, precision, logical structure, and color.

The Chicago Manual of Style, 14th edition, prepared by the Editorial Staff of the University of Chicago Press (Chicago: University of Chicago Press, 1993). This justly famous volume is the standard reference tool, essential guide, and primary authority for all authors, editors, copywriters, and proofreaders. Covers editing, grammar, style, usage, production, and printing. *The Chicago Manual* settles most disputes over usage and grammar and is called "the bible of the book business."

A Christian Writer's Manual of Style, by Bob Hudson and Shelley Townsend (Grand Rapids, Mich.: Zondervan Publishing House, 1988). A complete reference guide that covers all the basic rules of grammar, style, and editing that will be of immediate use to writers and editors in the religious field. Unique because the examples are taken from Scripture, church history, and Christian literature. This manual encourages those who work professionally with words to awake to the significant spiritual implications of our language.

The Complete Stylist, 3rd edition, by Sheridan Baker (New York: Harper and Row, Publishers, 1989). A justly famous textbook by a University of Michigan English professor on expository writing that has been used by many thousands of students since it originally appeared in 1966. From the larger concept of rhetoric to the more focused rhetorical problems of paragraphs, sentences, punctuation, and words. The text does many other things, like survey the advantages and pitfalls of logic and tour the library. An essential reference.

The Crossway Stylebook: A Brief Guide for Authors and Editors, written by the Editorial Staff of Good News Publishers/Crossway Books (Wheaton, Ill.: Crossway Books, 1995). A useful and creative reference guide for all those involved in Christian publishing, covering topics ranging from book production to the proper use of words to proofreading. The Crossway editors offer help and some inspiration in mastering the art and craft of writing.

Dictionary of Bias-Free Usage: A Guide to Nondiscriminatory Language, by Rosalie Maggio (Phoenix,

354

Ariz.: The Oryx Press, 1991). How to avoid sexist, racist, and ageist language, organized in alphabetical order.

A Dictionary of Modern English Usage, 2nd edition, by H. W. Fowler, revised by Sir Ernest Gowers (Oxford: Oxford University Press, 1965). Dated now, but still full of wonderful essays on grammar, style, and language use.

Dr. Grammar's Writes from Wrongs, by Richard Francis Tracz (New York: Vintage Books/Random House, Inc., 1991). As "Dr. Grammar," the author directs The Write Line, an English-language telephone hotline. This book is an excellent guide to the common and not-so-common rules of our language.

English Prose Style, by Herbert Read (New York: Pantheon Books, 1980). A classic on the art of good writing that is compulsory for all writers and editors as well as teachers of composition and rhetoric.

The Elements of Grammar, by Margaret Shertzer (New York: Macmillan Publishing Company, 1986). An authoritative and thorough guide to good grammar and a companion to Strunk and White's *The Elements of Style.* Hundreds of examples of correct grammar drawn from contemporary writers.

The Elements of Nonsexist Usage: A Guide to Inclusive Spoken and Written English, by Val Dumond (New York: Prentice Hall Press/Simon & Schuster, Inc., 1990). A brief handbook for anyone wanting to eliminate sexism from their spoken and written English. Good material on the way to circumvent sexist writing and good glossary of alternative terms.

The Elements of Style, 3rd edition, by William I. Strunk, Jr., and E. B. White (New York: Macmillan Publishing Company, 1979). The most acclaimed and indispensable small style manual. Always have it on hand.

Grammar Gremlins, by Don K. Ferguson (Lakewood, Colo.: Glenbridge Publishing, Ltd., 1995). Handles nagging grammar and usage questions to help writers and editors in punctuation, spelling, grammar, usage, pronunciation, etc. The information in this book was collected through various teachers' groups the author has addressed in many venues.

Guidelines for Creating Positive Sexual and Racial Images in Educational Materials, prepared under the direction of the Macmillan Publishing Company School Division Committee (New York: Macmillan Publishing Company, Inc., 1975). Alerts editors and writers to the mostly illegitimate world of symbols, signs, and signals that transmit detailed directions for the specific gender, class, and ethnic roles we are expected to play.

The Handbook of Nonsexist Writing for Writers, Editors and Speakers, 2nd edition, by Casey Miller and Kate Swift (New York: Harper & Row, Publishers, 1988). Useful and sensible suggestions on avoiding unconscious sexual bias and outright sexist connotations in writing.

The Harbrace College Handbook, 11th edition, by John C. Hodges, Mary E. Whitten, Winifred B. Horner, and Suzanne S. Webb, with Robert K. Miller (San Diego, Calif.: Harcourt Brace Jovanovich, 1990). A classic and easy-to-follow classroom text on grammar, punctuation, spelling, diction, and more.

The Harper Dictionary of Contemporary Usage, 2nd edition, by William Morris and Mary Morris (New York: HarperCollins Publishers, 1992). The authors were assisted by a panel of 136 distinguished consultants on usage. Informative, fascinating, and expert guidance on the latest trends in our constantly-changing language. Good discussion of sexism in language and of effective ways to deal with it. Hundreds of questions on usage, with sharp debates among the consultants.

Harper's English Grammar, revised edition, by John B. Opdycke (New York: Fawcett Popular Library, 1965). A clear and complete introduction to all phases of good grammar, with a blending of traditional rules and later developments. An excellent index allows the reader to go directly to specific entries.

How To Stop a Sentence (and Other Methods of Managing Words), by Nora Gallagher (Reading, Mass.: Addison-Wesley Publishing Company, 1982). A fun and foundational guide to good punctuation, useful for the novice as brush-up. The theme is on using punctuation as a matter of common sense—using the mark that feels right.

The Little Rhetoric and Handbook, by Edward P. J. Corbett (New York: John Wiley & Sons, 1977). From grammar, style, paragraphing, punctuation, and mechanics, to the overall process of effective writing. A great, basic aid.

MLA Handbook for Writers of Research Papers, 4th edition, by Joseph Gibaldi (New York: Modern Language Association, 1995). A new edition of the handbook that has been used by over three million writers. This authoritative manual to MLA style presents a comprehensive guide to preparing research papers, including information on using computers for research and writing and on citing electronic publications.

Miss Thistlebottom's Hobgoblins: The Careful Writer's Guide to the Taboos, Bugbears and Outmoded Rules of English Usage, by Theodore M. Bernstein (New York: Farrar, Straus & Giroux, Inc., 1991). By the author of *The Careful Writer.* Bernstein shows how Miss Thistlebottom and others who teach the "rules" of grammar are sometimes wrong about what makes good English, and especially wrong about accepting certain taboos that lack any historical, logical, or grammatical basis.

Modern American Usage: A Guide, by Wilson Follett, edited by Jacques Barzun (New York: Hill and Wang, 1966). All writers and editors should have this famous and wide-ranging volume on their shelf for constant reference.

The New York Times Manual of Style and Usage, revised and edited by Lewis Jordan (New York: Quadrangle/The New York Times Book Company, 1982). This is the stylebook used by the editors and writers of *The New York Times,* but it is a desk book for all editors and writers. A sure guide (especially for article writing and other non-book writing) for accuracy and consistency on matters of spelling, punctuation, English usage, overall writing quality, and much more.

On Language, by William Safire (New York: Times Books, 1981). Safire, political columnist for *The New York Times*, enlightens readers on proper English grammar and usage, correct pronunciation, slang, neologisms, jargon, the roots of our words, and much more. All taken from his famous column "On Language."

Pinckert's Practical Grammar: A Lively, Unintimidating Guide to Usage, Punctuation and Style, by Robert C. Pinckert (Cincinnati, Ohio: Writer's Digest Books, 1986). Sometimes the study of grammar, usage, and punctuation appears rule-ridden and stiff. This book offers helpful examples, lists, quizzes, and other devices that help clarify usage and reinforce strong sentences and paragraphs.

The Right Word at the Right Time: A Guide to the English Language and How to Use It, compiled by The Reader's Digest Association (London: Reader's Digest Association, 1985). This accessible guide treats usage, spelling problems, confusing words, etc.

Saying What You Mean: A Commonsense Guide to American Usage, by Robert Claiborne (New York: W. W. Norton and Company, 1986). A usage expert who gets behind why a given word or construction is good or bad.

The Scott, Foresman Handbook for Writers, 2nd edition, by Maxine Hairston and John J. Ruszkiewicz (New York: HarperCollins Publishers, Inc., 1991). Lively expert help for writers in mastering the conventions of standard English, including an overview of the writing process, and sections on style, mechanics, usage, research, and writing tools. The handbook has helpful marginal symbols that mark items of composition and usage on a research-based scale of priorities.

Style: Ten Lessons in Clarity and Grace, by Joseph M. Williams (Glenview, Ill.: Scott, Foresman and Company,

1981). Extremely valuable prescriptive help in eliminating the tangled, overly-complex type of prose and in communicating writing that is comprehensible, clear, and precise. The author is a professor of English at the University of Chicago who does not cover all the problems of form and composition but focuses rather on style.

Style Manuals of the English-Speaking World: A Guide, by John Bruce Howell (Phoenix, Ariz.: Oryx Press, 1983). Annotates 231 English-language style manuals from all over the world.

Take My Word For It, by William Safire (New York: Times Books, 1986). The author of *On Language* offers this second volume of advice on words and usage taken from his nationally syndicated "On Language" column in The New York Times.

The Transitive Vampire: A Handbook of Grammar for the Innocent, the Eager, and the Doomed, by Karen Elizabeth Gordon (New York: Times Books, 1884). Intelligent and whimsical guide out of the linguistic labyrinth. William Safire called this "a book to sink your fangs into."

21st Century Manual of Style, edited by The Princeton Language Institute (New York: Dell Publishing, 1993). An alternative style guide that is arranged in a convenient dictionary format and combines the information found in standard stylebooks. Rolls the essentials of the dictionary, thesaurus, and grammar book into one reference volume.

U. S. Government Printing Office Style Manual, revised edition (Washington, D.C.: U.S. Government Printing Office, 1984). For writers and editors who work for government publications, this is the standard guide. But all editors and writers will find it very useful, especially for the list of official government abbreviations.

Usage and Abusage: A Guide to Good English, by Eric Partridge, New Edition edited by James Whitcut (New York: W. W. Norton and Company, Inc., 1994). Packed with historical, cultural, and literary information, along with the basics of grammar, this book steers the reader away from confusions between words and toward clarity and directness of expression.

Webster's New World Guide to Current American Usage, by Bernice Randall (New York: Webster's New World/Simon & Schuster, Inc., 1988). A genuinely helpful book on usage, from grammar and punctuation to the different directions American English is taking into the twenty-first century. Covers the idioms and the slang that have come into the language and the linguistic principles of assimilation. Includes an extensive analysis of current trends.

Webster's New World Guide to Punctuation, by Auriel Douglas and Michael Strumpf (New York: Prentice Hall/ Simon & Schuster, Inc., 1988). All the rules you need to know to punctuate correctly.

Wiley Guidelines on Sexism in Language, prepared by the College Editing Department of John Wiley & Sons (New York: John Wiley & Sons, Inc., 1977). Brief but excellent guidelines for authors and editors to achieve equal treatment of both sexes in the writing of books.

Words and Women: New Language in New Times, by Casey Miller and Kate Swift (Garden City, N.Y.: Anchor Press/Doubleday, 1976). A summary of the question of sex stereotyping in language, with evidence drawn from the language itself.

Words Into Type, 3rd edition, by Marjorie E. Skillin, Robert M. Gay, and Others (Englewood Cliffs, N.J.: Prentice-Hall, Inc., 1986). All those connected to writing, editing, publishing, typesetting—in short, those connected with putting words into type—should have this volume, but especially copy editors will benefit from it. It is a treasure trove of information on countless things, like grammar rules, punctuation, style guidelines, preparing manuscripts, copy editing, typography, and printing, One reviewer called this about a half a dozen textbooks rolled into one.

The Wordsworth Book of Usage & Abusage, by Eric Partridge (Ware, Hertfordshire, Eng.: Wordsworth Editions,

Ltd., 1995). Condensed from the author's *Usage and Abusage: A Guide to Good English* and first published in 1954 as *The Concise Usage and Abusage* this is—as the cover tagline says—the famous guide to good English. A fascinating work by a famous philologist and lexicographer.

DICTIONARIES, THESAURUSES, AND OTHER REFERENCE BOOKS

A B C For Book Collectors, 7th edition, by John Carter, revised by Nicolas Barker (New Castle, Del.: Oak Knoll Press, 1995). Formerly published by Alfred A. Knopf, this is a highly entertaining and basic reference tool containing definitions and analyses of more than 450 technical terms having to do with bookmaking, book-collecting, and bibliography. The revisor is editor of *The Book Collector.*

The American Heritage Dictionary of the English Language, 3rd edition (Boston: Houghton Mifflin, 1992). Highly regarded for its word histories and regional notes. Considered more permissive than other dictionarries. Almost 200,000 main entries and over 500 separate notes on usage.

Bartlett's Familiar Quotations, by John Bartlett (Boston: Little, Brown, 1992). For checking the accuracy of quotations, this is the editor's first recourse. A very usable index that allows one to find a quotation with just a key word or phrase.

Biblical Words and Their Meaning: An Introduction to Lexical Semantics, by Moises Silva (Grand Rapids, Mich.: Academie Books, Zondervan Publishing House, 1983). A thorough, up-to-date exposition of the nature of biblical lexicology.

The Book of Jargon: An Essential Guide to the Inside Language of Today, by Don Ethan Miller (New York: Macmillan Publishing Company, Inc., 1981). Very useful in helping decode the "inside" jargon of fields such as medicine, legalese, rock music, motion pictures, public relations, computerese, business management, sports, and more. Covers more than 500 terms defining the vocabulary of 25 professions.

Books Children Love: A Guide to the Best Children's Literature, by Elizabeth Laraway Wilson (Wheaton, Ill.: Crossway Books, 1987). While this comprehensive guide is meant to help bring children and fine books together, it is extremely useful for writers and editors who work in the children's field and want to see excellently written and attention-holding books on a wide range of topics in both fiction and nonfiction.

A Browser's Dictionary and Native's Guide to the Unknown American Language, by John Ciardi (New York: Harper & Row, Publishers, 1980). The tagline on this book is its best description: A compendium of curious expressions and intriguing facts. Writer, editor, and poet Ciardi goes beyond the standard dictionaries and offers an enlightening and entertaining book for browsing, full of intimate conversation with words and phrases and their origins and shifting histories.

The Cambridge Thesaurus of American English, by William D. Lutz (New York: Cambridge University Press, 1994). A collection of more than 200,000 synonyms and antonyms.

Christian Words, by Nigel Turner (Nashville, Tenn.: Thomas Nelson Publishers, 1982). A dictionary of more than 450 biblical words showing how the early Christians gave new meanings to these terms. Turner shows what the early Christians did mean and did not mean when they wrote and spoke these words.

CIP Publishers Manual, 3rd edition, provided by the Library of Congress (Washington, D.C.: Library of Congress Cataloging in Publication Division, 1994). Introduction to the Cataloging in Publication (CIP) program designed to facilitate cataloging activities for the nation's libraries. Includes the scope of the program, how to join, how to apply for CIP data, and much other general information.

A Concise Etymological Dictionary of the English Language, by Walter W. Skeat (New York: Perigee Books/

G. P. Putnam's Sons, 1980). Over 12,750 entries by the University of Cambridge philologist and medieval scholar that was originally published in 1882. Still famous and valuable for all wishing to discover the origins of words. The word list contains primary words of most frequent occurrence, as well as others prominent in literature.

The Concise Oxford Dictionary of Current English, 8th edition, edited by R. E. Allen (Oxford: Oxford University Press, 1990). With British spellings and the British meanings for words, this is an accessible, authoritative and concise reference tool.

Crazy English: The Ultimate Joy Ride Through Our Language, by Richard Lederer (New York: Pocket Books/ Simon & Schuster, 1989). By the author of *Anguished English, Get Thee to a Punnery,* and *The Miracle of Language,* this book is a highly entertaining look at how logic and consistency are very often not a part of our language, but a crazy randomness is.

The Devil's Dictionary, by Ambrose Bierce (New York: Dover Publications, Inc., 1958). This work was originally published in 1911. It was begun in a weekly newspaper column in 1881 and continued at intervals until 1906. There are over 1,000 separate entries, listed in alphabetical order, and are almost all irreverent and sardonic jabs at the sacred, political, business, religious, literary, and artistic cows in our language.

Dictionaries: The Art and Craft of Lexicography, by Sidney I. Landau (New York: Cambridge University Press, 1989). The authoritative source on dictionaries and dictionary making.

Dictionary of American Slang, 2nd edition, compiled by Harold Wentworth and Stuart Berg Flexner (New York: Thomas Y. Crowell, Publishers, 1975). A vast number of entries on regionalisms and colloquialisms, supplied by Wentworth, with thousands of slang definitions from many different times and places (politics, entertainment, jazz, the underworld, the armed forces, business, teenagers, the sports world, the beat generation, etc.), supplied by Flexner. More than 22,000 definitions.

A Dictionary of Book History, by John Feather (New York: Oxford University Press, 1986). This is a handbook of 650 articles for scholars, editors, bibliophiles, research students, librarians, and booksellers on the history of books, book collectors and collecting, printing and bookselling. Includes notes for further research.

Dictionary of Problem Words and Expressions, by Harry Shaw (New York: McGraw-Hill Book Company, 1975). An alphabetical arrangement of problem words and expressions are described, discussed, and illustrated with examples from actual usage. Will alert readers to faulty writing habits.

The Dictionary of Publishing, by David M. Brownstone and Irene M. Franck (New York: Van Nostrand Reinhold Company, 1982). The peculiar language of publishing includes definitions from many fields, including printing, journalism, art, photography, computer science, sales, marketing, bookselling, the old and rare books field, business and finance, law, accounting, administration, distribution, insurance, library studies, etc. Here is an excellent reference aid to keep up.

A Dictionary of Synonyms and Antonyms, by Joseph Devlin, edited and enlarged by Jerome Fried (New York: Popular Library, Inc./Warner Books, Inc., 1982). Help in finding just the right word for fresh written and spoken expression. Includes 5,000 words most often mispronounced.

Dictionary of Word Origins, by Joseph T. Shipley (New York: Philosophical Library, 1945). Intriguing and authoritative history of words and their derivations for all word-lovers and those fascinated by language. Much entertaining anecdotal material from the editor of *The American Bookman.*

Directory of Historical Societies and Agencies in the United States and Canada, 12th edition, edited by Tracey

Lenton Craig (Nashville, Tenn.: American Association for State and Local History, 1982). This directory lists over 4,000 historical societies, archives, record centers, and the like. Marvelous for historical research.

Finding Facts Fast, by Alden Todd (Berkeley, Calif.: Ten Speed Press, 1979). This is one of the finest guides to fact-gathering techniques in a "how to do it" format.

The Grand Panjandrum and 2,699 Other Rare, Useful, and Delightful Words and Expressions, revised and expanded edition, by J. N. Hook (New York: Collier Books, 1991). All entries are real, existent useful rare words done in a chapter format (with different subject matter for each chapter) with part of the total list of words presented in alphabetical order within each chapter. The author is a verified verbidopterist.

Guide to Reference Books, 10th edition, by Eugene P. Sheehy (Chicago: American Library Association, 1986). Recommends the basic reference materials available throughout the world, with annotated listings.

Hammond Atlas of the World (Maplewood, N.J.: Hammond, 1992). Many think it is the best atlas.

The Harper Dictionary of Foreign Terms, 3rd edition, edited by Eugene Ehrlich (New York: Harper & Row, Publishers, 1987). This edition is based on the 1934 classic edition complied by C. O. Sylvester Mawson. Here one finds definitions of more than 15,000 foreign words and expressions from more than 50 different languages that Americans frequently use in their conversation and writing.

A Hog On Ice and Other Curious Expressions, by Charles Earle Funk (New York: Harper & Row, Publishers, 1985). Funk takes over 400 expressions and sayings that we use in everyday speech and traces the meanings back through the years. By the author of *Thereby Hangs a Tale.*

How and Where to Look It Up: A Guide to Standard Sources of Information, by Robert W. Murphey (New York: McGraw-Hill Book Company, 1958). Dated but still useful to the layperson and novice writer and researcher.

I Always Look Up the Word "Egregious": A Vocabulary Book for People Who Don't Need One, by Maxwell Nurnberg (Englewood Cliffs, N.J.: Prentice-Hall, Inc., 1981). An outstanding manual for people who want to improve their vocabularies. Instructive comments and entertaining anecdotes.

The International Thesaurus of Quotations, compiled by Roda Thomas Tripp (New York: Thomas Y. Crowell Company, 1970). One of the most useful book of quotations you can have. Look for an idea closest to your own thought, and you will find many quotations that put that thought into appropriate words. Arranged alphabetically.

The Joy of Lex: How to Have Fun with 860, 341, 500 Words, by Gyles Brandreth (New York: Quill/William Morrow and Company, Inc., 1983). For word freaks and lexicon lovers. Shows our language can be endlessly fascinating and fun.

Knowing Where to Look: The Ultimate Guide to Research, revised and updated edition, by Lois Horowitz (Cincinnati, Ohio: Writer's Digest Books, 1988). This book is a painless approach to using libraries, finding facts, locating rare and unusual sources, avoiding research traps and dead ends, tracking down statistics and quotes, finding answers to quick-and-dirty questions, and much more. An excellent resource for writers and editors.

Le Mot Juste: A Dictionary of Classical and Foreign Words and Phrases, edited by John Buchanan-Brown, and Others (New York: Vintage Books, 1981). This small lexicon carries hundreds of words and phrases from Greek, Latin, French, German, Italian, Spanish, Russian, and Yiddish that have been introduced into our language but which nevertheless are often confused and misused. For the writer tired of making faux pas and looking like a dummkopf. Phonetic spellings for proper pronunciation are included.

Literary Market Place: The Directory of the American Book Publishing Industry (New York: R. R. Bowker

Company, updated annually). This is an absolutely thorough listing of publishers, editorial services and agents, book manufacturers, publishing associations, book events, courses and awards, and markets. A massive volume and the best resource to the entire industry that you can find.

Merriam-Webster Collegiate Dictionary, 10th edition (Springfield, Mass.: Merriam-Webster, Inc., 1993). The 10th edition is based on a citation file of over 14 million examples of English words. Most publishing houses in the U. S. use this dictionary as their authority on the vocabulary of English, and all editors should have a copy of the most recent edition. It is especially good on capitalization, hyphenation, word division, and guidance on synonyms and usage.

Merriam Webster's Encyclopedia of Literature (Springfield, Mass.: Merriam-Webster, Inc., in collaboration with *Encyclopedia Britannica, 1995*). This comprehensive and authoritative guide combines the best features of a dictionary and an encyclopedia, all focused on the appreciation of the written word. It is an indispensable tool for students, teachers, writers, and editors. There are more than 10,000 entries for authors, works, terms, topics, and movements from all over the world, and includes coverage of all literary forms, including novels, poems, plays, essays, and literary criticism.

The Miracle of Language, by Richard Lederer (New York: Pocket Books, 1991). This book is in praise of English. The author calls it "a love letter to the most glorious of human achievements—our ability to utter words, write words, and receive words." Contains a wonderful gallimaufry on words about words for word lovers.

The Modern Researcher, 3rd edition, by Jacques Barzun and Henry F. Graff (New York: Harcourt Brace Jonanovich, Inc., 1977). This book is a standard in the field of research. The authors offer a thorough guide to fact-gathering and interpretation. Read this one.

More Than Words, by William Sydnor (San Francisco: Harper & Row, Publishers, 1990). This is a dictionary for professional and lay religious leaders, teachers, editors, and others involved in religious education, offering clear and concise definitions on terminology relating to the Christian faith. The book amounts to a primer on Christianity and provides insight, Scripture references, and illustrations.

New International Atlas (New York: Rand McNally, 1993). Another excellent atlas.

The New York Times Guide to Reference Material, by Mona McCormick (New York: Popular Library, 1982). McCormick offers a wealth of resource and reference material useful to any writer.

Not the Websters Dictionary, by Byron Preiss and Michael Sorkin (New York: A Wallaby Book/Simon & Schuster, Inc., 1983). For all who wonder "what does it all mean?" A listing of outrageous words that can be found nowhere else.

The Official Politically Correct Dictionary and Handbook, by Henry Beard and Christopher Cerf (New York: Villard Books, 1993). For both oppressors and victims, this book on the new appropriateness tells you exactly what's okay to say to whom, what you can't say, who says so, and why. It is hilarious, except that when one discovers all the entries come from actual use in magazines, books, speeches, etc., it becomes quite chilling. This book shows that "language is not merely the mirror of our society; it is the major force in 'constructing' what we perceive as 'reality.'" Changing our language means changing everything.

Our Own Words, by Mary Helen Dohan (New York: Alfred A. Knopf, 1974). Fascinating biography of the American language from its Anglo-Saxon roots to the American English we speak today.

Oxford American Dictionary, compiled by Eugene Ehrlich, Stuart Berg Flexner, Gorton Carruth, and Joyce M. Hawkins (New York: Oxford University Press, 1980). Compact guide to American English. Includes slang, informal words, and technical words and phrases.

Partridge's Concise Dictionary of Slang and Unconventional English, from the work of Eric Partridge and edited by Paul Beale (New York: Macmillan Publishing Company, 1990). This work is from the 8th edition (1984) of *A Dictionary of Slang and Unconventional English,* by Eric Partridge. Edmund Wilson said "this dictionary . . . is a masterful performance and ought to be acquired by every reader who wants for his library a sound lexicographical foundation."

The Penguin Dictionary of Troublesome Words, by Bill Bryson (New York: Penguin Books, 1985). Guidance handbook on the pitfalls and disputed issues in standard written English. Also includes a glossary of grammatical terms and an appendix on punctuation.

Playing With Words, by Joseph T. Shipley (Englewood Cliffs, N.J.: Prentice-Hall, Inc., 1960). Word games, semantic antics, rhymes, and puns.

Practical English: 1000 Most Effective Words, by Norman W. Schur (New York: Ballantine Books, 1983). For all who want to use common words correctly.

The Random House Basic Dictionary of Synonyms and Antonyms, edited by Laurence Urdang (New York: Ballantine Books, 1960). Over 80,000 words listed. Great for writers, editors, and speakers.

Random House College Thesaurus (New York: Random House, 1984). Each synonym is introduced in a sample sentence. This thesaurus uses the alphabetical arrangement.

Random House Dictionary of the English Language, 2nd edition unabridged (New York: Random House, 1987). Widely respected and up-to-date.

Random House Historical Dictionary of American Slang, edited by J. E. Lighter (New York: Random House, 1994). A monumental multi-volume dictionary that spans 300 years of American language history.

Random House Webster's College Dictionary (New York: Random House, 1991). Good all purpose dictionary.

The Reader's Quotation Book: A Literary Companion, edited by Steven Gilbar (Wainscott, N.Y.: Pushcart Press, 1990). This celebrates the reader by collecting hundreds of observations from very famous authors on the art of reading. The entries are all excellent sentences and paragraphs that should be turned around in the mind slowly.

Religious Books and Serials in Print: An Index to Religious Literature Including Philosophy (New Providence, N.J.: R. R. Bowker Company). Biannual publication.

Roget's International Thesaurus, 5th edition, revised by Robert L. Chapman (New York: HarperCollins Publishers, 1992). This is the classic thesaurus, compiled according to the plan devised originally by Peter Mark Roget (d. 1869); it is still considered the standard. The text is about 250,000 words and phrases, arranged in more than a thousand categories by their meanings. Also contains a comprehensive index.

Slang and Euphemism, by Richard A. Spears (Middle Village, N.Y.: Jonathan David Publishers, Inc., 1981). The book's tagline has it right: A dictionary of oaths, curses, insults, sexual slang and metaphor, racial slurs, drug talk, homosexual lingo, and related matters. A good reference for being aware of usually-prohibited words and subjects. 17,500 entries and 40,000 definitions.

The Story of English, by Robert McCrum, William Cran, and Robert MacNeil (New York: Viking Penguin Inc., 1986). The tale of the language that conquered the world and is now spoken by more than a billion people. This book is a popular and very entertaining history of the language and a companion to the PBS television series of the same name.

Studies In Words, 2nd edition, by C. S. Lewis (Cambridge, Eng.: Cambridge University Press, 1967; Canto imprint edition 1990). *Studies In Words* explores the nature and implication of language and the theory of meaning by taking a series of words and "teasing out their connotations using examples from a vast range of English literature, recovering lost meanings, and analysing their functions." This is a brilliant and entertaining study of the pleasures and problems of verbal communication. The point of view is philological, lexical, historical, and scholarly (but this is as absorbing as all Lewis' writing).

The Superior Person's Book of Words, by Peter Bowler (Boston: David R. Godine, Publisher, 1985). To provide the man or woman in the street with better verbal weapons so they can become superior people—whose vocabulary is "a badge of rank as compelling as a top hat or a painted forehead." 500 outrageous entries.

The Superior Person's Second Book of Weird and Wondrous Words, by Peter Bowler (Boston: David R. Godine, Publisher, 1992). 600 new words as outlandish as the ones in the previous volume.

The Survivor's Guide to Library Research, by William B. Badke (Grand Rapids, Mich.: 1990). A librarian shows that library research need not strike terror into one's heart. He helps researchers and writers overcome fear by providing simple guidelines that take control of the research process by working with the specific topic, organizing notes and bibliographical information, using a systematic strategy to approach the library, and actually doing the writing.

The Synonym Finder, revised edition, by J. I. Rodale and revised by Laurence Urdang, Nancy LaRoche, and Others (Emmaus, Penn.: Rodale Press, 1978). This has over 1,000,000 synonyms and makes a marvelous companion for writers, editors, speakers, students, and teachers. The book abounds, teems, flourishes, overflows with helpful entries.

Thereby Hangs a Tale: Stories of Curious Word Origins, by Charles Earle Funk (New York: Harper & Row, Publishers, 1985). Examines hundreds of words in common English that acquired their meanings in strange and unusual ways. Written by an authority on word and phrase origins.

Thesaurus of Alternatives to Worn-Out Words and Phrases, by Robert Hartwell Fiske (Cincinnati, Ohio: Writer's Digest Books, 1994). Help in getting rid of moribund metaphors, torpid terms, and wretched redundancies. This book offers many good replacements for shopworn expressions, with advice on how to keep your writing fresh.

United States Government Organizational Manual (Washington, D.C.: U. S. Government Printing Office, annual). Updated annually, this book gives background information on each of the government's various agencies. It has a list of names, addresses, and phone numbers of the press officers of those agencies.

Valsalva's Maneuver: Mots Justes and Indispensable Terms, by John Train (New York: Harper & Row, Publishers, 1989). The author himself describes this funny and essential little handbook as a guide to "elegant word-dropping." As for Valsalva's maneuver, it is when one holds one's nose and blows out one's cheeks in an elevator or airplane to relieve pressure in the ears.

Webster's New Biographical Dictionary (Springfield, Mass.: Merriam-Webster, Inc., 1988). Short biographies of nonliving persons. Excellent for quickly checking facts, dates, spellings, etc.

Webster's Ninth New Collegiate Dictionary (Springfield, Mass.: Merriam-Webster, Inc., 1983). The abridged version of *Webster's Third New International Dictionary of the English Language.*

Webster's New Dictionary of Synonym: A Dictionary of Discriminated Synonyms with Antonyms and Analogous and Contrasted Words, 2nd edition (Springfield, Mass.: Merriam-Webster, Inc., 1984). Every word discussed in an article is entered into its own alphabetical place, followed by a list of synonyms, and most often attended by quotations from classic as well as contemporary writers to illustrate their meanings.

Webster's New Geographical Dictionary, revised edition (Springfield, Mass.: Merriam-Webster, Inc., 1988). Handy reference for place names, alternative names, and former names.

Webster's New World Dictionary of American English, 3rd edition (New York: Prentice Hall/Simon & Schuster, Inc., 1991). Noted for its sharp and concise definitions.

Webster's Third New International Dictionary of the English Language, unabridged (Springfield, Mass.: Merriam-Webster, Inc., 1961). Extensive, comprehensive, and authoritative. Maybe the best unabridged dictionary.

When Is a Pig a Hog? A Guide to Confoundingly Related English Words, by Bernice Randall (New York: Prentice Hall/Simon & Schuster, Inc., 1991). The answer is, when it weighs more than 120 pounds. A pig is an immature swine weighing less. Answers hundreds of language questions.

Where to Go For What, by Mara Miller (Englewood Cliffs, N.J.: Prentice-Hall, 1981). Miller offers guidance on basic research skills and techniques, including how to use libraries, government information systems, and reference materials.

Word Mysteries and Histories: From Quiche to Humble Pie, by the Editors of The American Heritage Dictionaries (Boston: Houghton Mifflin Company, 1986). Intriguing and sometimes whimsical facts about the backgrounds of more than 500 English words.

Word Play, by Hans Holzer (San Francisco, Calif.: Strawberry Hill Press, 1978). The author says that "Word Play is not meant to replace the dictionary or the *Encyclopedia Britannica.* But it is intended to make their usage more difficult." Amaze and confound your friends with rather unique (read: made-up) definitions to hundreds of words.

Wordplay: Ambigrams and Reflections on the Art of Ambigrams, by John Langdon (Orlando, Fla.: Harcourt Brace Jovanovich, Publishers, 1992). A delightful book for lovers of words and art. Ambigrams are words so scripted that they are the same when read upside down, back to front, or in the mirror as well as left to right. Word ambigrams are cousins of picture ambigrams, such as faces that turn into other faces when inverted. The purpose? To present familiar concepts in an unfamiliar way, to stimulate one's imagination, and to see things in a new light.

Word Play: What Happens When People Talk, by Peter Farb (New York: Alfred A. Knopf, 1974). The author proposes that language represents twin systems of grammar and human behavior.

Word Watch: The Stories Behind the Words of Our Lives, by Anne Soukhanov (New York: Henry Holt and Company, Inc., 1994). From affluenza to zip code wine, this book covers the origins of intriguing words that make a statement about our society.

The Wordsworth Book of Euphemism, by Judith S. Neaman and Carole G. Silver (Ware, Hertfordshire, Eng.: Wordsworth Editions, Ltd., 1995). Milder options for crude, embarrassing and offensive terms. This originally appeared in 1983 as *Kind Words: A Thesaurus of Euphemisms.*

The Wordsworth Book of Spelling Rules, compiled by G. Terry Page (Ware, Hertfordshire, Eng.: Wordsworth Editions, Ltd., 1995). First published as *Harrap's English Spelling Rules,* this is a concise self-instruction manual to the sometimes tricky rules of English spelling, with a guideline for spelling improvement.

The Wordsworth Dictionary of Anagrams, by Michael Curl (Ware, Hertfordshire, Eng.: Wordsworth Editions, 1995). This was originally published in 1982 as *The Anagram Dictionary.* Anagrams have come to be associated with mystical properties. This reference source includes a history of anagrams from the Greeks and Romans, and lists 20,000 words which are arranged alphabetically, with all their known anagrams. For lovers of all word games.

The World Almanac and Book of Facts (New York: Newspaper Enterprise Association, annual). A chronology of each year's world events reported on many different fields.

11

A SAMPLE STYLE GUIDE FOR
AUTHORS AND EDITORS

Numbers in parentheses are cross-referenced with *The Chicago Manual of Style, Fourteenth Edition* (Chicago: The University of Chicago Press, 1993) for additional information and examples. That is the really essential guide all writers, editors, and proofreaders must have. In those cases that may be ambiguous, however, remember that this style guide is addressed to the unique problems of religious writers and writing, and that the house style of the publisher issuing any particular book usually predominates. Most of this brief stylebook I wrote several years ago, and it was included in the book *Writing Religiously: A Guide to Writing Nonfiction Religious Books* (Grand Rapids, Mich.: Baker Books, 1984). It is now revised and updated. I wish to thank Ted Griffin, Lila Bishop, Steve Hawkins, and Jill Carter for help in bringing this up-to-date for use in this book.

—L.G.G.

I. Book Production

Preparation of the Manuscript (2.3-52; 13.16-51)

1. It is the author's responsibility to provide copy that is clear, readable, and accurate. The manuscript must be typed and double-spaced. It should have wide margins (1 inch) on good-quality standard white bond paper 8-1/2 x 11 inches. Computer printouts are also acceptable, preferably printed by a laser printer. Colored paper or onion skin is not acceptable. Use only one side of the sheet.

2. The manuscript must be complete. Both additions and corrections are confusing and difficult to add once the manuscript has been accepted for publication. The author should include the following parts with book:

Title Page
Table of Contents
All Text Matter
Footnotes on separate pages
Tables or graphs on separate pages
Bibliography
Index (prepared by author after final proofs are available)

3. The manuscript pages should be numbered consecutively in the upper *right* corner. The author should *not* number them by chapter (3-1, 3-2, etc.). Sheets inserted after the manuscript has been paginated should carry the preceding page number with *a, b, c* added: *86a, 86b, 86c*. If a page is later removed, the preceding page should be double numbered: 106-107.

4. It is the author's responsibility to check all Scripture references and footnotes for accuracy.

Rights and Permissions (4.1-4.72)

1. The publisher will prepare the copyright page and also has the privilege to give permission to reprint excerpts in other publications.

2. If the author wishes to use a portion of a copyrighted work and there is some question whether the kind or amount of the material exceeds a fair use, permission should be requested. It is the author's responsibility to obtain permission to quote from other sources. Notice of the original copyright and permission to reprint must appear either on the copyright page of the book or in a footnote on the first page of the reprinted material or in a special list of acknowledgments. All permissions or copies of them must be sent to the publisher.

3. The author is further responsible for any fees charged by grantors of permission unless other arrangements are made by the author. When the publisher pays the cost of procuring permission rights, these costs are generally deducted from the author's future royalties.

4. Frequent use of modern Scripture versions may require permission.

Stages in Manuscript Production (2.129; 3.4-57)

1. An edited manuscript usually passes through the following eight stages in the production process:

Sample page and design
Typesetting
First proofs (copy sent to author)
Second and additional proofs (if necessary)
Final proofs

Camera copy
Platemaking
Press
Binding

2. Once page proofs (final proofs) are made, revisions are costly and should be minimal. Major changes at this stage in production are not acceptable. Corrections should be confined to substantive errors.

3. Authors will receive final proofs *only* if the book requires an index. In this case, the author will receive a deadline to complete the index, but manuscript revisions are not made at this time.

The Editor/Author Relationship

1. During the editorial process, the editors at most houses work with authors to produce books that are as excellent as they can be, both in terms of content and of quality. Editing is usually done on screen—sometimes only for house style, sometimes in a more comprehensive way, depending on the specific needs of a given manuscript.

2. Basically as the editor edits an assigned book, he or she corrects misspellings, mispunctuation, incorrect word usage, etc. and generally conforms the book to the house style. The editor also identifies and, in cooperation with the author, clarifies unclear writing, theological or historical inaccuracies, and other potential problems. Potentially offensive material is also addressed.

3. A good philosophy of editing is as follows:

Some see the editor as a super-critical, academic-monastic individual who cackles as he or she edits a manuscript so heavily writers can't recognize their own work. Others overidealize the editor as a knight in shining armor who will rescue a manuscript (or an author) from obscurity, make the work great, and bring huge success! The truth is somewhere in between.

In Christian publishing, the editor and the writer have the same goals and serve the same Lord, but they are coming to the task from different angles. This sometimes makes for a nebulous world in which "the rules" seem unclear. Ideally, author and editor will maintain a context of cooperation and teamwork, and within that context the editor fills necessary roles on behalf of both the publisher and the author. The editor and the writer are coworkers.

Throughout the editorial process, the editor gives honest feedback and offers constructive criticism. If some elements in the book do not work, or are offensive to the intended readership, or are theologically questionable, or . . . , it is up to the editor to work with the author to resolve the problem.

Trust is at the core of the editor/author relationship. The editor respects the writer's point of view, the purpose for the book, the style, etc. and so doesn't make the book the editor's rather than the writer's. On the other hand, the writer trusts the editor to tell him or her what the book is really like, its strengths and its weaknesses, and so on. The editor helps a writer focus on a reading audience, on the real purpose for writing the book (is one writing to communicate or to be published?), and on whether the story line, writing style, and vocabulary effectively reach intended readers. The editor helps the author remember that quality is just as important as content.

II.   Punctuation

The Period (5.7-5.16)

1. Use a period without parentheses after numerals or letters in a vertical listing.

1. a.
2. b.
3. c.

2. Numerals or letters in a list within a paragraph should either be enclosed in double parentheses or the numeral or letter could be followed by an end parentheses. In neither case should these be followed by a period.

Some of the earliest texts of the New Testament have been found in (1) Oxyrhynchus Papyrus 657, (2) Chester Beatty Papyrus II, and (3) Bodmer Papyrus II.

3. Omit the period after running heads, centered headlines, and signatures.

4. Periods should be placed within quotation marks except when single quotation marks are used to set off special terms.

The would-be theologian took up residence in a cave, thinking he would thus avoid succumbing to 'the social gospel'.

The teacher's favorite saying was, "there is no such thing as a dumb question."

Exclamation Point (5.17-5.20)

1. Use the exclamation point to mark an emphatic or sarcastic comment.

How beautiful is the girl in my arms!
He seems to enjoy being miserable!

2. The exclamation point should be placed within quotation marks, parentheses, or brackets when it is part of the quoted or parenthetical material; otherwise, it should be placed outside.

"Don't hang me," cried the captured rustler, "I'm innocent!"

The traitor betrayed everyone, including his "friends"!

Question Mark (5.21-5.28)

1. The question mark is used to pose a question or to express an editorial doubt.

What is the sound of one hand clapping?

The translation of the Bible made by Miles Coverdale (1488?-1569) was used to a great extent by the translators of the 1611 Authorized Version.

2. Questions within a sentence that consist of single words, such as *who, when, how,* or *why* do not require a question mark. It is better to italicize the word.

The question is not *how* but *when.*

3. The question mark should be placed inside quotation marks, parentheses, or brackets when it is part of the quoted or parenthetical material.

"Moses, did you tell him you can't talk worth beans?"

4. The question mark goes outside the quotation marks when the quoted material is not a question.

When you finish work, will you hear Jesus say, "Well done"?

The Comma (5.29-5.88)

A comma is used to indicate the smallest pause in continuity of thought or sentence structure. The modern practice is to pause infrequently, especially if the meaning is clear without an interruption. Aside from a few set rules, its use is a matter of good judgment.

1. Use a comma before the conjunction uniting two parts of a compound sentence unless both parts are very short.

Lila's homemade coleslaw is considered good, but her french fries are the best in the county.

2. An adjectival phrase or clause that is nonrestrictive and could be dropped without changing the reference of the noun is set off by commas.

The apostle Paul, a peace-loving man, was often the target of violence from nonbelievers during his ministry.

3. Use commas to set off interjecting transitional adverbs and similar elements that effect a distinct break in the continuity of thought.

All people of goodwill, therefore, must remain vigilant.

4. A word, phrase, or clause in apposition to a noun is usually set off by commas.

My wife, Carolyn, leads a woman's Bible study class.

However, if the appositive has a restrictive function, it is not set off by commas.

My son David is more studious than his friends.

5. Two or more adjectives should be set off by commas if each modifies the noun alone.

Timothy proved himself to be an honest, hard-working servant.

However, if the first adjective modifies the idea expressed by the combination of the second adjective and the noun, no comma is needed.

The hungry old tiger licked his chops when he saw the missionary stumble into the clearing.

[One method to determine this usage is to ask if the word *and* can be inserted between the two modifiers without changing the meaning of the sentence or making it awkward. If it cannot, no comma is required.]

6. In a series of three or more elements, place a comma before the conjunction.

According to legend, Vladimir studied Islam, Judaism, and Roman Catholicism before deciding to become a Christian.

7. Use commas to set off words identifying a title or position after a name.

Nero, the cruel and bloodthirsty emperor who murdered Christians, was also responsible for the burning of Rome.

8. Commas are used to indicate the date and to set off names of geographical places.

December 7, 1941 (preferred) but 7 December 1941

The author was born on December 31, 1947, in San Diego, California, and later moved to Arizona.

9. A dependent clause that precedes the main clause should usually be set off by a comma.

If you go to the store, please get some bananas.

10. A direct quotation or maxim should usually be separated from the rest of the sentence by commas.

"I am sorry," said the Grand Pooh-bah, "that I can be of no help."

However, if the quote is a restrictive appositive, or used as the subject or predicate nominative, it should not be set off with commas.

"When pigs fly" was a phrase he least expected.

Semicolon (5.89-5.96)

A semicolon marks a more important break in sentence flow than one marked by a comma.

1. Use a semicolon between two independent clauses not connected by a conjunction.

Bibles are steady moneymakers; particular sellers are the study Bibles.

2. The following adverbs—*then, however, thus, hence, indeed, yet, so*—should be preceded by a semicolon when used between clauses for a compound sentence.

Joseph says he intends to go to graduate school; yet he makes no definite plans.

3. Use a semicolon to separate a compound sentence when either part of the sentence has a comma break.

Donna is an intelligent, happy person; and she is well-adjusted.

4. Semicolons may be used for emphasis.

It was the best of times; it was the worst of times.

5. Semicolons should be used to separate references when they contain internal punctuation.

Luke 1:1-4; 2:14, 21; 5:12, 14, 16.

6. Semicolons always go outside of quotation marks and parentheses.

Luther once called the book of James "the epistle of straw"; yet he wrote a brilliant commentary on it.

Colon (5.97-5.104)

A colon marks a discontinuity of grammatical construction greater than that indicated by a semicolon but less than a period. Its one main function is to introduce material that follows immediately.

1. A colon may be used to emphasize a sequence in thought between two clauses that form a single sentence.

Many in the congregation helped with the bake sale: twenty of them, for example, made pies.

2. A colon may introduce a list or series.

Chicago's night life consists of three important pleasure points: Rush Street, the theater district, and Wheaton.

[If, however, the series is introduced by *namely, for instance, for example,* or *that is,* a colon should not be used unless the series consists of one or more grammatical complete clauses.]

3. A colon should be used between chapter and verse in scripture passages.

Matthew 2:5-13

The Dash (5.105-5.122)

1. An endash is used to indicate inclusive or continuing numbers, as in dates, page references, or Scripture references.

pp. 23-46
1861-65
Jan-May 1994
Acts 2:35-5:14

2. The em dash (—) denotes an abrupt break in thought that affects sentence structure.

The emperor—he had been awake half the night waiting in vain for a reply—came down to breakfast in an angry mood.

3. A 2-em dash (no space on either side) indicates missing letters in a word.

We ha——a copy in the library.

4. A 3-em dash (with space on each side) indicates a whole word has been omitted.

The ship left ——— in May.

Quotations (10.1-10.47)

1. Direct quotations must reproduce exactly the wording, spelling, and punctuation of the original. However, the initial letter may be changed to a capital or lowercase letter to fit the syntax of the text. Typographical errors may be corrected in modern works, but idiosyncrasies of spelling in older works should be observed.

2. It is the author's responsibility to check every quotation against the original for accuracy.

3. Quotations over eight lines are set in block quotes. Shorter quotations may be set within the text.

4. If the quotation, either run into or set off from the text, is used as part of the author's sentence, it begins with a lower-case letter, even though the original is a complete sentence and begins with a capital letter.

5. Direct conversation, whether run into or set off from the text, should always be enclosed in quotation marks.

6. Quoted material set off from the text as a block quotation should not be enclosed in quotation marks. Quoted material within a block quotation should be enclosed in double quotations mark, even if the source used single quotation marks.

7. Scripture used in block quotations must be followed by the reference in parentheses.

8. The words *yes* and *no* should not be quoted except in direct discourse.

Joshua always answered yes; he could not say no.

Parentheses (5.123-127)

1. Parentheses, like commas and dashes, may be used to set off amplifying, explanatory, or digressive elements. Commas, however, should be used if the two parts are closely related.

He had long suspected that the inert gasses (helium, neon, argon, krypton) could be used to produce a similar effect.

2. Expressions such as *that is, namely, e.g., i.e.,* and the element introduced may be enclosed in parentheses if the break in thought is greater than that signaled by a comma.

Bones from several animals (e.g., a dog, a cat, a squirrel, a pigeon) were found in the grave.

3. Parentheses should be used to enclose numerals or letters marking divisions or enumerations run into the text.

The anthropologist stated there were no inexplicable differences between (1) Java man, (2) Neanderthal man, and, (3) Cro-Magnon man.

4. Ending punctuation should be placed outside a closing parenthesis if the word or phrase in the parentheses interrupts or is interjected into a sentence. However, when a question mark or an exclamation point is part of the parenthetical matter, it may precede the closing parenthesis.

A consistent format should be followed (do not punctuate by ear).
A consistent format should be followed (never punctuate by ear!).

5. Ending punctuation is enclosed by parenthetical matter that is an entire sentence independent of another context.

Was this a desperate cry for help? (Or any one of a hundred other considerations?)

6. When quoting Scripture, place the period after the parenthesis containing the reference. If the quotation requires a question mark or exclamation point, place it with the text, and place the period after the parenthesis. When quoting Scripture that is set off from the text as a block quotation, the period should be placed after the Scripture text.

"In the beginning God created the heaven and the earth" (Genesis 1:1).
"Lord, are you going to wash my feet?" (John 13:6).

Brackets (5.128-132)

1. Brackets enclose editorial interpolations, corrections, explanations, or comments.

Jesus told Nicodemus, "Unless a man is born again [born anew, or born from above] he cannot see the Kingdom of God."

He [Robert E. Lee] died in 1870, never having received a pardon from the United States government.

2. Brackets may also be used to enclose the phonetic transcript of a word.

He attributed the light to the phenomenon called gegenschein [ga-gen-shin].

Ellipses (5.16; 10.48-63)

1. Any omission of a word, phrase, line, or paragraph from a quoted passage must be indicated by ellipsis points, with a space before and after each dot.

2. Three dots . . . indicate that material is deleted at the beginning or within a sentence.

"By faith Moses' parents hid him for three months . . . because they saw he was no ordinary child" (Hebrews 11:23).

3. Other punctuation may be used on either side of the three ellipsis dots if it makes the meaning clearer.

I wondered, was he the hapless dupe he was made out to be? . . . he seemed far too clever for that.

4. Three dots may indicate a break in thought, daydreaming, or hesitation. But a dash should be used to indicate an *external* interruption of speech or thought.

If he had only come sooner . . . if only . . . then perhaps everything would have been different. I—that is, we—yes, we wish he had come sooner.

5. Unless the content requires such, it is not usually necessary to use ellipsis points before or after a verse or a portion of a Scripture verse. Introductory words such as *and* and *for* may be omitted from a Scripture quotation without using ellipsis points.

"For God so loved the world . . . " (John 3:16) may read "God so loved the world . . . "

6. Four dots . . . . indicate that material is omitted at the end of a sentence (the extra dot accounts for the period). The missing material could be (1) the last part of a quoted sentence, (2) the first part of the next sentence, (3) a whole sentence or more, (4) a whole paragraph or more.

"All the believers were together and had everything in common. . . . Everyday they continued to meet together" (Acts 2:44, 46).

If the original quotation is punctuated with a question mark or an exclamation point, this mark is retained and the three dots used for the ellipsis.

"Now is my soul troubled; and what shall I say? . . . for this cause came I unto this hour" (John 12:27).

The Apostrophe (6.19-6.31)

1. The apostrophe is the mark of the possessive. The possessive case of singular nouns is formed by the addition

of an apostrophe and an *s*, and the possessive of plural nouns by the addition of an apostrophe only.

the book's cover
the puppies' tails

2. When it can be done without confusion, numbers and letters used as words form the plural by adding *s* alone.

the three Rs
four YMCAs
the early 1930s

3. However, abbreviations with periods, lowercase letters used as nouns, and some capital letters may require an apostrophe for clarity.

M.Div.'s
Ph.D.'s
x's and y's
S's, A's, I's

4. The general rule for common nouns is also used for proper names, including most names of any length ending in sibilants.

Peter's boat
Cheryl's baby
Rosses' house
Burns's poems

Exceptions: the names Jesus and Moses are traditional exceptions to the general rule for forming the possessive.

Jesus' disciples
Moses' staff

Solidus, also known as slash, slant, or virgule (5.122)

1. Related to the dash and the hyphen in form and function, the solidus (/) is sometimes used to indicate alternatives and alternative word forms or spellings and replaces *and* in some sentences.

Boys and/or girls may play in the park district's volleyball league.
Qu'ran/Koran
Sales figures rose dramatically in the June/July period.

2. A solidus with no spaces before or after can indicate that a time period spans two consecutive years, though the endash is preferred.

Winter 1910/11 Winter 1910-11

3. When poetry or text from songs is run into the text, a solidus is used to show line breaks.

As Thomas Gray once observed, "Full many a flower was born to blush unseen/And waste its sweetness on the desert air."

Diacritical Marks and Special Characters (9.10|9.146)

English is one of very few languages that can be set without accents, diacritics, or special alphabetic characters for native words. Editors and typesetters may recognize the more common marks used in foreign words such as *g, á, è,* or *ñ,* but may not be familiar with ones used in other languages (i.e., classical Greek, Hebrew, or Chinese). Authors need to mark their manuscripts clearly when they use such a mark or notify the editor if there will be a need to use a special typeface.

III. Spelling and Proper Use of Words

Italics (6.63-72, 10.67-68)

1. The author may underline a word or phrase to emphasize it with italics.

But the *actual* cause of the accident is yet to be determined.

2. Technical terms, especially when accompanied by definition, may be set in italics the first time they appear.

Tabular matter is copy, usually consisting of figures, that is set in columns.

3. Isolated words or phrases in a foreign language should be italicized.

Caveat Emptor!
au revoir
sine qua non

But foreign expressions used so commonly that they have become a recognized part of the English language do not need to be italicized.

per se
ad lib

4. A person's thought in contrast to verbal discourse may be set in italics for clarity.

I looked over the unarmed bushwhacker who was attempting to rob me. *He can't be serious,* I thought to myself.

5. References to words as words are italicized.

The word *faith* has often been confused with hope.

6. Italics are to be used for book titles, movies, ships, and for radio or TV programs in continuing series. Titles of individual programs not in continuing series should be set in Roman type and quotation marks.

Screwtape Letters
USS Yorktown
Gunsmoke
"Beverly Sills Sings at the Met"

Hyphenation (5.120|121; 6.32|58)

1. Hyphens are to be used cautiously. Most compound words do not require a hyphen. Most noun combinations which were formerly hyphenated are now written as solid words: butterfat, willpower. Others are still hyphenated: well-being. Some that were once hyphenated are now two words: water supply. Keep a copy of *Merriam-Webster's Collegiate Dictionary: Tenth Edition* on hand so as not to hyphenate by intuition.

2. A word or phrase used as an adjective is often hyphenated.

born-again Christian
soul-winning program
born again (noun)
Soulwinning was...(noun)

References (15.4-15.426)

1. Footnotes should be numbered consecutively throughout each chapter of the book, beginning with the number 1 in each new chapter.

2. Footnotes should be typed on sheets separate from the text, be double-spaced, and have generous margins.

3. Notes are usually printed at the end of the book, not at the end of each chapter or at page bottoms. The decision will be made by the publisher.

4. Each footnote should include the following information:

Author's full name
Complete title of book
Editor, compiler, or translator, if any
Edition, if other than the first
Number of volumes
Facts of publication—city where published, publisher, date of publication
Volume number (if any)
Page number(s) of the particular citation (The abbreviation p. or pp. should be omitted from citations.)

5. When citing an article from a periodical as the source, the following information should be given:

Author's full name
Title of the article
Name of the periodical
Volume (and number) of the periodical
Date of the volume or issue
Page number(s) of the particular citation

6. After the first reference to a particular work in each chapter, subsequent references in the same chapter should be shortened. The shortened reference should include only the last name of the author and the short title of the book, in italics, followed by the page numbers of the reference.

1. Harold G. Henderson, *An Introduction to Haiku: An Anthology of Poems and Poets from Basho to Shiki* (New York: Doubleday Anchor Books, 1958), 124.

2. Fyodor Dostoevsky, *The Possessed* (New York: Signet Classics, 1962), 224.

3. Henderson, *An Introduction to Haiku,* 78.

7. *Ibid.* may be used to refer to a single work cited in the note immediately preceding. It takes the place of the author's name, the title of the work, and the succeeding identical material. Incidentally, Roman type should be used for Latin words and abbreviations (Ibid., et al., op cit., and idem.).

11. C. S. Lewis, *The Allegory of Love: A Study in Medieval Tradition* (Oxford: Clarendon Press, 1936), 259
12. Ibid., 360.

8. It is the author's responsibility to include complete and accurate footnotes as part of the manuscript, prior to editing.

Scripture References (7.87-90; 14.34-35, 15.294-295)

It is the author's responsibility to provide accurate and complete references to the Bible.

1. Books of the Bible should not be abbreviated when the reference is cited without chapter and verse.

2. In block quotations, the names of Bible books may be properly abbreviated. (See **Abbreviations and Scripture References.**)

3. Arabic numerals will be used to cite all references to Scripture.

2 Chronicles
2 Peter
3 John

4. The names of Bible versions may be abbreviated when citing a reference. **(See Abbreviations and Scripture References)**

5. When quoting Scripture, place the period after the parenthesis containing the reference. If the quotation ends in a question or exclamation point, place it with the text and place a period after the parenthesis.

"Finally, my brethren, rejoice in the Lord" (Phil. 3:1).
"Jesus saith unto him, If I will that he tarry till I come, what is that to thee?" (John 21:21).

Abbreviations (14.1|14.57)

1. Abbreviations should not be used for given names.

William not Wm.

2. When a civil or military title is used with the surname alone, the title must be spelled out.

General Eisenhower
Lieutenant Jenkins

If the full name is used, however, the title may be abbreviated.

Sen. Sam Nunn
Col. Jack Papworth Goss

3. Abbreviations are always used for Mr., Mrs., Ms., and Dr.

4. The title *Reverend* should be accompanied by the article *the*. When it is abbreviated, the article can be dropped, but it should be accompanied by a full name.

The Reverend Billy Sunday
The Reverend Mr. Sunday
Rev. Billy Sunday

5. The names of government agencies, organizations, associations, and other groups may be abbreviated. Such abbreviations are usually set in capitals without periods.

NATO
ECPA

The same applies to famous persons known by their initials only.

FDR
JFK

6. The names of states, territories, and possessions of the United States should always be spelled out when standing alone.

7. The names of countries should be spelled out in the text. (United States is preferred over U. S. United States may be abbreviated to U. S. in informal writing, i.e. U. S. currency)

8. Names of the months should be spelled out in the text, whether alone or in dates. They may be abbreviated in chronologies or footnotes.

Jan.	July
Feb.	Aug.
Mar.	Sept.
Apr.	Oct.
May	Nov.
June	Dec.

9. The days of the week should be spelled out.

10. Parts of a book may be abbreviated for use in footnotes or bibliographies.

appendix	app.
book	bk.
figure	fig.
folio	fol.
notes(s)	n. (pl. nn.)
number	no.
page(s)	p. (pl. pp.)
paragraph	par.
volume	vol. (pl. vols.)

Abbreviations and Scripture References (7.87-90; 14.34-35; 15.294-295)

1. In text, references to whole books of the Bible or whole chapters are spelled out.

The opening chapters of Ephesians...
Genesis, chapters 1 and 2, records the creation of the world.

2. Biblical references may be abbreviated when enclosed in parentheses. In some scholarly or reference works, they may be abbreviated in the text.

Old Testament

Gen.	2 Chron.	Dan.
Ex.	Ezra	Hos.
Lev.	Neh.	Joel
Num.	Est.	Amos
Deut.	Job	Obad.
Josh.	Ps. (pl Pss.)	Jonah
Judg.	Prov.	Mic.
Ruth	Eccl.	Nah.
1 Sam.	Song	Hab.

2 Sam.	Isa.	Zeph.
1 Kings	Jer.	Hag.
2 Kings	Lam.	Zech.
1 Chron.	Ezek.	Mal.

New Testament

Matt.	Eph.	Heb.
Mark	Phil.	James
Luke	Col.	1 Peter
John	1 Thess.	2 Peter
Acts	2 Thess.	1 John
Rom.	1 Tim.	2 John
1 Cor.	2 Tim.	3 John
2 Cor.	Titus	Jude
Gal.	Philem.	Rev.

Books of the Bible should be referred to with the title used in the version cited. For example, Song of Solomon is Song of Songs in the *New International Version* and is not abbreviated.

3. Arabic numerals are used for all references. If the reference begins a sentence, the number should be written out.

in 1 John
First John 3:16 says...

4. Versions of Scripture may be abbreviated in references and set in small caps without periods.

AV	*Authorized (King James) Version*
RV	*Revised Version*
NEB	*New English Bible*
ASV	*American Standard Version*
JB	*Jerusalem Bible*
KJV	*King James Version* (also known as *Authorized Version*)

LB	*Living Bible*
MLB	*Modern Language Bible/New Berkeley*
NASB	*New American Standard Bible*
NCV	*New Century Version*
NIV	*New International Version*
NKJV	*New King James Version*
NRSV	*New Revised Standard Version*
RNASB	*Revised New American Standard Bible*
RSV	*Revised Standard Version*
TEV	*Today's English Version*
Phillips	
AMP	*Amplified*

5. The abbreviation for verse is v. and for verses, vv.

v. 23
vv. 24-26

IV. Use of Numbers in Text

General Rules for Numbers in Text (8.1-8.80)

1. If the word following the number is not a measurement, numbers under 100 are written as words and numbers 100 and over are written as numerals (see rule 5 below).

Our five editors work tirelessly 24 hours a day.

2. Exact numbers of less than one hundred and round numbers in hundreds, thousands, or millions should be spelled out.

Sixty children
four billion
3.6 billion
2,486
237

3. Two exceptions to this rule are year numbers and numbers referring to parts of the book.

44 B.C.
page 7

4. Initial numbers at the beginning of a sentence should be spelled out.

One hundred forty...
Twenty-five percent...

5. When numbers precede units of measurement, they are written as numerals and the units may be abbreviated.

3 cubic inches
76 pounds
11 lb.
22 ft.
6 gal.
12 percent
60 volts
32° F.
9 hr.

6. Percentages and decimal fractions (including academic grades) are set in figures in literary as well as scientific copy.

A grade point average of 3.9 is considered outstanding.

In scientific and technical copy use the symbol "%" for a percentage; in literary copy, use the word percent.

Of the citizens polled, more than 82% are in favor of the referendum.

The loan has an interest rate of 7 percent.

Numerals should be used for percentages for statistical or technical use.

The author claims that only 10 percent of evangelicals define themselves as doctrinal people.

7. Numbers applicable to the same category should be consistent throughout a paragraph. If the largest number contains three or more digits, use figures for all.

8. Where there are two adjacent numbers, spell out one of them.

sixty 12-in. rulers
200 thirty-two-cent stamps

9. Use a period without parentheses after numbers in a vertical listing.

1.
2.
3.

10. Numerals in a list within a paragraph should be enclosed in parentheses and should not be followed by a period.

There were three areas of concern for the new product division: (1) production, (2) marketing, and (3) distribution.

11. Percentages should be spelled out when they begin a sentence and when they are used in a literary or informal way.

Ninety-nine percent of all editors think they are woefully underpaid.

Currency (8.23-31)

1. Isolated references to money in United States currency are spelled out or written in figures according to general rules for numbers.

I'll give five dollars for the fund.

403

Each employee received $42.20 for wages, $11.44 for benefits, and $2.40 for cost-of-living.

2. Substitute million and billion for zeros, but use zeros for sums in thousands.

$6 million
$10,000

Dates and Times (8.33-50)

1. Spell out (lowercase letters) references to particular centuries and decades.

nineteenth century
sixties and seventies (but 1940s)

2. Dates should be consistently written in one of the following forms. Never use st, nd, rd, or th after figures in dates.

14 October 1964
Saturday Review, 12 October 1968, p. 32
The third of June, 1943
June 9 (never June 9th)

3. Times of day are usually spelled out in the text.

The church meeting wasn't over until four-thirty.

However, figures may be used to emphasize the exact time.

The train arrived at 3:20.

4. Figures are used in designations of time with A.M. or P.M.

2:00 P.M.
8:25 A.M.

5. House numbers or street addresses are given in figures.

814 Evergreen Street
Interstate 57
However: Fifth Avenue

6. In figures of one thousand or more, commas should be used between every group of three digits.

56,925
2,414

Exceptions to this rule are page numbers, addresses, and year numbers of four digits, which are written in figures without commas.

V.   Capitalization (7.2-161)

Titles of Offices (7.16-27)

1. Civil, military, religious, and professional titles are capitalized when they immediately precede a personal name.

President McKinley
General Patton
Emperor Maximilian
Queen Elizabeth
Cardinal Newman

2. In text matter, titles following a personal name or used alone in place of a name are, with few exceptions, lowercased.

Abraham Lincoln, president of the United States
President Lincoln, the president of the United States
the president, presidential, presidency

General Ulysses S. Grant, commander in chief of the
Union army
General Grant
the commander in chief
the general
George VI, king of England
the king of England, the king
the bishop of London
Charles H. Weatherly, Doctor of Law
Jeremy Feingold, M.D.

Kinship Names (7.31)

A kinship name is lowercased when not followed by a
given name, but capitalized in direct address or when the term
is substituted for a personal name.

his father
my brothers and sister
Uncle Ed
Aunt Sara
Marjorie is Mother's middle name.

Political Divisions (7.36-41; 7.57-59)

In general, words designating political divisions of the
world, a country, state, city, and so forth are capitalized when
following the name or an accepted part of it.

Roman Empire; the empire under Diocletian; the empire
Washington State; the state of Washington

Organizations (7.50-60)

1. Names of national and international organizations,
movements and alliances, and members of political parties are
capitalized, but not the words *party*, *movement*, *platform* and
so forth.

Communist party; Communist(s); Communist bloc
Common Market
Loyalist(s)
Republican party, Republican platform; Republicans(s)

2. Nouns and adjectives designating political and economic systems of thought and their proponents are lowercased, unless derived from a proper noun.

bolshevism
communism
democracy
democrat (a general advocate of democracy)
republican (a general advocate of republicanism)
Marxism

3. Words derived from personal or geographical names are lowercased when used with a specialized meaning.

dutch oven
french fries
india ink

Holidays/Seasons (7.32; 7.74-75)

1. The four seasons are lowercased except when personified.

Then Winter—with her icy blasts—subsided.

2. The names of religious holidays and seasons are capitalized.

Christmas Eve
Easter Day
Pentecost
Passover

3. Secular holidays and other specially designated days are also capitalized.

Fourth of July; the Fourth
Mother's Day
Thanksgiving Day

Religious Terms (7.21; 7.77-95)

1. The names of the one supreme God are capitalized.

God
Abba
Adonai
Logos
Jehovah
the Word
the Redeemer
Yahweh
the Savior
Master
Son
Holy Spirit
Christ

2. The style of many Christian publishing houses differs from *The Chicago Manual of Style* and many other publishers in that they often capitalize pronouns referring to God (but: who, whom).

Trust in Him.
God gives man what He wants.
Jesus and His disciples.
Jesus knew He was the one who must die on the cross.

3. Though the names of specific places in Scripture are normally capitalized, *heaven, hell,* and *hades* are lowercased.

4. Capitalize adjectives derived from proper names—e.g., Mosaic dispensation; Christian era; Maccabean period; Messianic age.

5. The following list of biblical and religious terms are capitalized or lowercased according to house style:

Abyss, the
Advent, the
Advent season
Almighty, the
almighty God, the
Alpha and Omega (Christ)
angel
angel of the Lord
Angel of the Lord (if theophany)
ante-Nicene fathers
Antichrist, the
anti-Christian
Apocalypse, the (Revelation)
Apocrypha, the
Apostle, the
the Apostle Peter et al.; Peter the Apostle
apostles
Apostle to the Gentiles (Paul)
apostolic age
apostolic council
Apostles' Creed
archangel
ark, the (Noah's)
ark of the covenant
Ascension, the
Ascension Day
ascension of Christ, the
atheism
Atonement, the
atonement of Christ, the
Augsburg Confession

baby Jesus
baptism
Baptism, the (of Christ); but: Christ's baptism
Battle of Armageddon
Beast, the (Antichrist)
Beatitudes, the
Betrayal, the (of Christ)
Bible, the
Bible school
biblical
body of Christ (the church)
Book, the (Bible)
book of Genesis et al.
Book of the Law
Bread of Life (Bible or Christ)
Bridegroom, the (Christ)
bride of Christ (the church)
burnt offering
Calvary
Canon, the (Scripture)
canon of Scripture, the
Captivity, the
Catholic church (Roman Catholic)
charismatic movement, the
charismatics
cherub, cherubim
chief priest
children of Israel
chosen people, the
Christian
Christlike
Christmas Day
Christmas Eve
christological
Christology
Church (body of Christ; universal)
church (building; service; local)
church fathers

city of David
Comforter, the (Holy Spirit)
commandment (first, et al.)
Communion (Lord's Supper)
covenant, the
covenant of grace
covenant of works
Creation, the
creation of man, the
Creator, the
Cross, the (event, not object)
Crucifixion, the
crucifixion of Christ
Crusades, the
Day of Atonement
Day of Judgment
Dead Sea Scrolls
Diety, the (God)
deism, deists
Deity, the
devil, a
Devil, the (Satan)
Diaspora
disciples
Dispensation of the Law
dispensationalism, -ist
Dispersion, the
divine
Divinity, the (God)
Door, the (Christ)
Dragon, the
Earth (planet)
earth (dirt or ground)
Easter Day
Eastern church
ecumenism
eleven, the
end times, the

epistle (John's epistle, et al.)
Epistle to the Romans
Epistles, the (apostolic letters)
eternal God, the
eternal life
Eucharist, the
Evangel
evangelicals
Evangelist (Gospel writer)
evangelist (one who evangelizes)
Exile, the
Exodus, the
exodus from Egypt, the
faith, the (Christian)
Fall, the
fall of man
False Prophet (of Revelation)
Fathers, the (church fathers)
Feast of the Passover (Tabernacles, Dedication, Unleavened Bread)
First Advent, the
Flood, the
fundamentalists, -ism
Garden of Eden
gehenna
Gentile
gentile laws
Gethsemane, Garden of
Gnosticism
God
Godhead (essential being of God)
godhead (godship or godhood)
godless
Godlike
godly
God-man
godsend
God's house

Godspeed
God's Word
Golden Rule, the
Good News
Good Friday
Good Samaritan
Gospel, the (specific New Testament concept of the Good News or God's redemption)
  gospel (John's, et al.)
  gospel (adj.)
  Gospels, the
  grace
  Great Commission, the
  Great High Priest, the
  Great Judgment, the
  Great Physician, the
  Great Shepherd, the
  Great White Throne, the
  Hades (mythological)
  hades (hell)
  heaven
  heavenly Father
  Heidelberg Catechism
  hell
  High Church (Anglican)
  High Priest, the (Christ)
  high priest, a
  Holy Bible
  Holy Ghost
  Holy Land
  Holy of Holies
  Holy Scriptures
  Holy Spirit
  Holy Trinity
  house of the Lord
  Incarnation, The
  incarnation of Christ, the
  Jordan River (but river Jordan)

Judaic
judges, the
Judgment Day
judgment seat of Christ, the
kerygma
kingdom, the
kingdom of God
kingdom of heaven
King of Kings (Christ)
koinonia
lake of fire
last days, the
Last Judgment, the
Last Supper
law (as opposed to grace)
Law, the (OT)
Lord's Day, the
Lord's Supper, the
Lord's Table, the
Love Chapter, the
Low Church (Anglican)
Magi
Mass, the (sacrament; lowercase for service)
Masoretic
mercy seat
messianic
millennial
Millennium, the
minor prophets (people)
Minor Prophets (the books)
Mishna
Mount of Transfiguration, the
Muslim (preferred)
Muhammad (preferred)
Nativity, the
nativity of Christ, The
New Age movement, the
New Covenant

new heaven and new earth
New Jersulam
Nicene Creed
non-Christian
northern kingdom
Old Covenant
orthodoxy
Palm Sunday
papacy
paradise (heaven)
Paradise (Garden of Eden)
Passover
Passover feast
Pentateuch
Pentacost
Pentacostal, -ism
Pharaoh, the Pharaoh
piety, pietism, pietists, pietistic
pillar of fire
pope, the (past)
Pope, the (reigning)
Pope John Paul II
Prince of Peace
Prison Epistles
Prodigal Son, the
Promised Land
prophet Isaiah, the
prophets, the (people)
Prophets, the (books of OT)
Protestant (ism)
Providence (God)
providence of God
psalm, a
psalmist, the
rabbi, rabbinical
Rapture, the
rapture of Christ (or the Church), the
Real Presence (of Christ), The

Reformation
Reformed theology
Resurrection, the
resurrection of Christ, the
Sabbath (day)
saints, the
Saint Peter (et. al.)
Satan
satanic
Satanism
Savior
scriptural
Scripture(s)
Second Adam, the (Christ)
Second Coming, the
second coming of Christ, the
Second Person of the Trinity
Septuagint (LXX)
seraph, seraphim
Sermon on the Mount
Serpent, the (Satan)
Seventieth Week
shekinah
Son of God
Son of Man
sonship of Christ
southern kingdom
sovereign Lord
Sunday school
synagogue
synoptic Gospels
the Synoptics
tabernacle, the (building)
Talmud
temple, the (at Jerusalem)
Ten Commandments (but the second commandment)
Ten Tribes, the

ten tribes of Israel, the
Testaments, the
Thirty-nine Articles, the (Anglican)
Time of the Gentiles, the
tomb, the
Tower of Babel
transfiguration, the
tribulation, the
Trinitarian, -ism
Trinity, the
Twelve, the
twelve apostles, the
Twenty-third Psalm
unchristian
un-Christlike
universal church
unscriptural
Upper Room, the
Upper Room Discourse
Vine, the (Christ)
Virgin Birth, the
visible church
wise men
Way, the (Christ)
Western church
Word, the (Bible or Christ)
Word of God (Bible)
Word of Life

VI. Miscellaneous Information

Elements of nonsexist use of language

Women should receive the same treatment as men in all areas of writing. Physical descriptions, sexist references, demeaning stereotypes, and condescending phrases should not be used.

References to humanity in general should use language that includes women. Instead of using words such as man or mankind, attempt to use words such as *people, persons,* or *humanity.*

The use of *he* as the pronoun for nouns embracing both genders has been the accepted usage for centuries. Inserting *he* or *she* or *his* or *her* is not the solution. "An editor must maintain good rapport with his or her authors," is obviously awkward. If possible, revise the sentence. For example, "Editors must maintain good rapport with their authors."

Recommended Dictionaries

The American Heritage Dictionary of the English Language, 3rd Edition

The Concise Oxford Dictionary of Current English, 8th Edition

Mirriam-Webster Collegiate Dictionary, 10th Edition

Random House Dictionary of the English Language, 2nd Edition

Webster's New World Dictionary of American English, 3rd Edition

Webster's Third New International Dictionary, unabridged

Miscellaneous Preferred Usage (Watch out for these)*:

A/An before "H" Words Usage depends on whether or not the *h* is pronounced. We would not call something "an historical event" just as we would not say "an home run." We would, however, call someone "an honest person," because the *h* is silent.

A.D./B.C. Abbreviation for eras are set in small caps with periods, A.D. should always precede the year number (i.e., A.D. 33). C.E. and B.C.E. are sometimes used instead of B.C., but we prefer the latter designation referring to the advent of Christ.

African-American or black (Chicago Manual of Style recommends using either)

AIDS (Not Aids or A.I.D.S.)

Farther/Further *Farther* can be used only when speaking of distance. *Further* can be used in this way and in the sense of additional, as in further details.

Fewer/Less *Fewer* refers to *a number of individual things. Less* refers to *a quantity or amount of one thing.* Use fewer if the word it modifies is plural. Use *less* if the word it modifies is singular. (i.e., Because of automation, *fewer* workers are needed. *Less* rain has fallen this season than was predicted.)

Hopefully Avoid using *hopefully* when you mean *it is to be hoped.* "Hopefully, Christmas will soon be upon us." It is not Christmas that is doing the hoping.

Incomplete Sentences In fiction, you may use for effect or in dialogue. For nonfiction, however, use sparingly.

Infinitives "To be or to not be. That is the question." An infinitive is *to + verb* such as to *write, to edit, to play,* and it functions in a sentence as a noun. This once was an unbreakable rule enforced by grammar teachers and editors with harsh punishment. Now, while splitting an infinitive still should be avoided, it is acceptable if it makes the sentence read better than any of the alternatives. Splitting an infinitive with the word *not*, however, still should be avoided.

Use Of The Word *It* Avoid more than one use of the word *it* in a sentence unless the context makes perfectly clear who or what each *it* refers to.

Koran See **Qu'ran.**

Mohammed See **Muhammad.**

Moslem See Muslim.

Muslim This is the preferred spelling for a follower of Muhammad (not Mohammed).

Muhammad Preferred over Mohammed.

Poetry/Verse When fewer than four lines of poetry or verse are quoted, set in roman type and enclose in quotation marks within the same paragraph. Separate each line of poetry or verse with a slash (solidus, diagonal), and a thin, but equal, amount of space on either side: "Build thee more stately mansions, oh my soul,/While the swift seasons roll."
   When four or more lines are quoted, set in italics and center the entire block on the longest line. If the lines are longer than the coumn width in which they are to be set, indent the beginning of each new line 1 em instead, and bring the remainder of the line out to the left margin.

P.M./A.M. These abbreviations are always set in small caps (not lowercase) with periods and with no space between.

Qu'ran This is now considered the more accurate contemporary spelling instead of *Koran* (i.e., just as *Beijing* is now accepted instead of *Peking*).

Saint Spell out in text. Abbreviate in parenthetical use, in addresses, in names of cities, and in any tabular use.

shall, will In formal writing, the future tense requires *shall* for the first person, *will* for the second and third. To express the author's belief regarding future action or state *is I shall; I will* expresses the author's determination or consent. Today, however, the distinction between the two has blurred and generally either is accepted as proper usage.

Sunday School and Sunday school Do not capitalize school unless you are referring to a particular Sunday school.

"He teaches a class at Suburban Evangelical Sunday School";
but: "He teaches Sunday school at Suburban Evangelical
Church."

teenager Although still hyphenated in some dictionaries,
it's more common usage is as one word.

that, which *That* is a defining, or restrictive pronoun,
which is a nondefining, or nonrestrictive prounoun. i.e., "The
copy machine that is broken is down the hall." (Tells which
one) "The copy machine, which is broken, is down the hall.'
(Adds a fact about the copy machine in question)
 A way to check is to ask yourself if this needs a comma.
If so, insert it and leave *which*; if not, change *which* to *that*.

Trademarks/Servicemark/ Registered Brand names
Please make every effort to find out if a specific term is a
trademark and capitalize it as is dictated.

Band-Aid
Dacron (but polyester)
Dr Pepper
Kleenex (but tissue)
Scotch Tape
Styrofoam (but *foam* cups—the Styrofoam company does
not make cups)
Technicolor movies
TelePrompTer
Vaseline (but petroleum jelly)
Xerox (but photocopier)

which, that See that, which.

Who/Whom Use *who* and *whom* for references to human
beings and to animals with a name. Use *that* and *which* for
inanimate objects and animals without a name.

421

Who is used when someone is the subject of a sentence, clause, or phrase. (i.e., The man who bought the book forgot it on the counter. Who is it?)

Whom is used when someone is the object of a verb or preposition. (i.e., The man to whom the book was sold forgot it on the counter. Whom do you wish to see?)

worshiped, worshiping American usage spells these words with a single p.

*It is usually helpful to keep a good grammar textbook handy to help you with questionable words, usage, or punctuation. There probably is not an editor's bookshelf in the country that doesn't have at least one on it. (Be sure to check the "Grammar, Style, and Usage" section of the Selective Bibliography in Chapter 10 of this book!) In some instances these grammar books may not agree with this style guide or with *The Chicago Manual of Style;* in cases such as this, the author should probably adhere to this style guide or *The Chicago Manual of Style, Fourteenth Edition.*

Author's Checklist

____   Manuscript is typed, double-spaced on white bond with wide margins.

____   Manuscript is complete and includes:
        Title Page
        Table of Contents
        Text
        Footnotes at end of book
        Tables or graphs on separate pages
        Bibliography

____   All Scripture references have been checked for accuracy.

____   All footnotes have been checked for accuracy.

____ All quotations have been checked for accuracy.

____ All notes are complete.

____ Permission has been granted for quotes from other sources. Copies of the permissions are available for the publisher.

____ Except for changes made by the editor, the manuscript stands complete and ready for publication.

Disk accompanying the manuscript is either Macintosh or IBM-compatible. (Check with publishing house, most use only IBM-compatible computers.)

VII. Proofreading and Editing Marks and Explanations (3.19-36)

Deletions and Indentations

Delete and close-up

Delete, take out

◻ Indentation or em quad space

Insert space (more space)

stet. Let it stand—(all matter above dots)

Position and Paragraphing

Align horizontally

‖ Align vertically

⟧⟦ Center

⁋ Begin new paragraph

[[Move to left

] Move to right]

flush ⁋ ⊢No paragraph indentation

no ⁋ No paragraph.

Run in.

⌐ Move up

⌐ Move down

tr. Transpose encircled matter

tr. Transpose characters in/word

Punctuation

∀ Apostrophe or 'single quote'

∀ Close quotes

:/ Colon

;/ Semicolon

⋀ Comma

M — em dash

N — en dash

!/ — Exclamation point

set — Question mark **?**

= — Hyphen

ⱽ — Open quotes

(|) — Parenthesis

⊙ — Period

Miscellaneous

✗ — Broken type; remove blemish

••• — Ellipsis

ᓂ — Invert (upside-down type)

ok w/c — OK "with corrections"

sp. — Spell out

Spacing

ᒍ — Close-up completely; no space

— Insert space

‿ — Less space between words

eq # — make space between words equal

hr # — Insert hairspace

ls. — Letterspace

Type Style

bf. — Set in **bold face**

lf. — Set in light face

ital. — Set in *italic*

rom. — Set in roman

sc. — SET IN small capitals

caps v lc. — Lower Case with initial Caps

caps — SET IN capital letters

lc. — Set in LOWER CASE

wf. — Incorrect type style